Reading Tocqueville

Also by Raf Geenens

DE STEM VAN HET VOLK: Democratie als Gesprek
(editor, with Ronald Tinnevelt)

Reading Tocqueville

From Oracle to Actor

Edited by

Raf Geenens

and

Annelien De Dijn

palgrave
macmillan

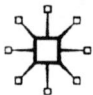

First published in 2007 by
PALGRAVE MACMILLAN
Houndmills, Basingstoke, Hampshire RG21 6XS and
175 Fifth Avenue, New York, N.Y. 10010
Companies and representatives throughout the world.

PALGRAVE MACMILLAN is the global academic imprint of the Palgrave
Macmillan division of St. Martin's Press, LLC and of Palgrave Macmillan Ltd.
Macmillan® is a registered trademark in the United States, United Kingdom
and other countries. Palgrave is a registered trademark in the European
Union and other countries.

ISBN-13: 978–0–230–52746–1 hardback
ISBN-10: 0–230–52746–9 hardback

A catalogue record for this book is available from the British Library.

A catalog record for this book is available from the Library of Congress.

10 9 8 7 6 5 4 3 2 1
16 15 14 13 12 11 10 09 08 07

Printed and bound in Great Britain by
Antony Rowe Ltd, Chippenham and Eastbourne

Contents

vi *Contents*

9 Tocqueville, European Integration and Free Moeurs   143
Larry Siedentop

10 Tocqueville and European Federalism: A Reply
to Larry Siedentop   155
Wilfried Swenden

Bibliography   176

Index   185

Acknowledgements

Bringing together diverse insights, ideas and perspectives into one single volume, is an endeavor that one does not undertake alone. The editors of this book would therefore like to thank a number of people. First of all, we are immensely grateful to the authors, who kindly contributed previously unpublished material to this volume. Their confidence in our project, their patience throughout the sometimes lengthy editing process, as well as their heartfelt encouragements are unequaled. (Un très grand merci à tous!) Furthermore we would like to thank, at the University of Antwerp and the Catholic University of Brussels: Peter De Graeve, Tim Heysse and Fernand Tanghe. Without their inspiration and encouragement, this book would not be what it is. We owe a special debt to Sarah Allen, who was initially called upon as a translator (she translated Agnès Antoine's, Serge Audier's and Jean-Louis Benoît's original manuscripts into English) but turned out to be much more than that. Apart from her accurate translations, her additional research and relentless attention to details contributed considerably to the book as a whole. Most importantly, though, we would like to thank UCSIA (University Centre Saint Ignatius Antwerp/www.ucsia.org), who generously supported the production of this book. Although rooted in a Christian tradition, UCSIA offers an open, tolerant and interdisciplinary platform for scholarly debate on issues related to religion, culture and society and especially on fundamental issues affecting justice in society. In particular, we would like to thank UCSIA's Geert Van Haverbeke, Chris Timmerman, Barbara Segaert, Walter Nonneman and Luc Braeckmans. Without their unremitting support and the personal confidence they gave us, this book would never have come to fruition. Although Alexis de Tocqueville had never been the focus of their work, the UCSIA-team enthusiastically agreed, very soon in the process, that his ideas and insights are not just valuable but might well be indispensable to their mission of holding up a democratic culture in a multireligious and multicultural society. Their liberal commitment to the creation of this book commands admiration.

Notes on Contributors

Agnès Antoine
Agnès Antoine, a doctor in political sciences, currently holds a professorship at the Ecole des Hautes Etudes en Sciences Sociales (Paris). Her research focuses on the tension between the individual and society, between contemplation and action, between religiosity and democratic citizenship. Antoine is the author of *Maine de Biran. Sujet et politique* (PUF, 1999) and *L'Impensé de la démocratie. Tocqueville, la citoyenneté et la religion* (Fayard, 2003), for which she won the *Prix de thèse Auguste Comte* and the *Prix Gegner de l'Académie des Sciences morales et politiques*.

Serge Audier
Serge Audier is a doctor in philosophy and currently lectures on moral and political philosophy at the Sorbonne University (Paris IV). His publications include: *Les Théories de la République* (La Découverte, 2004), *Raymond Aron. La démocratie conflictuelle* (Michalon, 2004), *Machiavel, conflit et liberté* (Vrin/EHESS, 2005) and *Le socialisme libéral* (La Découverte, 2006). In his widely acclaimed *Tocqueville retrouvé. Genèse et enjeux du renouveau tocquevillien français* (Vrin/EHESS, 2004) he carefully rereads the Tocqueville interpretations provided by Raymond Aron, François Furet, Claude Lefort and many other French intellectuals.

Jean-Louis Benoît
Jean-Louis Benoît received a graduate degree in moral and political philosophy from the Sorbonne University (Paris IV) and defended his PhD thesis, *Tocqueville Moraliste*, at the University of Caen. He was a lecturer at the University of Caen and a teacher in pre-university classes. The majority of his research has been devoted to Tocqueville, on which he has published the following works: Tome XIV of the *Oeuvres Complètes. Correspondance familiale de Tocqueville* (Gallimard, 1998), *Tocqueville, textes essentiels* (Agora/Pocket, 2000), *Tocqueville moraliste* (Champion, 2004), *Tocqueville, textes économiques* (with E. Keslassy, Agora/Pocket, 2004), *Comprendre Tocqueville* (Armand Colin, 2004), *Tocqueville, un destin paradoxal* (Bayard, 2005) and *Tocqueville, notes sur le Coran et autres textes sur les religions* (Bayard, 2007).

Paul Cliteur

Paul Cliteur is a professor of Jurisprudence at the University of Leiden, where he is also coordinator of the research programme on social cohesion and the function of law. His fields of interest are: human rights, religion, life- and worldviews, multiculturalism, the rule of law, constitutionalism and constitutional change. His books include *De filosofie van mensenrechten* (Ars Aequi, 1999) and *Moreel Esperanto: naar een autonome ethiek* (De Arbeiderspers, 2007).

Annelien De Dijn

After stints as a fellow at the Remarque Institute, and as a visiting fellow at Columbia University and Cambridge University, Annelien De Dijn was appointed as a postdoctoral researcher at Leuven University. Her research focuses on nineteenth-century French liberalism and Alexis de Tocqueville, on which she has published in several scholarly journals. Her book *Political Thought in France from Montesquieu to Tocqueville: Liberty in a Levelled Society* will be published by Cambridge University Press.

Raf Geenens

Raf Geenens studied at the universities of Brussels, Leuven and Paris VIII, was a visiting student at the New School for Social Research and is currently a researcher for the Political Philosophy Research Group of the Catholic University of Brussels. He is preparing a PhD thesis on the role of power in democracy, taking its point of departure in the works of Jürgen Habermas and Claude Lefort. Together with Ronald Tinnevelt, he edited an introductory volume to deliberative democracy: *De stem van het volk. Democratie als gesprek* (LannooCampus, 2007).

Ringo Ossewaarde

Ringo Ossewaarde is a lecturer in sociology at the University of Twente. In 2002 he completed his PhD, titled *Tocqueville's Catholic Liberalism*, at the London School of Economics. A rewritten version was published as *Tocqueville's Moral and Political Thought: New Liberalism* (Routledge, 2004). Besides his participation in Tocqueville scholarship, his research interests include public sociology, dialectics, self-government, individual responsibility, cosmopolitanism, governance, sovereignty and subsidiarity. He is also the author of *Maatschappelijke Organisaties* (Boom, 2006).

Jennifer Pitts

Jennifer Pitts is an assistant professor of politics at Princeton University whose research interests in modern political and social thought include British and French thought of the eighteenth and nineteenth centuries, empire, international law and international justice. She is the author of *A Turn to Empire: the rise of imperial liberalism in Britain and France* (Princeton University Press, 2005) and editor and translator of *Alexis de Tocqueville: Writings on Empire and Slavery* (Johns Hopkins University Press, 2001).

Larry Siedentop

Larry Siedentop, Professor Emeritus at Keble College, University of Oxford, is an expert on the history of political thought. His publications include *Tocqueville* (Oxford University Press, 1994) and the highly influential *Democracy in Europe* (Allen Lane, 2000). In the latter book, Siedentop rigorously analyses the weaknesses of the European institutions. He warns of a looming crisis of legitimacy and argues in favour of a less centralist and more democratic Europe.

Wilfried Swenden

Wilfried Swenden is a lecturer in Politics at the University of Edinburgh. He primarily teaches and researches on comparative federalism, regionalism, devolution and intergovernmental relations. His work has been published in several scholarly journals. His most recent book is *Federalism and Regionalism in Western Europe. A comparative and thematic analysis* (Palgrave Macmillan, 2006).

Cheryl Welch

Cheryl Welch, professor and chair of the Department of Political Science and International Relations at Simmons College, is the author of *Liberty and Utility: The French Idéologues and the Transformation of Liberalism* (Columbia University Press, 1984), *Critical Issues in Social Theory* (with M. Milgate, Academic Press, 1989) and *De Tocqueville* (Oxford University Press, 2001). She is also the editor of *The Cambridge Companion to Tocqueville* (Cambridge University Press, 2006). Welch has written widely on nineteenth-century French and British political thought, liberalism and democracy. She is currently working on a study of liberal philanthropy and politics in post-revolutionary France.

1
Tocqueville Today? Contexts, Interpretations and Usages

Raf Geenens and Annelien De Dijn

From Oracle to Actor

Over the past decade or so, both public and scholarly interest in the writings of Alexis de Tocqueville (1805–1859) has increased exponentially. In the United States, this revival was triggered by Robert Putnam and other political scientists, who looked at Tocqueville as the first major theorist of the value of civil society to democracy.[1] In France, intellectuals such as Raymond Aron brought Tocqueville back to attention as a critic of French exceptionalism, of the illiberal tendencies in French political culture.[2] The result has been an explosion of research into Tocqueville, marked by new editions and translations of his writings as well as a number of new biographical and scholarly studies. The bicentenary of Tocqueville's birth, which took place in 2005, was, moreover, celebrated with multiple conferences in France, the United States, Belgium and even Japan.[3] The 'Tocqueville revival' now looms so large that it has become a subject of study in and of itself.

Characterizing how this explosion of research has deepened our understanding of Tocqueville and his political thought is not an easy task. Here, we will outline a few of the most important trends, with a focus on how these have informed the essays collected in this volume. The main challenge of contemporary Tocqueville research has arguably been to reach beyond and underneath the iconic understanding of Tocqueville as an 'oracle'. Indeed, Tocqueville's long-standing image is that of an almost prophetic political thinker, the 'Nostradamus of democracy' (as Caleb Crain put it), who correctly predicted many political trends and developments. As is well known, the pages of *De la démocratie en Amérique* include vivid insights into the self-expanding logic of the welfare state (written before there even was such a thing as

1

a welfare state) and lucid warnings against the risk that democracy might deteriorate into totalitarianism. Similarly, Tocqueville is credited with having anticipated mass society, consumerism, materialism and other possible downsides of democracy at a time when other political thinkers were still struggling with the very notion of democracy. And in the very last chapter of the first volume Tocqueville famously formulated what is without any doubt the earliest forecast of the Cold War and its causes.

Yet no matter how powerful and remarkable these aspects of Tocqueville's work are, recent scholarship has successfully defied this image of Tocqueville as an oracle, and we have learned to see him rather as an historical actor. Before being a prophet or a seer, Tocqueville was a writer and a politician whose work inevitably positioned him within a field of forces that outlined the contours of his intellectual task. More particularly, Tocqueville has been reclaimed as a 'French' thinker, whose ideas were positively shaped by the debates and problems that had come to confront his compatriots in the wake of the revolutions of 1789 and 1830. This approach to Tocqueville's writings, pioneered by François Furet and Larry Siedentop, has greatly increased our understanding of the sources of Tocqueville's thought.[4] It has by now become clear that the questions Tocqueville posed in his *De la démocratie en Amérique* were to an important extent informed by the political issues of the Restoration period. How to reconcile liberty and democracy, how to make up for the disappearance of aristocratic checks on central power – these were all problems actively debated by major and minor figures of the Restoration period. The study of hitherto unexplored material, such as Tocqueville's letters and the notes he took while attending the lectures of one of the most famous liberal historians of the Restoration period, François Guizot, has enabled us to see that he followed these debates quite closely. Thus, it has become clear that a large part of Tocqueville's conceptual framework was already in place before he set foot on American soil.

While such exercises in contextualization have greatly increased our understanding of the sources of Tocqueville's thought, they have also allowed us – and that is perhaps the more important result – to come to a better understanding of the answers he gave to them. Tocqueville, it is worth emphasizing, sought to be an active politician, not just by running for parliament, but also by inspiring his compatriots to action through his writings and speeches. As a result, his *vita contemplativa* was always deeply intertwined with his *vita activa*. Looking at Tocqueville from this perspective, seeing him as an *actor*, allows us to gain more insight into one of the most important puzzles in Tocqueville scholarship: the existence of profound internal contradictions in his work. Identified in 1969 by Seymour Drescher as the problem of the 'two Tocquevilles' (although a case could be made that there are in fact three or four Tocquevilles) many scholars have tried to explain these contradictions away. But by seeing Tocqueville's work as shaped by the political *milieu* in which he was writing, it becomes clear that, while his overriding concern as a politician stayed the same – how to reconcile liberty and democracy – the solutions he provided were not always consistent with one another because of changing audiences and circumstances.

That is, in very general terms, the lesson which can be drawn from Jennifer Pitts's and Cheryl Welch's contributions in this volume. Both authors focus not on Tocqueville's major writings, but on the products of his activities as a politician, his parliamentary speeches and reports. Jennifer Pitts discusses Tocqueville's position vis-à-vis the colonization of Algeria, an issue close to his heart, on which he wrote several parliamentary reports and gave a number of speeches. Interestingly enough, Tocqueville, who in all other matters was an avowed humanist, did not just condone imperialism, but even violent conquest. Pitts argues that Tocqueville adopted the position he did, although it was in direct conflict with his avowed humanitarianism, because he believed that the colonial enterprise would have a beneficial effect on the declining public spiritedness in France.

In her contribution, Cheryl Welch discusses a related topic, namely Tocqueville's views on slavery. Here, Tocqueville can be encountered in a more familiar guise, as an enthusiastic abolitionist. Welch explains how Tocqueville's discourse in this respect was formed by the debates of the Restoration period. She then explains how Tocqueville's awareness of the difficulties entailed in the abolitionist position – the danger that former slaves were by no means ready for freedom – led him to adopt an uncharacteristically positive attitude towards the state. Tocqueville hoped that the state would create the conditions in which the abolition of slavery would become possible without violence or oppression.

Reading Tocqueville

If Tocqueville has been reclaimed as an historical agent, embedded in his time and context, scholars have similarly been led to historicize the reception of his works. Tracing the interpretation of Tocqueville's writings over time and place has in fact become a well-established sub-discipline in Tocqueville scholarship, especially since the publication of Françoise Mélonio's *Tocqueville et les Français* (1993)[5] and Serge Audier's *Tocqueville retrouvé* (2004).[6] In an 1835 letter (discussed by Jean-Louis Benoît later on in this volume), Tocqueville expressed mixed feelings concerning the popularity of his recently published *De la démocratie en Amérique*:

> I please many people of conflicting opinions, not because they understand me, but because they find in my work, by considering it only from a single side, arguments favorable to their passion of the moment.[7]

The same remained true, it seems, throughout the entire history of Tocqueville's reception. As Benoît and Audier convincingly argue in their respective contributions to this volume, most Tocqueville readers have been selective and some even deliberately misleading in their presentation of Tocqueville's ideas.

Jean-Louis Benoît points out that Raymond Aron not only single-handedly launched a massive renewal of interest in Tocqueville in France but did so with a clear agenda, using a number of Tocqueville's ideas to defend his own, not particularly Tocquevillian, flavour of liberalism. At the same time, Aron overlooked Tocqueville's writings on war and the military (or downplayed them as mere opinion), because they were difficult to blend with his own position. More recently, Marcel Gauchet's appropriation of Tocqueville falls victim to a similar onesidedness. According to Benoît, Gauchet exaggerates the distance between Tocqueville's allegedly consensualist idea of democracy as a finished 'product' and, on the other hand, his own view of democracy as a conflictuous process that can in essence never be completed. In general, Benoît attributes the French understanding of Tocqueville as a classical liberal to the fact that Tocqueville was forgotten by the end of the nineteenth century. According to Benoît, Tocqueville was only reestablished in France by Aron in the 1950s, hence the still dominant liberal image.

Serge Audier, by contrast, disagrees with this received conception of the 'forgetting' of Tocqueville in France, which he argues to be nothing but a myth. Not unlike what Matthew Mancini has recently demonstrated with regard to Tocqueville's American legacy,[8] Audier shows that Tocqueville has never really been absent from the French intellectual scene. He cites a number of influential Tocqueville interpretations, such as Antoine Rédier's and Jacob Peter Mayer's, which largely preceded Aron's reading.

Moreover, these authors pictured a very different Tocqueville, one who uncovers the internal connection between massification and atomization, and could thus be cast in their criticism of modernity. As Audier explains, this permanent heritage of Tocqueville in France (the continuation of which can be seen in the work of Gilles Lipovetsky, among others) has been overshadowed and pushed into oblivion by the myth of Aron's Tocqueville revival.

However, Benoît and Audier do agree on one important point. They both argue that there is a gulf separating the French and the American receptions of Tocqueville. Despite the different fashions to which Tocqueville was subjected in France, he was always read as a prophet of modern *individualism* – with varying positive and negative connotations. In the United States, by contrast, Tocqueville was from the very outset seen as the one author to have understood, better than anyone else, that the New England town meetings were the quintessential locus of popular sovereignty and the perfect school for the civic virtues proper to democracy. As a result, Tocqueville continues to inspire those democratic theorists who emphasize the importance of associations and citizen participation. Benoît and Audier show that Tocqueville is frequently cited by American political philosophers across a wide spectrum: from communitarians (Michael Sandel, Charles Taylor) and civic republicans (Robert Putnam, Richard Sennett) to deliberative democrats (Benjamin Barber, James Fishkin).

Democracy and religion

A study of the history of Tocqueville's reception also helps to remind us how instrumental Tocqueville has been in shaping our present-day vocabulary. For, it is important to remember, the present Tocqueville revival is by no means the first. In the United States, for instance, sociologists and political scientists have been reaching back to Tocqueville to warn their compatriots of the dire consequences of declining civic associationism since at least the 1950s, as is illustrated by the work of David Riesman and Richard Sennett.[9] And even in France, the present Tocqueville revival is not without its precedents. A study of the reception of Tocqueville thus makes it clear that if his work still speaks to us, this is not because he was not of his time, but because his legacy has continued to inspire political thinkers and sociologists throughout the twentieth century. The rise of modern mass media, for instance, is not a trend Tocqueville discussed or anticipated in his works. But his analysis of democratic individualism has been applied by many a sociologist to precisely this phenomenon. Similarly, Tocqueville's discussion of the growth of a new, democratic despotism still continues to inspire many political thinkers in France today.[10]

But to point to the continuing influence of Tocqueville is also to raise a question: isn't it time we went on and did our thinking for ourselves? That task is taken up in the five remaining chapters collected in this volume, in which a dialogue is constructed around the question of the contemporary relevance of Tocqueville's ideas. Can Tocqueville's writings and insights be brought to bear on a number of today's pressing problems?

A first case that will be explored is the relationship between religion and democracy. Ringo Ossewaarde, Paul Cliteur and Agnès Antoine, in their respective contributions, bring Tocqueville to bear on the question as to what role, if any, religion is to play in democratic societies at the outset of the twenty-first century.

The discussion is opened by Ringo Ossewaarde who, in an unconventional interpretation, argues that Tocqueville's insights in the Christian underpinnings of democratic ideas should be kept in mind, even today, as they might foster the civic virtues of democracy. In Ossewaarde's view, the Puritan mindset of the American settlers was crucial in the establishment of the town meetings and thus for the success of democratic self-government. Losing sight of this Christian heritage (and that means, according to him, keeping in mind that democracy is a 'providential fact') might open the door to the many pathologies of democracy identified by Tocqueville.

Paul Cliteur, by contrast, argues that Tocqueville's ideas on religion, although in line with his own time, are of no direct use to our pluralist, multireligious societies, in which religion has lost its unifying and integrating potential. However, this does not entirely eradicate the importance of Tocqueville's insights, for, as Cliteur reveals, there is a certain ambiguity in Tocqueville's writings. Although Tocqueville sometimes stresses that the polity, if it is to remain bound together, needs a set of shared religious beliefs, many other passages suggest that what is needed is simply *some* shared beliefs, not necessarily *religious* ones. In this regard it might be helpful to think of Habermas's notion of *constitutional patriotism*, which equally points to the need for a thin loyalty to the public decision-making procedures – a loyalty without which democracy cannot fulfil its integrative function.[11] Cliteur shows not only that Tocqueville was already aware of this at certain points but also uncovers a passage in *De la démocratie en Amérique* where Tocqueville strongly condemns Connecticut's Puritan lawmakers, who intended to literally translate a number of harsh and crude imperatives from the Old Testament into public law. The fact that Tocqueville does so in the name of religious freedom, clearly contradicts the idea that his writings on the intrinsic connectedness of democracy and religion ought to be interpreted literally. Instead, Cliteur claims, they should first and foremost be seen as a recognition of the need for a shared, public morality.

Agnès Antoine, in a third contribution to this discussion, reveals that Tocqueville had a sharp awareness of the tension between 'the liberal sentiment' and the 'religious sentiment'.[12] Moreover, the very challenge Tocqueville wanted to address in his work, a challenge he himself described as 'one of the most beautiful enterprises of our times',[13] was precisely to bring both these sentiments into harmony. While Tocqueville recognizes perfectly well that religion, as a source of authority and political legitimacy has become obsolete once and for all, he maintains that religious feelings continue to matter as a counterbalance to some of democracy's self-undermining tendencies. Religion not only creates a sense of moral stability, it also, and more importantly, introduces a temporal dimension that surpasses the narcissist emphasis on the present that tends to prevail in democratic times. Accordingly, Antoine argues, Tocqueville should be seen as the one author who carries out most successfully the difficult balancing act of civic humanism and religious humanism.

Tocqueville in Europe?

A second test case for the contemporary relevance of Tocqueville's writings is the European Union. It has been argued that Europe is currently going through a 'Tocquevillian moment'.[14] Not only because it is a continental-scale democracy in the process of coming into being, but also because it is unpleasantly suspended between its elitist inception and its democratic future. Moreover, many European citizens and politicians alike believe that the spectre of centralization looms large over Brussels. But are Tocqueville's nineteenth-century precepts really relevant to the contemporary European Union and its incremental process of integration? That is the issue discussed by Larry Siedentop and Wilfried Swenden in their contributions to this volume. Larry Siedentop argues first of all that Tocqueville's analysis of the danger of centralization is still applicable to the shaping of the European Union. The primacy of EU law, effected by the Luxembourg Court, clearly creates an enormous potential for power in the centre. At the same time, the transfer of decision-making to Brussels entails a risk of weakening the (in many cases already weak) national democratic cultures, and of generating too strong a central bureaucracy. Second, Siedentop argues that the economic lexicon in which European integration has thus far proceeded is detrimental to the development of political commitment and free institutions. By reducing liberalism to economic liberalism and making the satisfaction of consumer needs its primary concern, the European Union has done little to foster a sense of European citizenship. What is needed then, according to Siedentop, is the stimulating of *free moeurs* and a *constitutional sense*. Inspired by Tocqueville, he goes on to formulate a number of formal and informal solutions, from a common public language and shared moral beliefs to the institution of a bicameral system.

Siedentop's analysis, however, is seriously questioned by Wilfried Swenden, who emphasizes the crucial ways in which twenty-first-century political problems differ from those Tocqueville was addressing. Rather than retain his conclusions, we should be faithful to Tocqueville's method of enquiry, which was comparative in nature, and mostly characterized by a continuous two-way movement between empirical evidence and abstract assumptions. Proceeding in exactly this way, Swenden comes to very different conclusions than Tocqueville or Siedentop. For instance, Swenden's detailed institutional analysis reveals that the danger of centralization is largely overestimated. The causes that Tocqueville identified as leading towards a concentration of power, are absent in Europe. Swenden concludes that the European Union is far from developing towards a 'bureaucratic tyranny'. He also strongly denies that the EU has been reduced to an economic or 'utilitarian' arrangement. It can be shown that the EU is successfully pursuing a number of goals in the fields of justice and civil rights, and even in such domains as higher education and military intervention. Finally, Swenden puts forward a different set of institutional suggestions. Before there can be any real constitutional sense, Swenden argues, a further politicization of the EU's daily business is needed. Rather than commitment to grand constitutional questions, we should seek to improve involvement in Europe's 'micro-politics'. This could be achieved, for instance, by improving the transparency and accountability of the current procedures. More importantly, Swenden argues for more democratic competition within EU decision-making, so that legitimate opposition towards certain policies can be voiced and channelled without automatically turning into opposition against the EU as such.

Tocqueville today

As it will have become clear by now, the texts collected in this volume draw on a multitude of perspectives and methodologies, and they do not quite lead to a single, clear conclusion. Yet they do have a common goal. What this volume in its entirety wants to show, is that a 'naive' reading of Tocqueville is no longer possible.

First of all, this is because it would be wrong to see his works as disembodied studies in political theory. Tocqueville always wrote in tangible political circumstances, and more often than not with a specific political purpose. This is true not only for the texts that deal with concrete issues like slavery or France's opportunities in Algeria. His 'analytic' writings can be read in this way as well. Claude Lefort, for instance, has shown that many chapters of the second *Démocratie* contain hardly masked strikes at Guizot's policies: numerous passages purposely target the repressive measures taken by Guizot in 1935, Guizot's strategic invoking and exaggerating of the risks of revolution and anarchy, and the anti-liberal tendencies of his government in general – yet without naming them.[15]

Second, it should be clear that translating Tocqueville's ideas to contemporary issues is a risky undertaking. His views on religion, for instance, are ambiguous and sometimes even contradictory. Likewise, his writings on federalism and centralization lead to controversy when set against the background of current European politics. And the specific flavour of liberalism Tocqueville defended, fits uncomfortably in today's categories.

Yet this should not dissuade anyone from reading Tocqueville. Quite the contrary: the debates in this book should decidedly be seen as a sign of the richness of Tocqueville's writings. Tocqueville's œuvre still triggers and most likely always will trigger debate. And that might well be how Tocqueville himself wanted it. Even though he was a vivid actor, he clearly sensed that his sharp eye and political intelligence came nowhere better to the fore than in his writings. In a letter to Gustave de Beaumont, he notes: 'I thought a hundred times that if I have to leave some trace in the world, it will be what I will have written, rather than what I will have done.'[16] And in that sense as well he remains an important actor. Although Tocqueville would have celebrated his 200th birthday a few years ago, his presence is still felt on the stage of contemporary political debate.

Notes

1 Robert Putnam, *Bowling Alone. The Collapse and Revival of American Community* (New York: Simon and Schuster, 2000).
2 Raymond Aron, 'Tocqueville retrouvé', *The Tocqueville Review/La Revue Tocqueville* 1(1) (1979), pp. 8–23.
3 To name but a few: the international conference 'Tocqueville entre l'Europe et les Etats-Unis' held at the Centre culturel international de Cerisy-La-Salle;

the conference, 'Alexis de Tocqueville. An international conference commemorating the bicentennial of his birth' at the Yale Beinecke library; the conference at the University of Tokyo commemorating Tocqueville, 'La France et les Etats-Unis, deux modèles de démocratie?': in Antwerp, the conference 'Condemned to democracy? Tocqueville 1805–2005', on which the present volume of essays draws.

4 François Furet has been instrumental in resituating Tocqueville in his French context, see in particular his essay, 'The Intellectual Origins of Tocqueville's Thought', *The Tocqueville Review/La Revue Tocqueville*, 7 (1985–6) pp. 117–29; Larry Siedentop provides a careful reconstruction of the Restoration debates which shaped Tocqueville's thought in his *Tocqueville* (Oxford University Press, 1994).

5 Françoise Mélonio, *Tocqueville et les Français* (Paris: Aubier, 1993). Translated as: *Tocqueville and the French*, trans. Beth G. Raps (London: University Press of Virginia, 1998).

6 Serge Audier, *Tocqueville retrouvé* (Paris: Vrin/EHESS, 2004). Other examples of this 'sub-discipline' are Claire Le Strat and Willy Pelletier, *La canonisation libérale de Tocqueville* (Paris: Editions Syllepse, 2006) and Matthew Mancini, *Alexis de Tocqueville and American Intellectuals: From His Times to Ours* (Lanham: Rowman and Littlefield Publishers, 2006).

7 Letter from Tocqueville to Eugène Stoffels, 21 February 1835, *Selected Letters on Politics and Society*, ed. Roger Boesche, trans. James Toupin and Roger Boesche (Berkeley/Los Angeles/London: University of California Press, 1985), pp. 99–100.

8 Matthew Mancini, *Alexis de Tocqueville and American Intellectuals*.

9 David Riesman, *The Lonely Crowd: A Study of the Changing American Character*, in collaboration with Reuel Denney and Nathan Glazer (New Haven: Yale University Press, 1950); Richard Sennett, *The Fall of Public Man* (New York: Knopf, 1977).

10 For the link between democracy and totalitarianism, see for instance: François Furet and Mona Ozouf, introduction to *A Critical Dictionary of the French Revolution* (Cambridge, MA: The Belknapp Press of Harvard University Press, 1989).

11 On the notion of constitutional patriotism (*Verfassungspatriotismus*), see Jürgen Habermas, 'Popular Sovereignty as Procedure', in Habermas, *Between Facts and Norms*, trans. William Rehg (Cambridge: Polity Press, 1996), pp. 463–90, see pp. 465–66 in particular. See Jürgen Habermas, 'Citizenship and National Identity', in *Ibid.*, pp. 491–515, see pp. 498–500 in particular. And see Jürgen Habermas, *The Inclusion of the Other*, ed. Ciaran Cronin and Pablo De Greiff (Cambridge, MA: MIT Press, 1998), see pp. 117–8 and pp. 224–6.

12 Letter to Claude-François de Corcelle, 17 September 1853, *Selected Letters on Politics and Society*, p. 295.

13 Letter to Eugène Stoffels, on his love of freedom and new kind of liberalism, 24 July 1836, in *The Tocqueville reader. A Life in Letters and Politics*, ed. Olivier Zunz and Alan S. Kahan (Malden, MA: Blackwell, 2002), p. 152.

14 Kalypso Nicolaïdis, 'UE: un moment tocquevillien', *Politique étrangère*, 3 (Autumn 2005) pp. 497–509.

15 Claude Lefort, 'Préface', in Alexis de Tocqueville, *Souvenirs*, ed. Luc Monnier, J.P. Mayer, and B.M. Wicks-Boisson (Paris: Gallimard, 1999), pp. I-L, see pp. XV–XIX in particular.

16 'J'ai pensé cent fois que si je dois laisser quelques traces de moi dans le monde, ce sera plutôt par ce que j'aurai écrit que par ce que j'aurai fait.' Alexis de Tocqueville, *Oeuvres complètes*, ed. J.-P. Mayer (Paris: Gallimard, 1951-) 8.ii, p. 343. Also quoted by Claude Lefort, *Préface*, p. IV.

2
Liberalism, Democracy and Empire: Tocqueville on Algeria

Jennifer Pitts

Introduction

Tocqueville, who was always alert to the originality of his times and of his own ideas, announced the need for a new political science in his introduction to the first volume of *De la démocratie en Amérique* (1835).[1] He had in mind the great political transformations in Europe, in 'the Christian nations of our day', the halting but inexorable advance of democracy and social equality. But he could have been speaking of the equally revolutionary developments in Europe's relations with the non-European world. Tocqueville himself felt these phenomena were little understood in Europe. Like democracy, the growing European empires of the nineteenth century called for analysis by someone who appreciated their novelty and who understood that they would profoundly affect not just the conquered peoples but European societies themselves.[2]

Tocqueville believed the study of empire was central to his work as a politician and an observer of politics and society. His views on empire also present the struggles of a complex and perceptive thinker as he attempted a difficult balancing act: that of reconciling a belief in human equality with a defence of the subjugation of other societies. Tocqueville's support for the violent conquest and settlement of Algeria must be read in light of his own avowed belief in human equality. He understood himself, after all, as a humanitarian, a defender of the principles of 1789, and as one who practised an equitable and honourable international politics.[3]

It is difficult to reconcile Tocqueville's avowals of human equality and the right of nations, his sympathy for the Amerindians, and his disgust at 'European tyranny' in America, with his own often ruthless support for European conquest of Algeria and India. Tocqueville's liberalism did not, it is true, rest primarily on a theory of natural rights. But he often referred to such rights as though they were a matter of consensus and did not need to be defended. His support for empire stood in tension with his own avowed commitments as well as with what we might call liberalism's centre of gravity, its insistence on the moral equality of all human beings. And yet Tocqueville's imperialism also arose out of his liberalism, for it emerged directly from his concern to build a durable liberal political order in France.

Tocqueville argued for the maintenance and expansion of the French empire primarily for two reasons, I would suggest: he believed that such a grand enterprise could build political solidarity and engagement among the French population, and he feared that France would lose its international position and reputation if it continued to fall behind Britain in the quest for overseas possessions. Tocqueville was convinced for most of his political career that his parliamentary colleagues under-valued French colonies and their political worth for France. He devoted such energy to the question of colonization because he felt he had grasped the historic importance of conquest as few Frenchmen in his day had done.

Tocqueville's writings on America and France were animated by his worry about the dangers of what he termed 'individualism'. This was, in short, the worry that modern individuals were retreating from politics into the private world of family and business, leaving a political vacuum that the state would fill all too eagerly. For citizens to abandon political activity in this way, he believed, was both a form of moral debasement and a great danger to basic liberties. Politics in modern commercial societies would have to reckon with modern individualism without allowing it to destroy the social fabric.

Such problems, he believed, were particularly acute in France. Tocqueville feared that France, more than other European nations, and especially in contrast to Britain and America, lacked a solid foundation as a political community. For too many centuries, the French had been apolitical, and their government had been over-centralized. French citizens were used to depending on the state for everything. In New England, when a road or a church roof needed mending, the citizens of a town would raise the funds and get the work done. All over France, in contrast, villagers would turn to Paris for help whenever they faced a need, however small.

Tocqueville also deplored the apathy of the French public about national politics, and the mediocrity and pettiness of politicians under the July Monarchy. The sort of great public actions that had distinguished the Revolutionary era and that seemed largely out of reach in his own day were essential, in his view, to a vibrant democratic politics. He worried that there were few occasions any longer for great political enterprises that might draw people out of their narrow individual lives and into the realm of concerted action and the display of public 'virtue'. As he wrote to a friend, in admiration of the French soldiers fighting in the Crimean War, 'Are you not astonished with me, Madame, upon seeing spring from a nation that appears so devoid of public virtues, an army that demonstrates itself to be so full of virtue? So much egoism here, so much self-sacrifice there.'[4]

Tocqueville looked to both the abolition of slavery and colonial expansion as opportunities for the French nation to demonstrate that it was still capable of great political deeds. In the case of emancipation, what Tocqueville called 'the execution of vast plans' that would raise French politics above its usual pettiness and mediocrity was happily compatible with France's vocation as the national home of freedom and human equality. Tocqueville could ask, in an essay on slavery, 'Will France, the democratic country *par excellence*, remain the sole European nation to support slavery? When all inequalities disappear at her word, will she keep part of her subjects under the weight of the greatest and the most intolerable of all social inequalities?'[5]

In contrast, there was a deep tension between those revolutionary principles and Tocqueville's advocacy of the subjugation of Algeria. While he sometimes suggested that European rule might benefit backward peoples, he believed Europeans had consistently failed in their *mission civilisatrice*.[6] As he wrote in an 1840 letter to his friend Francisque de Corcelle, for instance: 'I think that we will never do all the great things we set out to do in Algeria, and, all things considered, we have quite a sad possession there. But, on the other hand, I remain more convinced than ever: 1st that there is no middle ground between complete abandonment and, I don't say conquest, but total domination; 2nd that this domination ... is quite practicable'.[7] Tocqueville never shared the unalloyed confidence of his British liberal contemporaries that such a civilizing project was politically possible or even wholly desirable, and with his sense of the complex interdependence of all aspects of a society, he doubted the feasibility of any such effort at radical change. And yet Tocqueville deliberately distanced himself from Corcelle's own insistence that the French, because of their revolutionary history, had a particular obligation to treat native Algerians with decency and respect.

I want to suggest that Tocqueville's anxieties about France's halting and perilous transition to democracy and his often bleak account of modern European society led him to embrace imperial politics despite his recognition of its perils. Although Tocqueville never forgot or denied the violence of imperial conquest, he oscillated between daringly accepting it as the price that France had to pay for empire and expressing horror at imperial brutality. While he argued that to repeat the atrocities of the Spanish and Anglo-Americans in the New World would be an inexcusable violation of the laws of humanity, he also defended General Bugeaud's infamous attacks on Algerian civilians.[8] He wrote, 'I have often heard men in France whom I respect, but with whom I do not agree, find it wrong that we burn harvests, that we empty silos, and finally that we seize unarmed men, women, and children. These, in my view, are unfortunate necessities, but ones to which any people who want to wage war on the Arabs are obliged to submit'.[9] With an uncomfortable marriage of clear-sightedness and willful callousness, Tocqueville acknowledged, as British liberals such as Mill did not, the violence that imperial conquest required.[10]

Scholars have often remarked on the tension between sociological analysis and moral judgment in Tocqueville's writings on America and France. Tocqueville's sociological work is always driven, at least in part, by a distinctly moral goal. As he wrote in the preface to the *Ancien Régime*, 'I wanted to discover not only what illness killed the patient, but how the patient could have been cured. My purpose has been to paint a picture both accurate and instructive.'[11] Tocqueville studied America with the idea that democracy is more just than aristocracy and more appropriate in the modern world, and that American democracy might provide the only model that preserves the liberty, once found among aristocrats, without which democracy becomes tyranny. And yet in Tocqueville's reflections on empire, his rich sociological analysis of colonial societies often appears disjointed from his normative claims – cut off from both his defence of colonization, and his criticism of colonial injustices. Because Tocqueville was committed to the idea that sociological analysis is inextricable from moral prescription, his apparent willingness to separate them in his writings on empire is all the more puzzling.

Tocqueville himself never confronted his own ambivalence, or acknowledged the contradictions that his commitment to the conquest of Algeria imposed on his thought.[12] I want to suggest that Tocqueville's anxieties about the difficulty of maintaining political engagement in France in an age of democratization led him to approve of the exercise of French power in Algeria and elsewhere — India, for instance, if possible — and largely to ignore the claims of those France sought to dominate.

The evolution of Tocqueville's views about Algeria

Tocqueville followed the French colonization of Algeria, which he later described as '*la plus grande affaire de ce pays*', from its inception. In 1833, three years after the French army captured Algiers from the Ottoman Empire, the twenty-seven-year-old Tocqueville and his cousin Louis de Kergorlay, who had participated in the conquest, seem briefly to have considered purchasing land in Algeria and becoming settlers. Tocqueville sketched a list of questions, including: 'Is spoken Arabic a difficult language to learn? How long would a man of average abilities and devoting himself to it exclusively require to acquire enough for it to be useful in everyday life?'[13] Though he soon abandoned any plans to settle in Algeria, he continued to study Algerian history and culture, investigate the Turkish administration of Algeria, and read the Quran.

Tocqueville had also begun, when he was travelling in America, to think about why the French seemed to be less successful colonizers than the British, and he concluded that significant differences of national character had led France to fall behind in the race for colonies and international power.[14] The Anglo-Americans had long-established habits of self-reliance and self-government; they had succeeded in turning thousands of miles of wilderness into farms and cities. Tocqueville had discovered log cabins deep in the woods of the American frontier whose inhabitants read newspapers and kept up with the latest developments on the east coast and in Europe.[15] The French, used to passivity in the face of their powerful central government, did not have the initiative and self-discipline, Tocqueville feared, that was necessary to colonize a hostile land. But he allowed himself to hope that the Algerian colony itself might serve as a laboratory for the sort of local self-government that would be needed throughout France if liberal democracy was to succeed.

Tocqueville placed French colonialism at the centre of his political agenda from the beginning of his legislative career. In 1837, during his first, failed, effort to win a seat in the Chamber of Deputies, he published two 'Lettres sur l'Algérie', the first product of his study of the country.[16] It is telling that Tocqueville chose to write about Algeria as he made his first bid for public office; and it was an accurate foretaste of the considerable attention Tocqueville would pay to the French empire as a legislator. What is most striking about these letters is their optimism about the future of French-Algerian relations.

He criticized the Turks for remaining aloof from the native population and for failing to establish a real government in Algeria; the Turkish regime was just the continued 'violent exploitation of the conquered by the conquerors'.[17] The French, he argued, should aspire to a very different sort of empire: a government that would at first respect the Arabs' laws, customs, and religion, with the hope of reconciling the Algerians to their new rulers, and eventually of assimilating the native and European populations. The influence of Tocqueville's observations about America is apparent here. He had faulted the Anglo-Americans precisely for forcing the indigenous peoples too quickly to live under European laws, and for not permitting them to become 'sedentary' at least partly on their own terms.[18] These early articles also express a plea for humility on the part of the French: if they went into the country believing they had everything to teach the natives, they would fail not only the conquered people but also their own interests.

Nonetheless, even at this early stage, Tocqueville argued that the French must crush any early signs of national political organization by the Algerians. Unlike his British contemporaries like John Stuart Mill, who maintained that barbarous peoples were essentially incapable of political organization, Tocqueville understood only too well that the *marabout* Abd el-Kader, a 'sort of Muslim Cromwell' who skilfully combined 'sincere and feigned' religious enthusiasm to sustain opposition to the French, represented an emerging national political force and a formidable obstacle to French designs.[19]

Tocqueville made his first trip to Algeria in 1841, two years after he won a seat in the Chamber of Deputies representing the Norman district of Valogne, which included the ancestral town of Tocqueville. His travelling companions were his brother Hippolyte, and his close friends and fellow deputies Francisque de Corcelle and Gustave de Beaumont.[20] Tocqueville considered direct observation crucial for an understanding of the colonial project, and his two visits to Algeria left him firmly convinced that its colonization was essential to France's interests.[21] His two trips to Algeria gave him great insight into the vices of imperial governance, and he was critical of both the civilian and the military leadership in Algeria. But his concern remained largely with the injustices done to French settlers, rather than to Algerians. Much of Tocqueville's perceptive critique thus was devoted to the problems of the colonists: his sharp criticism of the government's arbitrary and high-handed treatment of the French *colons* is far more elaborate than his consideration of French–Arab relations.[22]

Tocqueville's first voyage took place just as the French began the total conquest and active colonization of Algeria. When he arrived in Algeria, he set out to understand the country much as he had America and

Ireland in the previous decade, beginning with impressions about the society drawn from its architecture and visual aspect, and interviewing military officials, civilian administrators, doctors, lawyers, bishops, and prominent citizens. Already we see his interest shift from Algeria's indigenous inhabitants to the new colonial society. His immediate impression, noted in his journal and early letters, was of restless activity reminiscent of the American frontier and a racial and cultural mixture even more bewildering. Tocqueville allowed himself a romanticism in his first responses to the country that would be short-lived: for the moment, it was a '[d]elicious country, Sicily with the industry of France'. 'Astonishing contrast', Tocqueville observed: 'the Sahel the image of nature cultivated by industry and the most advanced civilization; the plain: *wilderness*'.[23] Of Algiers he wrote,

> First appearance of the town: I have never seen anything like it. Prodigious mix of races and costumes, Arab, Cabyle, Moor, Negro, Mahonais, French. Each of these races, tossed together in a space much too tight to contain them, speaks its language, wears its attire, displays different mores. This whole world moves about with an activity that seems feverish. The entire lower town seems in a state of destruction and reconstruction. On all sides, one sees nothing but recent ruins, buildings going up; one hears nothing but the noise of the hammer. It is Cincinnati transported onto the soil of Africa.[24]

Tocqueville's writings on Algeria share with all his other major works a fascination with new societies and an eagerness to analyse their social and political development. It was when he studied the development of laws and mores under dramatically new circumstances that Tocqueville displayed most clearly his singular blend of sociological observation and moral purpose. He explored with great insight the creation of new polities out of diverse groups newly thrown together, and the mediation between existing customs and consciously developed practices.

Tocqueville was especially drawn to the idea of the colony as a laboratory for ideas of governance. He worried that the French had exaggerated ideas about the proper role of government, and he grew ever more wary of the active interventions of the colonial administration into colonization. The Algerian settlements, he said, reminded him of Potemkin villages. Tocqueville argued that the French government had gone about colonization entirely the wrong way, dropping the urban poor on Algerian farmland one by one, 'the way one plants asparagus'. It is absurd and ridiculous, he wrote, for the government 'to take a poor man in France, bring him to Algeria ... build him a house, clear a field, and then go find another poor devil to put next to him'.[25]

The dangers of a powerful central state had preoccupied Tocqueville from the time of his earliest writings on France and America. Here, for the first time, he outlined his ideas for a new society in the face of France's tendency to centralization. Tocqueville believed that Algeria suffered from both too little centralization and too much. On the one hand, nobody was accountable for problems, because responsibility for Algerian affairs was scattered among so many ministries in Paris and Algiers. But on the other hand, endless centralizing, bureaucratic regulations kept communities in Algeria from taking charge of their own affairs.[26] As it was, a town had to apply to the Paris ministries for funds to fix the church roof. The Parisian bureaucrats, he argued, must give up their aesthetically pleasing, uniform designs and allow authorities and settlers on the spot to tailor policies to local conditions. Eventually, however, Tocqueville came to doubt the capacity of the European settlers to sustain a vigorous local self-government.

It was on his first visit to Algeria that Tocqueville first recognized the real violence of colonial warfare and its likely consequences for both Frenchmen and Algerians.[27] He wrote of the abundant fertile territory that it would be a 'promised land, if one didn't have to farm with gun in hand'.[28] In America, Tocqueville had observed the brutalizing effects of colonial rule on both the indigenous people and their occupiers. His resolute defence of further conquest and occupation in the face of this knowledge indicates the degree of his commitment to the expansion of the French empire.

The voyage convinced Tocqueville that the French would never be able to gain the willing cooperation of the Algerians, and that the relationship between the two peoples would be one of perpetual hostility. He had, that is, rather quickly given up the hope that French rule might be more than just the 'continuation of conquest' that Ottoman rule had been.

Tocqueville tried out some of his central views on the question of the 'domination of the Arab people' in a long and revealing letter to General Lamoricière, which he wrote as he prepared for an important parliamentary debate in 1846 about the status and future of French Algeria. Arguing that conquest is 'nothing new in the world', Tocqueville looked to other empires in history for lessons about what he called 'the chemistry of conquest'.[29] That is, how could conquerors best dissolve existing social ties in a society and, as he put it, 'divid[e] the molecules of the social body to dominate some with the aid of others'? Tocqueville's ideas about how to create a 'social revolution' that would help to secure

French rule in Algeria are at once theoretically sophisticated and coldly cynical. He argued, for instance, that the French should take advantage of the fact that individual Arab property owners had long been vulnerable to the confiscation of their land. He asked, 'Why not give these lands to other Arabs, who, being usurpers like us and because of us, would then see their cause as linked to our own?' The French could thus 'use the ambition of some to counter the hostility of others'. Having committed the great violence of conquest, Tocqueville added, the French must not recoil from all the smaller acts of violence (*violences de détail*) that were necessary to consolidate their power.

Several weeks later, in the parliamentary debate itself, Tocqueville explicitly distanced himself from the view that decent treatment of the indigenous Algerians should be a paramount concern. Tocqueville's ally Corcelle was the only member, during several days of debate, to speak at length about indigenous Algerians and the moral duty of the French to treat them with humanity and decency. Corcelle eloquently denounced the 'murderous', indeed genocidal, sentiments expressed in all the French Algerian newspapers.[30]

But Corcelle also singled out for rejection a position that sounds strikingly like Tocqueville's own. He wanted to refute, he said, those who professed to being pained to see the repression of the indigenous Algerians, but resigned themselves to it on the grounds that history proved it to be inevitable. 'The people I'm talking about console themselves for the cruelty of the repression with erudition,' he said. With their 'historical fatalism', they exonerated everyone who bears real responsibility for French atrocities, and that included 'each one of us', he suggested. Such people, Corcelle said, ask how the French could possibly save the indigenous Algerians when the Americans could not save the native Amerindians. Corcelle replied, 'We have had the honour of carrying out the French Revolution, and this is the nineteenth century.'

Tocqueville certainly shared Corcelle's distaste for colonists' racism and, in his own speech to the chamber the following day, Tocqueville praised his friend's 'noble expression of such noble ideas'. But he distanced himself from what he portrayed as Corcelle's extreme idealism. He made it clear that France's posture towards the Arabs should not be one of cooperation and conciliation. 'I want no more than [my honourable friend] does to expel the natives. Above all, I do not want to exterminate them, as has been, if not proposed, then at least suggested or insinuated several times … . But I think that to trust to the good will of the natives to keep us in Africa: that is a pure illusion to which it would be insane to attach ourselves.'[31]

In both his letter to Lamoricière and his parliamentary speech, as in so many of his writings on Algeria, Tocqueville seized the ground of realism by declaring the need to accept a certain degree of violence. Tocqueville positioned himself on this question, as he so often did, as a pragmatist and a moderate. He rejected both General Lamoricière's view that peaceful domination over the Arab tribes was impossible, and Corcelle's contrary belief that the French must seek Arab cooperation. Although he claimed that genuine Arab support for French rule was a chimera, Tocqueville wanted to achieve something beyond perpetual war. Drawing on his study of the British in India and America, Tocqueville hoped instead that the French might be able to subdue Algeria politically, by manipulating social cleavages within Arab society.[32]

As Tocqueville travelled around Algeria several months later, he assured Corcelle that he was keeping in mind his friend's great concern for the indigenous people; but he continued to insist that this concern must not eclipse the broader goal of securing the colony for French settlement. In a letter written from Marseilles just before he embarked for the colony, Tocqueville wrote, 'You tell me, my dear friend, that the great question in Africa is to know how to arrange our relations with the natives. I am of your opinion that this is one of the great sides of the question and nothing will attract my attention more vividly. All the same, it is, in my view, only a part of the question. The question of Africa itself, in all its variety and its grandeur, for me can be summarized thus: how can we manage to create in Africa a French population with our laws, our mores, our civilization, while still preserving vis-à-vis the indigenous people all the considerations that justice, humanity, our interest well understood, and, as you have said, our honour strictly oblige us to preserve? The question has these two sides. One cannot usefully imagine the first without seeing the second'.[33]

By 1847, when Tocqueville wrote two reports for a parliamentary commission on Algeria, he had been chastened by the wanton violence of the French army and had concluded that the government in Algeria was disorderly, tyrannical, and 'profoundly illiberal'. The reports articulated the widespread discomfort in Paris and the Chamber with Bugeaud's strategies, especially his insistence on military rather than civilian colonization, and his brutal punitive expeditions against the Kabyles, whom Tocqueville had long insisted should be conquered 'peacefully' and through commerce.[34] In contrast to Tocqueville's earlier writings, which actively advocated conquest in the face of official indecision and general indifference, his 1847 reports spoke of the conquest, and the settlement, of Algeria as a fait accompli. The task now was to rule securely without having to continue the dramatic troop escalations of the past decade, to develop a proper legal system for the existing European population and to promote its growth, and to govern the Arabs as a society apart, encouraging them to adopt certain aspects of Western civilization while keeping them in their place.

Tocqueville preserved a hope that European rule over the indigenous Algerians would become regularized, sustained through custom and a recognition of French authority rather than remaining 'accepted only as the work of victory and the daily product of force'. But he also insisted that Muslims were not fellow citizens or equals; moreover, it was just to treat them as inferiors, since that was what they expected from French domination. In sum, the French owed the Arabs good government and 'exact, but rigorous, justice ... when they act reprehensibly toward us'.[35] Plans for the assimilation of Arabs, such as Tocqueville earlier had supported, and efforts to transplant 'European civilization' to North Africa, were, he now believed, futile and misguided. At best the French could hope to weaken indigenous hostility to French rule and win the population's support, not through ideas but by demonstrating their common interests.

Moments of caution in the reports indicate a retreat from the harshness of Tocqueville's earlier and quite ruthless 'Travail sur l'Algérie'. The intervening years had been those of Bugeaud's governor-generalship in Algeria: an era of what Tocqueville had come to see as increasing military arrogance and intransigence, of growing hostility between soldiers and civilian settlers, and of the brutal razzias that had terrorized the Arab population without subduing them.[36] Tocqueville, along with many in Paris, had by this point turned against Bugeaud and his tactics, and the first report indicated that new restraint with a typically accurate Tocquevillian prediction:

> If on the contrary we were to demonstrate by our behaviour – without saying so, for these things are often done but never admitted – that in our eyes the old inhabitants of Algeria are merely an obstacle to be pushed aside or trampled under foot, if we surrounded their populations, not to lift them in our arms towards well-being and enlightenment but to destroy and smother them, the question between the two races would be that of life or death. Algeria would become, sooner or later, a closed field, a walled arena, where the two peoples would have to fight without mercy, and where one of the two would have to die. May God save us, gentlemen, from such a destiny!

Let us not, in the middle of the nineteenth century, begin the history of the conquest of America over again.[37]

The humanity of this passage must not be exaggerated, however. It was underpinned by Tocqueville's new confidence that France's 'domination' over Algeria had never been more secure. Still, in these parliamentary reports, the last extended treatment Tocqueville would give to the question of empire, we glimpse as well his increasing disillusionment with the colonial experiment. As Tocqueville's explicit involvement in the Algerian question drew to a close at the end of the 1840s, he seems to have become more sensitive to the moral problems of empire, without relinquishing any of his earlier faith that a French colony could and should be maintained in Algeria.

There is a certain tragedy in the development of Tocqueville's engagement with Algeria. He began, filled with national pride and fierce determination, by imagining a French bastion in North Africa that might establish France's international reputation as a great power. He overcame his early ambivalence about the conquest with resolutions to see it through. Tocqueville's hopes for what might be achieved in Algeria constantly diminished over the course of his career.[38] If he dreamed at the beginning of an intermingling of French and Arabs, he soon came to insist on the need for European settlement to consolidate rule. In the end, his fear that settlement only worsened the antagonism between conquerors and subjects prompted still deeper ambivalence on Tocqueville's part about the viability of colonial empires. These were misgivings that he seems not to have pursued in relation to Algeria, about which he wrote almost nothing after 1847, as he turned his attention to France's pressing domestic troubles and then to French history, in his lifelong effort to craft a historical vision and a political order for France that could bear the weight of modern democracy.[39]

The Sepoy rebellion that took place in British India in 1857–8 seems to have led Tocqueville to think deeply about empire as he had not for nearly a decade and in particular to revisit his doubts about the wisdom of attempting to consolidate imperial rule with European settlement. He wrote to his English friend Henry Reeve that whenever Europeans settle among less civilized peoples, European superiority, both real and pretended, proved so 'mortifying to the self-respect of the indigenous people that more anger resulted from that than from any political oppression'.[40] The Sepoy rebellion was not an uprising against oppression, Tocqueville wrote, but 'the revolt of barbarism against pride'.

Tocqueville told Reeve he would go so far as to prohibit the purchase of land by European settlers in India: a far cry from his earlier projects for giving state lands in Algeria to colonists to encourage settlement. The equivocations of one letter offer a particularly stark display of Tocqueville's ambivalence about colonial expansion. In 1857, as the rebellion was going on, he wrote to Lord Hatherton, a British former MP, that he 'never for an instant doubted your triumph, which is that of Christianity and of civilization'.[41] Still, Tocqueville told Hatherton, after as careful a study as he could make without visiting India, he had concluded that England had done little more in the colony than take the place of indigenous governments and rule with the same methods, if somewhat more mildly and equitably. He wrote,

> I admit to youthat the thought still stays with me from this study that the English had not in a century done anything for the Indian populations that might have been expected from their enlightenment and their institutions. I think that more could have been expected from them.[42]

He described the British 'task' as 'not only to dominate India, but to civilize it. These two things, indeed, are closely connected.'[43] It should be noted that Tocqueville's letters to English correspondents consistently display a tone rather different from that of his other writings on empire, in that they treat empire as a *collective* European, or Christian, project and emphasize its civilizing aspect. Even when thus deploying the rhetoric of the *mission civilisatrice*, however, Tocqueville registered doubts, rarely shared by his English correspondents, about whether any European empire had ever benefited its subjects. As in his Algeria writings, Tocqueville was unwilling, in his late observations on British India, to rule out violent domination as an imperial tool. This letter thus displays three recurrent modes of Tocqueville's writings on empire: a vague hope that European empire will civilize the rest of the world; a doubt, based on careful study of administrative records, that European governments ever actually succeed in improving their colonial subjects; and an acknowledgement of violence as a necessary element of colonial rule.

Conclusion

Tocqueville was convinced that France's power and reputation within Europe would rely, increasingly, on its colonial possessions. I have suggested that Tocqueville's concern for French glory and reputation in

Europe, and his desire that the nation join in collective enterprises in order to preserve its liberty, lay behind his enthusiasm for the colonization of North Africa, even if Tocqueville himself never articulated the argument quite so explicitly.[44] Tocqueville felt deeply the imperatives of nation building, and every one of his works attested to his fear that French liberty was fragile, far more vulnerable than the liberty of America or Great Britain. Tocqueville's fear that Frenchmen in his day were dangerously apolitical, preoccupied by their petty personal affairs, was exacerbated by the thought that there were no longer opportunities for glorious action. He saw large-scale empires– both glorious military conquest and prosperous settlement – as among the only arenas for grand political gestures in his day. Two pursuits that seemed to him worthy of a great nation were imperial expansion and the abolition of slavery in the French West Indies.[45] His fierce sense of rivalry with Britain, which competed with his admiration for the country's political and social institutions, encouraged his belief that national projects that earned British respect– as both empire and abolition were likely to do – would be of a particularly valuable kind.

Tocqueville feared that the spread of democratic social and political culture would compromise other values, including, most importantly, the liberty that he believed was characteristic of aristocracies, and which he worried would be difficult to replicate under conditions of equality. Although Tocqueville believed that democracy was providential and just, he also confronted the emergence of democratic society with trepidation. This was especially so in France, where that process had involved revolution and dictatorship and would see both return before the end of Tocqueville's life. Tocqueville responded to such anxieties, in part, by turning to the conquest of Algeria as a political experiment that might lend dynamism and confidence to a weak French public.

To build a cohesive, stable and liberal domestic political order after the collapse of the *ancien régime*, revolutionary upheaval, and continuing political turmoil was Tocqueville's self-appointed task as a political thinker and actor. The notion of a proud French presence in Algeria, a vibrant and glorious new America filled with prosperous farms and engaged settler-citizens, played an important if long-overlooked part in Tocqueville's nation-building project. That Tocqueville recognized and accepted the violence of empire, despite his failure to develop a theoretically satisfying justification for it, testifies both to his clear-sightedness about the moral costs of the policies he recommended, and the moral callousness with which Tocqueville was willing to legitimate imperial exploits. The suggestion of Tocqueville's writings on Algeria, then, is that the development of a stable and liberal democratic regime might require the exploitation of non-European societies, might legitimate suspending principles of human equality and self-determination abroad in order to secure, first, glory and, eventually, virtue and stable liberty, at home, in France. In choosing to pursue national glory through empire, Tocqueville condoned – and indeed advocated – the subjugation of the Algerians for the sake of French national consolidation.

Such views constituted in an important sense a moral abdication on Tocqueville's part. But they also attest to his struggle, as a liberal political thinker, with one of the key questions of nineteenth-century politics. How were European societies to make the transition from the old autocratic regimes to republics without succumbing to anarchy or state terror? Tocqueville's arguments for French imperial expansion demonstrate forcefully the degree to which a concern to place the modern democratic nation on secure footing drew French liberals of his day into an exclusionary and violent international politics that so many of their predecessors, from Diderot to Condorcet to Constant, would have seen as a betrayal of liberal humanitarianism.

Notes

1 Alexis de Tocqueville, *Oeuvres complètes*, ed. J.-P. Mayer (Paris: Gallimard, 1951-), 1.i, p. 5 (hereinafter cited as OC). Translated as *Democracy in America*, trans. George Lawrence, ed. J.P. Mayer (New York: Harper & Row, 1966), p. 12 (hereinafter cited as Lawrence).
2 See, e.g., his remarks on the British conquest of India: 'For those who study the facts attentively, the event remains great, but it ceases to be inexplicable.' Tocqueville, OC 3.i, p. 443. All translations are mine unless otherwise noted.
3 For Tocqueville's claim that he sought, as foreign minister, to develop a 'liberal' foreign policy that lived up to the 'principles of our Revolution: liberty, equality, and clemency', see his *Souvenirs*. (*Recollections*, trans. George Lawrence, ed. J.P. Mayer and A.P. Kerr (New Brunswick: Transaction, 1995), p. 240, n. 6.
4 OC 15.ii, p. 263. It is telling that the specific examples Tocqueville provided of such displays of public virtue in France often involved military action rather than domestic political efforts of the kind he applauded in America.
5 OC 3.i, p. 89; Tocqueville, *Writings on Empire and Slavery*, ed. and trans. Jennifer Pitts (Baltimore: Johns Hopkins University Press, 2001), p. 70 (hereinafter cited as *Empire and Slavery*).
6 A few readers have emphasized Tocqueville's arguments that European rule would civilize Asia and Africa: see George Frederickson, *The Comparative Imagination: On the History of Racism, Nationalism, and Social Movements* (Berkeley: University of California Press, 1997), p. 113; and Roger Boesche, 'The Dark Side of Tocqueville: On War and Empire', *Review of Politics*, 67

(2005), pp. 737–52; though see Boesche on Tocqueville's Montesquieuian sense of social complexity.

See Françoise Mélonio on the 'duplicity' of Tocqueville's appeal to a civilizing mission; 'Nations et nationalismes', *The Tocqueville Review/La Revue Tocqueville*, 18(1) (1997), pp. 61–75 at p. 70.

7 Letter to Francisque (Claude) Corcelle, 26 September 1840; OC 15.i, p. 151.

8 Tocqueville himself recognized that some of his views would be ascribed to latent sympathy for the old-regime aristocracy, but he denied the bias, perhaps too confident in his intellectual independence: 'Democratic or aristocratic prejudices are alternatively attributed to me; I would perhaps have had one or the other had I been born in another century and country. But accident of birth has left me free to defend both … . The aristocracy was already dead when I was born, and democracy had not yet come into being. My instincts could not therefore be drawn blindly toward either one or the other,' he wrote in a letter to his friend and future translator Henry Reeve (22 March 1837) in OC 6.ii, pp. 37–8.

9 OC 3.i, pp. 226–7; *Empire and Slavery*, p. 70. Tocqueville also described Bugeaud's system of razzias as 'excellent' and wrote of Bugeaud, 'C'est le seul homme de ce pays' (Letter to Louis Kergorlay, Algiers, 23 May 1841; Tocqueville, *Lettres choisies; Souvenirs*, ed. Françoise Mélonio and Laurence Guellec [Paris: Gallimard, 2003], p. 477).

10 Seloua Luste Boulbina has noted that Tocqueville, animated rather by a concern to limit French risks than by principle, repeatedly attempted to steer a 'third way' between what he depicted as the excesses of the colonists and the anti-colonialists: ' "Neither … nor": that was his slogan.' He foundered, she suggests, on the insoluble challenge of creating a liberal, republican French government in a country at war: 'Présentation', in *Tocqueville: sur L'Algérie*, ed. Seloua Boulbina (Paris: Flammarion, 2003), pp. 36–8.

11 François Furet and Françoise Mélonio (eds), *The Old Regime and the Revolution*, trans. Alan S. Kahan (Chicago: University of Chicago Press, 1998), p. 86; Jack Lively, *The Social and Political Thought of Alexis de Tocqueville*. (Oxford: Clarendon Press, 1962), p. 29. See *Ibid.*, chapter 2 (especially pp. 42ff.), for a discussion of Tocqueville's beliefs about the moral import of historical and sociological study.

12 Melvin Richter has noted that only a commitment to French national interest above everything else or a blindness to the 'moral choices inherent in any colonial adventure' could have enabled Tocqueville to persuade himself that territory conquered through the razzia would ever be administered in the interest of the defeated, in 'Tocqueville on Algeria', *Review of Politics*, 25 (1963), pp. 362–98. Cheryl Welch has deepened our understanding of that blindness with her psychologically subtle reading of Tocqueville's violations or evasions, in his treatments of Algeria, of many of his own moral commitments and intuitions, and his 'efforts to make colonial violence absent to his imagination', in 'Colonial Violence and the Rhetoric of Evasion', *Political Theory*, 31.2 (2003) p. 257.

13 See Chevallier and Jardin, 'Introduction', OC 3.i, pp. 12–13; the questionnaire is undated, but the editors surmise it dates to around 1833.

14 'Some ideas about what prevents the French from having good colonies' (1833), OC 3.i, pp. 35–9; *Empire and Slavery*, pp. 1–4.

15   *Democracy*, vol. I, part 2, chapter 9. Also see Tocqueville's evocative 'Quinze jours dans le désert,' OC 5:i, p. 342–87. Translated by George Wilson Pierson as 'A fortnight in the wilderness', in *Tocqueville in America* (Baltimore: John Hopkins University Press, 1996 [1938]).

16   OC 3.i, pp. 129–153; *Empire and Slavery*, pp. 5–26. On Tocqueville's early electoral bids, see André Jardin, *Tocqueville: A Biography*. Trans. Lydia Davis (New York: Farrar Straus Giroux, 1988), pp. 279–96. Jardin notes the significance of Tocqueville's choice to write about Algeria as he formally entered elective politics. The articles were anonymous by custom, but their authorship was widely known. *Ibid.*, p. 320.

17   'First letter', OC 3.i, p. 138, *Empire and Slavery*, p. 12.

18   See *Democracy*, vol. I, OC 1.i, pp. 350–1, Lawrence, p. 335.

19   'Essay on Algeria', OC 3.i, p. 221, *Empire and Slavery*, p. 64.

20   *Le Moniteur universel* announced their arrival in Algiers in May 1841; see OC 5.ii, p. 199, and Mary Lawlor, *Alexis de Tocqueville in the Chamber of Deputies* (Washington, DC: Catholic University of America Press, 1959), p. 133.

21   Tocqueville has been called one of the 'artisans of [France's] colonial renaissance'; René Valet, *L'Afrique du Nord devant le parlement au XIXme siècle* (Alger: Imprimerie 'La typo-litho', 1924), p. 145.

22   Tocqueville was critical of not just the civilian government, especially its failure to protect property rights, but also the military leadership and in particular Bugeaud's consistent refusal to assist civilian colonization; see Jean-Louis Benoît, *Tocqueville: un destin paradoxal* (Paris: Bayard, 2005), pp. 269–71.

23   OC 5.ii, p. 192, *Empire and Slavery*, p. 37; 'wilderness' is in English. In a letter to his wife of 9 May, quoted by his French editor, Tocqueville wrote, 'Beyond the last outposts, war and desert begin. I say desert in the sense of *wilderness* and not desert.' For the complete letter, see OC 14, p. 419.

24   Entry of 7 May 1841. OC 5.ii, p. 191; *Empire and Slavery*, p. 36. Timothy Mitchell argues that Tocqueville, like other European visitors of Middle Eastern societies in his day, too readily took the 'visible exterior' of Algiers to be 'a representation of the invisible *vie intérieure*'; *Colonising Egypt* (Cambridge: Cambridge University Press, 1988), pp. 56–8.

25   Letter to Lamoricière, Paris, 5 April 1846, Tocqueville, *Lettres choisies*, p. 566.

26   *Essay on Algeria*, OC 3.i, p. 252; *Empire and Slavery*, p. 91; also see *Empire and Slavery*, pp. 95–6 for Tocqueville's argument that there is 'at once too little and too much centralization' in the administration of Algeria.

27   OC 3.i, pp. 315–16; *Empire and Slavery*, p. 135.

28   OC 5.ii, p. 192, *Empire and Slavery*, p. 37.

29   See letter to Lamoricière, Paris, 5 April 1846, *Lettres choisies*, p. 562.

30   'The newspapers in Algeria publish the most odious maxims against the indigenous people,' Corcelle said. Citing such passages as 'The extinction of this guilty race is a harmony,' Corcelle said, 'I am astonished that such provocations to the murder of an entire people are permitted in Algeria.' *Moniteur Universel*, 9 June 1846, p. 1716.

31   OC 3.i, pp. 293–4; *Empire and Slavery*, p. 118.

32   The weaknesses and vices of Indian institutions and princes, Tocqueville argued, had proven an 'inexhaustible fund' from which the British East India Company drew, sometimes even inadvertently, to enhance its power; see OC 3.i, p. 458.

33 Letter to Corcelle of 10 October 1846, OC 6.ii, p. 127; also see Chevallier and Jardin, 'Introduction', 3.i, p. 32. Corcelle's own concern about the effects of the conquest on indigenous Algerians seems to have impressed itself upon Tocqueville, for his letters to Corcelle include some of Tocqueville's most thoughtful and ambivalent remarks on the subject.

34 OC 3.i, p. 361; *Empire and Slavery*, p. 172; see his similar remarks of 1837 at 20. Jean-Louis Benoît argues that Tocqueville saw colonial war as a means to a political end and turned against Bugeaud as it came to seem, especially during the assaults on Kabylia, that for Bugeaud war was an end in itself; *Tocqueville: un destin paradoxal*, pp. 275–6.

35 OC 3.i, p. 323; *Empire and Slavery*, p. 141.

36 On Bugeaud's conquests, see Charles-André Julien, *Histoire de l'Algérie contemporaine* (Paris: Presses Universitaires de France, 1964), I, pp. 167–269; Antony Thrall Sullivan, *Thomas-Robert Bugeaud* (Hamden: Archon, 1983), pp. 77–93, and the collection of Bugeaud's letters and documents *Par l'épée et par la charrue*, ed. Paul Azan (Paris: Presses Universitaires de France, 1948).

37 'First report', OC 3.1, pp. 329–30; *Empire and Slavery*, p. 146.

38 Jean-Louis Benoît has rightly insisted on the importance of a 'diachronic' interpretation of Tocqueville's thought on Algeria during this highly volatile period of the colony's inception and expansion; *Comprendre Tocqueville* (Paris: Armand Colin, 2004), p. 126.

39 Tocqueville, who served as foreign minister in 1848–9, was president of a parliamentary sub-commission on Algerian legislation; his papers include a large collection of government documents on Algeria from that time, concerned primarily with facilitating civilian settlement. See Papiers Alexis de Tocqueville, *Archives de la Manche*, AT 2688.

40 Letter to Henry Reeve of 30 January 1858; OC 6.i; *Selected Letters*, p. 363.

41 27 November 1857. *Oeuvres complètes*, ed. Gustave de Beaumont (Paris: Michel Lévy-frères, 1864–6), VI, p. 422 (hereinafter cited as OCB), *Selected Letters*, p. 359. Todorov quotes the second sentence of this passage, but in ignoring the rest of the letter, he overstates Tocqueville's belief that European imperialism was a civilizing project, even while he concedes that in the cases that Tocqueville knew well, he did not believe that civilization had occurred in practice. Todorov, *On Human Diversity: Nationalism, Racism, and Exoticism in French Thought* (Cambridge, MA: Harvard University Press, 1994), p. 194.

42 He recommended that the British parliament abolish the East India Company and assume direct administrative responsibility for the country: as his anti-slavery articles suggest, Tocqueville believed that the greatest problems of colonial government stemmed from a lack of metropolitan interest in the colonies.

43 OCB VI, pp. 422–3, *Selected Letters*, pp. 359–60.

44 Michael Hereth argues that Tocqueville 'never applied his knowledge of the evil consequences of foreign rule to Algeria' because in this context he adopted an 'exclusively French viewpoint', one that demonstrates the 'limits of Tocqueville's understanding of politics and freedom' but that also attests to Tocqueville's belief that politics must appeal to the passions of the people. Hereth, *Alexis De Tocqueville: Threats to Freedom in Democracy* (Durham: Duke University Press, 1986), pp. 161–2.

45 Tocqueville cited the British abolition of slavery as one great event of his day that suggested that the decadence of his age was not yet total. 'We are often unjust towards our times. Our fathers saw such extraordinary things that, in comparison with their accomplishments, all those of our contemporaries seem commonplace. Still, the world today offers some great spectacles that would astonish us if we were not weary and distracted'; 'The emancipation of slaves', OC 3.i, p. 79; *Empire and Slavery*, p. 199.

3
Creating *Concitoyens*: Tocqueville on the Legacy of Slavery

Cheryl Welch

Introduction

From his entry into the Chamber of Deputies in 1839 to his principled withdrawal from political life a decade later, Tocqueville was guided by his deep-seated desire to negotiate a practical transition to democracy without sacrificing liberty. But he never managed to carve out a leading political role in the July Monarchy; instead, he steered an independent and uncertain course among the opposition. He was most visible not as a party leader or follower, but as a neutral expert on philanthropic and foreign policy issues: prison reform, public charity, military affairs, North African policy, and the abolition of colonial slavery. Of these, the cause that Tocqueville thought most clearly transcended 'petty politics' was slave emancipation in the French colonies. It also posed the most stubborn and frustrating of dilemmas. Abolition offered French policy-makers the chance to promote liberty, but in circumstances decidedly not of their choosing. Indeed, to borrow a phrase from Marx, those circumstances 'weigh[ed] like a nightmare on the brain of the living'.[1] Under the pressures of the democratic revolution, ties of mutual loyalty among equal citizens had come to have an important role in self-government. Yet the introduction of modern slavery had created exclusionary identities in which democratic majorities shunned and dehumanized subordinated groups, who in turn fashioned solidarity out of victimization.

The problem of democratic identity in the context of formerly slave societies may seem like a peripheral subject in Tocqueville studies. I argue in this essay, however, that Tocqueville's attempts to free democratic societies of the nightmare of modern race slavery illuminate both a central theme of his major works and a characteristic aspect of his style. His acceptance of the challenge of emancipation illustrates Tocqueville's preoccupation with distinguishing what is fated or determined in social life from what is responsive to political action and choice. He treads this line both in his abolitionist rhetoric and in his speculations on the possibility of turning ex-masters and ex-slaves into a society of fellow citizens (*semblables*) who share ideas, practices, and sentiments. These writings also employ a pattern of argumentation evident in his more analytical work: the tendency to think in 'contrasting pairs'.[2] The portraits of post-emancipation societies in the United States and in the French Caribbean, I argue, mirror each other in rhetorical tension: the first a distorted doppelgänger of history gone awry, the second a hopeful image of a future shaped by wise leadership. Finally, in addition to revealing these distinctive approaches to political analysis, Tocqueville's reflections on race and slavery – like so many of his texts – raise questions that are still central to liberal democratic theory. How do the tendencies of modern democracy interact with identity politics? And to what extent can the state intervene to defuse tensions between 'peoples', thus creating a new society of *concitoyens*?

This chapter proceeds as follows. The first section outlines the moral discourse of anti-slavery among French liberals in the Restoration and the July Monarchy, using Tocqueville's colleague Charles de Rémusat as an example. The second situates Tocqueville within this moral and political landscape. The third and fourth contrast Tocqueville's projection of the nightmare of post-emancipation America with his dream of creating a stable and prosperous society in the French sugar colonies. Finally, I consider Tocqueville's success in thinking about how to refound societies fractured by the legacy of slavery and racial antipathy.

Rémusat and the moral case against slavery

Much of the secondary literature about Tocqueville and slavery rightly focuses on the American case, for Tocqueville and his American travelling companion Gustave de Beaumont first confront the interpenetration of slavery and democratic society in the United States.[3] Nevertheless, they approach the problem of race and slavery in America with the general sensibilities of French philanthropic anti-slavery reformers, a movement whose themes are already set in the Restoration in connection with the *Société de la morale chrétienne*. Founded at the end of 1821 and active throughout the 1820s, the Society was led by a small number of liberal Catholics and French Protestants.[4] Officers or committee members included the leading lights of the liberal opposition, from the 'centre' to the 'extreme left' (among them Victor de Broglie – the first president – and Benjamin Constant, François Guizot, Charles Comte, Charles Dunoyer, Prosper de Barante, J.-D. Lanjuinais, Charles de Montalembert, Adolphe Thiers, Casimir Périer, and Charles Rémusat). The most active committee of the society was concerned with ending the slave trade, and indirectly with the abolition of slavery itself.

The key event for anti-slavery activists in France during the July Monarchy was the British Parliament's abolition of colonial slavery, which officially took effect in August 1834. As a direct result of British events, French supporters of emancipation in the Chamber of Deputies formed the *Société française pour l'abolition de l'esclavage*. Tocqueville and Beaumont were charter members of this elite association. Thus, just as he was completing the first *Démocratie*, Tocqueville joined a relatively small group of intellectuals and politicians struggling to move French debate and public opinion towards abolition.

In contrast to the situation in England, economic, political, and diplomatic factors conspired to make abolition seem risky and imprudent to a significant portion of the French elite. Whereas English reformers eventually appealed to the masses, mobilizing opinion in one of the first popular democratic reform movements, the minority of the French elite who favoured abolition was reluctant to disturb the indifference of the French masses. Ever conscious of the dangerous lessons of the French Revolution and of the example of Saint-Domingue, their fear of popular mobilization fed a politics of postponement.[5] A series of abolition initiatives sparked dilatory debates, requests for further study, and tabled reports. By the mid-1830s there was no need for the French pro-slavery lobby to make principled arguments against emancipation. They could rely on the complete success of delaying tactics to render legal emancipation a moot point for the foreseeable future.[6]

Despite the political paralysis surrounding abolition, or perhaps because of it, high-minded condemnation of the evils of slavery was a staple of liberal argument during the Restoration and July Monarchy. The writings of Charles de Rémusat give a particularly good sense of the characteristic features of this anti-slavery rhetoric: first, the rejection of reason or natural rights as an argument against slavery in favour of Christian teaching and, second, the frequent analogy between the pernicious effects of colonial slavery – on both masters and slaves – and the spiritual anarchy impeding the development of free political *moeurs* in France.[7]

In *L'habitation de Saint Domingue ou l'insurrection*, an unpublished but widely read play written in 1825, Rémusat fictionalizes the slave revolt in Saint-Domingue, drawing out the connection between religion and anti-slavery in a liberal morality tale for his own generation.[8] The dramatic action centres on the slave Hélène, her 'husband' Timur, who eventually leads a slave insurrection, and the planter's son Léon, whose casual rape of Hélène and later moral epiphanies precipitate much of the action. Other stock figures are the brutal overseer, the kindly *curé*, and the cynical emissary from revolutionary Paris, M. de Tendale.

A caricature of the *philosophe*-become-revolutionary, Tendale spouts a combination of superficial indictments of slavery based on abstract natural right and brutal justifications of immoral acts committed in the name of popular sovereignty.[9] The point is clear and unsubtle: revolutionary ideology untethered to faith leads to violence and terror. Political action based on reason alone cannot bring about either the end of colonial slavery or the regeneration of metropolitan political life. Not the shallow rationalist Tendale, but rather the semi-heroic figures of a redeemed Léon and a converted Timur are the moral exemplars in Rémusat's play. Both are transformed by exposure to the *curé*, a nineteenth-century *vicaire savoyard* who represents the reconciling power of Christian morality. At the beginning of the play Léon has no difficulty articulating his belief in Rousseau, Voltaire, and the rights of man even as he espouses an extreme theory of the planters' right to despotic rule. In a nice touch, he names his personal slave Jean-Jacques. Yet Léon cannot maintain his belief in the legitimacy of his own privilege and at the same time open himself to the power of Christian teaching about equality. On this view, the contradiction between slavery and Christianity counts for more than the contradiction between slavery and the rights of man.

French abolitionist rhetoric, then, concentrated on revealing the contradictions between slavery and an allegedly universal consensus on Christian moral teaching. Slavery was an evil so obviously shocking to the conscience that it could have no moral defenders. In a report on the work of the *Société de la morale chrétienne* written in the same year as Rémusat's play, Charles Coquerel describes the sacrilegious trafficking in fellow souls as a practice that encourages 'perfidy, theft, murder, greed, and avarice', a practice 'made conspicuous in the annals of evil by the hateful distinction of gathering all crimes into one ultimate crime.'[10] During the July Monarchy, abolitionists continue to recoil in horror before an unnatural phenomenon whose name, in the words of Rémusat in his 1838 parliamentary report, 'is odious in Europe'.[11] In its modern guise of black chattel slavery, slavery not only contradicted both justice and humanity but also constituted a sacrilegious forgetting of the slave's status as a fellow soul.[12]

If Rémusat and other anti-slavery reformers portrayed the enslavement of fellow children of God as a sinful process that perverted the nature of Christian societies, what did they propose as redress for this 'crime?' In the case of the slave trade, the practical issues appeared to be uncomplicated. Confidence that the trade could safely be outlawed immediately was bolstered by the belief that masters would then treat existing slave populations more humanely, if only because of their need to guarantee reproduction among the workforce. But the question of the institution of slavery itself appeared more intractable, precisely because of the assumption that slavery had created two sets of moral monsters: masters and slaves. Abruptly severing the legal ties that bound them together, leaving them free to act on their brutalized instincts, would lead only to monstrous acts. The moral and political duty to abolish slavery, then, seemed to require attention to spiritual regeneration: both masters and slaves must be transformed before they could be trusted with freedom. The rhetoric of spiritual enlightenment (to promote the recognition of fellow souls) and spiritual discipline (to restrain the impulse to retaliate) paralleled the larger post-revolutionary quest for a *pouvoir spirituel* that would enter politics covertly by influencing private conscience.

The need for a spiritual transformation of both oppressors and oppressed is a central theme of Rémusat's anti-slavery play. The heroic self-redemption of the planter's son, Léon, shows how Christian inspiration can restrain the greed for sugar profits and the desire to tyrannize over equals even as it promotes noble action. On this account, it is above all Christianity's veneration of law, work, and marriage that effects these transformations among the ruling elite. Leon's moral epiphany comes when he realizes that the slave leader Timur wants vengeance as a dishonoured husband: 'Timur did ... what any man of conscience [*homme de cœur*] would have done, what I would doubtless have done in his place.'[13] Reframing his own actions as sinful and acceptance of Timur as a fellow moral creature emerge together. This litany of the uplifting moral force of the new trinity – law, work, and marriage – also underlies the hope that slaves can be morally regenerated. Exposure to Christian teaching both restrains the slave leader Timur and stimulates orderly habits. He first exercises mercy when his wife Hélène reminds him that the *curé* had recognized the couple's humanity by encouraging them to form an exclusive union. And he emerges as an enlightened leader because he has grasped both the sanctity and utility of work and self-restraint.[14] Indeed, Rémusat suggests that the planters were quite correct to fear that true Christian teaching would ultimately undermine their hegemony. It would turn slaves into moral agents and thus free men.

By effecting an inner calibration of judgement, then, a purified Christianity – both in the world of anti-slavery rhetoric and post-revolutionary liberalism more generally – could restrain and empower both elites and masses. During the July Monarchy, when abolition of slavery forever hovered on the political horizon, the dynamic of restraint and empowerment implicit in *moralization* appeared in some form in every project of slave emancipation.

Tocqueville and the moral case for abolition

I have argued that French abolitionists made an uncompromising religious case against slavery, but embroiled themselves in an immobilizing rhetoric of 'not yet' in part because of their anxious perception that those deformed by the slave relationship must be morally transformed before the relationship could be ended. They all agreed, more or less, on how this transformation could be effected: by encouraging marriage and the formation of families and by spreading basic religious instruction, especially regarding the universal duty to work and to obey a law superior to individual passions, an *autorité sainte*.[15] In 1839, at the beginning of his parliamentary report on slavery, Tocqueville echoed this familiar rhetoric – 'enlighten [the slave's] religion, regularize his mores, create a family for him, extend and fortify his intelligence so that he can conceive of the future and develop foresight'[16] – even as he deplored its cooptation by the pro-slavery lobby and its unfortunate tendency to paralyze the efforts of fellow abolitionists.

Like others in the philanthropic reform movement, Tocqueville's conviction that slavery was unjust and unjustifiable is rooted in the moral claims of Christianity and *humanité*. Slavery represented a denial of the providential unfolding of Christian ideals of universality and equal fellowship. Indeed his faith in the compatibility between religion and democracy fuelled his hope that in a democratic future people would both recognize each other as equals (*semblables*) and exercise the free will implicit in the Christian notion of responsibility for one's soul. As notions of caste are progressively eradicated and people become more alike – Tocqueville uses the verbs *se confondre, s'assimiler, s'amalgamer* – each person is freed to act as an independent moral agent. This equality and this freedom do not stop at the artificial boundaries of race. Read in the context of increasingly racialized debates about human equality in the 1820s, 30s and 40s, Tocqueville emerges clearly as a Christian monogenist on the egalitarian end of what Martin Staum has called an emerging 'spectrum of racial theory'.[17]

If Tocqueville recognized the justice of a world in which all claim liberty on the basis of their spiritual equality, he nonetheless feared the new dangers inherent in such a uniform world – spiritual isolation, individualism, and absorption in material life. These fears led him to validate the persistence of a sense of difference among particular peoples or nations that could inspire resistance to the drag of democratic uniformity. Tocqueville noted that the apparently natural limitation of strong normative obligations to one's own people was not necessarily a bad thing, for a sense of justice rooted solely in duties to humanity as a whole was unlikely to produce selfless actions. Our identification with others grows weaker as it is extended.

At first glance it seems that those moralists, above all among the Christians, who apparently forget duty to country in order to think only of humanity, who forget the fellow-citizen [*concitoyen*] for the fellow-man [*prochain*], it seems, I say, that they are right. It is in fact by taking a detour that we discover that they are wrong. Man, as God has created him (I don't know why), becomes less devoted as the object of his affections becomes larger. His heart needs the particular, it needs to limit the object of its affections in order to grasp the object in a firm and lasting embrace.[18]

Identification with fellow citizens promoted mutual trust and joint action.

Patriotic solidarity, then, could have a positive relationship to democratic liberty. But how far should the claims of particular groups extend? While valuing one's own particular fragment of humanity (*patrie particulière*[19]) helped to combat the ills of individualism, Tocqueville recognized no transcendent grounding for nations or peoples other than the likelihood of promoting liberty.[20] Democratic majorities are not morally omnipotent within their borders; their laws can be overridden by the universal claims of humanity, which limit the power of majorities to oppress and exclude. Tocqueville usually employs such vague caveats as '[j]ustice therefore sets a limit to the right of each people'[21] or majorities should be 'well directed by reason and morality'.[22] The deliberate enslavement, objectification, or destruction of a people surpasses the justifiable power of a sovereign majority. Given Tocqueville's religious belief in the essential oneness of the human community, in the divine injunction to preserve human life, and in the duties of Christian charity, the portraits of exclusion, isolation and social death associated with modern slavery are inevitably judged to be deeply unjust.

Like other French liberals, then, Tocqueville saw slavery as a glaring evil inconsistent with the spiritual sources of his liberalism. The institution of black chattel slavery was an 'accursed seed' that had unexpectedly flourished in democratic soil.[23] Yet, also like those liberals, the construction of the master–slave relationship as an extreme form of arbitrary power and servile degradation simultaneously committed him to a cautious view of emancipation. Debate over slavery appeared to be imprisoned in a vicious circle: slavery was the *summum malum* of the modern age, but hasty abolition might be worse. When Tocqueville and Beaumont first confront the interpenetration of slavery and democracy in the United States, they view it from within this rhetorical universe of moral certainty and practical immobility and are most receptive to informants who read the American situation in a similar way.[24] Indeed, they struggle to vanquish the fear that some historical situations may present only bad choices. The peaceful amalgamation of ex-masters and ex-slaves into one society may be impossible due to a deadly combination of particular and general causes. This flirtation with despair could be indulged in writings about America – especially if those circumstances could be construed as 'American not democratic'. But such fatalism would be strenuously resisted in the context of French politics, not least because acceptance of colonial slavery seemed to jeopardize (at least rhetorically) the possible rejuvenation of liberty in France itself.

American nightmares

Tocqueville and Beaumont spent little time in the American South and observed very few slaves or masters. Indeed, they departed with a conviction that the true evil of modern slavery was the complex legacy of racial antipathy and exclusion that apparently prevented the assimilation of ex-slaves into the civic polity. Beaumont subtitled *Marie, Slavery in the United States*, but his novel does not analyze slavery itself; rather it tells the story of free citizens, a brother and sister who discover that they are socially 'black' by virtue of an African ancestor, and who are then plunged into the lawless underworld of an apartheid society. This pervasively racist public opinion is the subject of the novel: '[i]t is above all these secondary consequences of an evil [slavery] whose first cause has disappeared which I have endeavored to develop.'[25]

Tocqueville and Beaumont describe an America where peoples of different races cannot be blended or fused (they consistently use the verb *se confondre*) but remain at once intermingled and separate.[26] Arthur Goldhammer has pointed to the important place of this verb in the rhetorical universe of Tocqueville's *Democracy in America*; it connotes a commingling in which substances merge and lose their distinctiveness. He therefore translates *se confondre* as 'blended' rather than 'intermingled' to capture the distinction that Tocqueville maintains throughout his discussions of the results of contact and conflict among peoples. Peoples who are intermingled or intermixed (*entremêlés*), or who live side by side (*côte à côte*), retain their distinctiveness and remain separate and potentially isolated. If two peoples are *confondus* or *assimilés*, however, they lose their particular identities and become merged in a new one.[27]

The paradigmatic case of such a process of fusion is the breakdown of caste barriers, which dissolve over generations with the lessening of economic distance and the increase of daily contact and common interests.[28] When visible signs such as colour demarcate castes, however, the process of blending slows and becomes infinitely more difficult. Consequently, formerly subordinated peoples may be shunned or driven out before they can be assimilated. Indeed, in the northern states, freed Africans are economically exploited, prevented from exercising civil and political rights, socially isolated, and gradually eliminated – a misery empirically confirmed in their allegedly high mortality rate.[29] Given his assumptions about exclusionary tendencies, Tocqueville believed that emancipation in the southern states would lead to a race war that could mean the expulsion or massacre of whites.

In America, certain social psychological effects of both democratic equality and democratic liberty thwart the natural civilizing processes of commerce and *sociabilité*, thus unnaturally halting the assimilation of ex-slave populations. Because democratic equality leads to generalized anxiety about status, it increases the fear of sinking 'below the level of [one's] neighbors' and the psychological propensity to validate one's relative worth by depressing the status of others.[30] If all one has is one's citizen status, the notion of fraternizing with former slaves becomes abhorrent. In such situations the anxieties produced by equality denature democratic liberty – in an ideal world a universal attribute – by intensifying the fusion of democratic pride with racial heritage. Thus Tocqueville notes that pride of origin 'is markedly increased ... by the individual pride born of democratic liberty'.[31] Beaumont notes that democratic liberty is fragile; Anglo-Americans fear that it would be contaminated or polluted by the blackness associated with slave status.[32] Hence both Tocqueville and Beaumont note the paradox that racial exclusion is more virulent in the north, where democratic equality and liberty were more entrenched. 'Racial prejudice seems to me stronger in the states that have abolished slavery than in those where slavery still exists, and nowhere is intolerance greater than in states where servitude was unknown.'[33] Tocqueville also speculated that racism – the idea that the 'invisible influence of race' condemns 'some to freedom and others to servitude' was a materialistic idea, and materialism was a 'natural vice of the human mind' in democratic times, against which one must struggle.[34]

The dilemma presented by slavery was different in the southern states, where emancipation seemed to threaten not the rapid extinction of blacks, but rather the retaliatory annihilation of whites. Tocqueville assumes that there is no obvious place to which freed southern slaves can emigrate.[35] Schemes of gradual emancipation would never be implemented by whites because of fears of retribution by a black majority; moreover such schemes would not work because of resentment on the part of slaves who remained in bondage while others were freed.[36] African slaves, then, would have to be emancipated en masse, and would *ipso facto* become the majority before undergoing any economic and religious apprenticeship to liberty. Like the French peasant in the eighteenth century, however, the southern slave would not forgo this sudden opportunity for retaliation against former masters: 'there is no way to prevent him from learning enough to appreciate the extent of his afflictions and conceive a vague idea of the remedy. More than that, a singular principle of relative justice lies deep within the human heart.'[37] In Beaumont's *Marie*, like Rémusat's *L'habitation*, injustice leads to revenge and revolution.

> It is true that according to law a Negro is not a man; he is a chattel, A thing. Yes, but you will see that he is a thinking thing, an acting thing, that can hold a dagger! Inferior race! So you say! ... You are mistaken ... [I]n that brutish head there is a compartment that contains a powerful faculty, that of revenge – an implacable vengeance, horrible but intelligent.[38]

Tocqueville draws the following conclusion: '[i]f we assume that Whites and emancipated Negroes are to occupy the same land and face each other as foreign peoples, it is easy to see that the future holds only two prospects: either Negroes or Whites must blend altogether [*se confondre*] or they must separate'.[39] Tocqueville assumed that the North would not come to the aid of the southern white minority in a war to maintain slavery. Hence the strength of southern blacks (a combination of superior numbers and the emergence of a self-conscious reactionary fraternity) would lead to a black victory. In an ironic response to arguments about the inherent suitability of Africans to labour in the southern climate, Tocqueville notes that this victory would leave them dominant and unrestrained in a land 'apparently destined by Providence to be theirs'.[40] Tocqueville never abandoned this pessimism about the likely consequences of emancipation in the American South. As he followed the crises that would lead to the Civil War, he allied himself to 'free soilers', that is to those who combated the spread of slavery into new territory, but despaired of abolition in the southern states.[41]

One of the clearest lessons of *De la démocratie en Amérique* was that democracy – if immoderate and unrestrained – leads to tyranny of the majority. Given the combination of particular and general causes leading to a racist and exclusionary public opinion in the United States, the subjection of freedmen in the North and the potential for reactionary black despotism in the South were stark illustrations of such tyranny. '[Of] all governments, those that have the least power over mores are free governments.'[42] The central image of Beaumont's *Marie* is the irrationality of these American mores in the matter of race – Americans perceive an illusory colour where it does not exist – but Beaumont proposes no mechanism of reform. Both Marie's resignation and George's rebellion in an aborted alliance with Amerindians lead to spiritual and physical annihilation.[43] Similarly, Tocqueville's exaggerated racial scenarios are warnings about the fusion of majority opinion and majority power in situations where one cannot count on either internalized mores or external pressure to restrain majorities from exceeding moral limits. One can then expect only 'unprecedented atrocity, which by itself reveals some profound perturbation in the laws of humanity'.[44]

What most excited Tocqueville's condemnation of the legacy of slavery in America was the complete surrender to democratic 'interest and pride' on the part of the Anglo-Americans, a surrender that led to a reckless trespassing of the bounds of civilized humanity.[45] Given the particular and general causes conspiring to support democracy's worst tendencies, and absent any inhibiting force from another people or from a higher authority, such a surrender, he argued, was perhaps inevitable. '[A]n entire people cannot rise, as it were, above itself.'[46] Indeed, in America tendencies towards tyrannical excess had grown to such unmanageable proportions that Tocqueville and Beaumont adopt a tone of mournful inevitability about man's inhumanity to man. Yet this tone serves also to reinforce rhetorically the implicit reminder: it is too late for them, but not – *à Dieu ne plaise!* – for us. Indeed, Tocqueville never succumbed to fatalism in the French case. When British emancipation seemed to open a window of opportunity for French abolitionists, he attempted to unsettle the politics of postponement with a bold state initiative.

Caribbean dreams

The essence of Tocqueville's hope to control and moderate the pernicious legacy of slavery in the French colonies can be glimpsed in his comment that a despot might succeed in mixing peoples in America, or in the contrast (also made by Beaumont) between the different patterns of racial integration in Protestant and Catholic churches.[47] Because Protestant ministers are elected, they come under the sway of tyranny of majority opinion. Hence Protestant congregations replicate the patterns of exclusion characteristic of the society in which they are embedded. Catholic priests, however, impose law, rather than conforming to it. Under the benevolent despotism of the priest who preaches the equality of Christian souls, an integrated religious confraternity may emerge. Let me turn, then, to the political analogue of this religious example.

The counter-type to nightmares of racial isolation or extermination is the dream of deliberately blending different populations into a new whole. Such societies foster a common civic identity and enough mutual recognition to sustain a common life. What makes Tocqueville's vision of social unity the opposite of oppression or race war is neither the absence of political force nor any presumed parity of influence between peoples in a multicultural community. Indeed, outside political force is necessary to create unity, and one people or nation will usually dominate. What distinguishes the positive images of new societies from the negative image of oppression and conflict is the relatively unresisted nature of the amalgamation (achieved by self-restraint on the part of the powerful and voluntary acculturation on the part of the weak) and the gradual emergence of a sense of shared fate. None of Tocqueville's accounts of successfully fused communities are purely natural and voluntary; all involve the maintenance — long or short – of a tutelary power that holds the collectivity together while a process of assimilation occurs, a power that enables peoples to mix 'in such a way as to derive the same benefits from the state of society'.[48]

Considered apart from the failed fraternization with Amerindians and Africans, the society of white Anglo-Americans, dominated by the North, is perhaps the closest approximation to a new people founded spontaneously through voluntary contact.[49] A more apt example for relations among civilized and 'savage' or 'barbarian' peoples, however, was the case of the barbarian kingdoms that absorbed and replaced the Roman Empire – a forced mixture of peoples that spawned a new and greater civilization. The key element here was long interaction in the same geographic space under steady political pressure. It is this model of transformation from above that underlies Tocqueville's hopes for the post-emancipation societies of the French Caribbean, countering his pessimistic predictions of exclusion or race war in the United States.

In 1845 Tocqueville rose to speak in the Chamber in support of yet another modest proposal to commence abolition in the sugar colonies. Against an opponent who charged Tocqueville with inconsistency, recalling the pessimistic alternatives presented in *De la démocratie en Amérique* concerning emancipation in the southern states, Tocqueville insisted that he had not changed his views. '[I]t is precisely because I thought that then, and still think it today, that I believe that the necessary prelude to any kind of emancipation is to first place the state in a superior and dominant position.'[50] If the French state exerted the proper force, it could impose itself between planters and ex-slaves and 'force the two refractory elements to combine themselves in some way in order to form one and the same people'.[51] Control by the metropole would prevent planters from imposing a racial despotism over ex-slaves and ex-slaves from rising up against their erstwhile masters.

Tocqueville's parliamentary efforts to bring about emancipation in the French Antilles are at once less overtly moralistic and more resolutely abolitionist than his discussion in *De la démocratie en Amérique* or Beaumont's in *Marie*. Tocqueville treated the moral case against slavery as accepted and beyond dispute.[52] Indeed, in a situation in which even the French planter lobby did not often defend the legitimacy of slavery, Tocqueville was impatient with rhetorical moral posturing that appeared to be contributing to political paralysis.[53] The key questions were all pragmatic: how to convince all parties that immediate emancipation was in their interest and in the long-term interest of France, and how to manage the transition to a society with free labour. In a ploy familiar from the *Démocratie*, he asserts that the process of change in the colonies is inevitable and already far advanced. Statesmen must master the forces of change, not resist them or allow the nation to drift into disaster. In an implicit and parallel response to his own analysis in the *Démocratie*, he argues that there is no constellation of particular and general forces preventing a regeneration of society in the West Indies. Hence acquiescence in the status quo is not caution but cowardice. Or, as he says elsewhere about the possibility of creating a new society in North Africa, 'God is not stopping it.'[54]

The *Rapport fait au nom de la commission chargée d'examiner la proposition de M. DeTracy, relative aux esclaves des colonies* (1839), which advocated the immediate and simultaneous emancipation of all French colonial slaves, was Tocqueville's first major political intervention after taking his seat in the Chamber of Deputies. The centrepiece of the report was a scheme of planter indemnification (carefully worded to deny that this was payment for expropriated property, since fellow souls could never have been rightfully owned) and the recommendation that the French state assume heightened political and economic controls during the period of transition.[55] He argued that the French were faced with an opportunity to 'regenerate and save' colonial society; the state could impose a transitional regime with new laws, new administrative rulings, and new functionaries; it could take charge in a 'firm and prudent' manner; exerting 'energetic and moderate power'.[56]

Although Tocqueville praised the objectives of the British attempt to ease the transition between slave and free societies by creating a system of temporary apprenticeship to former masters, he argued that in practice this policy had sown confusion among ex-slaves and ceded too much power to planters, who presumably could not be expected to 'rise above themselves'.[57] In the French colonies, it must be made clear that planters have no sovereign right over ex-slaves, but merely a transitory influence borrowed from the state. For a time the state would become the guardian of ex-slaves, a 'guide and a liberator' inculcating in these temporarily indentured subjects 'the hard-working and virile practices of liberty' and establishing social guarantees for those who could not work.[58] Since Tocqueville also believed that particular fears of race-mixing were less marked in the French national character, and that the history of French colonization was more favourable to assimilation, he hoped that the deadly combination of particular and general causes that doomed American race relations could be avoided in the French colonies.[59]

Tocqueville proposes a plan in which both the economic factors associated with a civilized economy and the psychological tendencies towards exclusion and domination associated with democratic liberty would be controlled or defused by the state. A proper understanding of the economic consequences of British emancipation, and a prudent analysis of the sugar industry, he argued, revealed that slave emancipation was economically necessary to save the French empire in the Caribbean.[60] Planters would not be able to hold on to their workforce if slaves could escape and migrate to free British colonies, and free labour represented the best hope of productivity in the future. Central to this understanding was a belief in the long-term benefits of the European plantation economy to ex-slaves as well as to white planters and metropolitan French. It was assumed – by Tocqueville no less than by other liberals – that Christianizing and educating the ex-slaves would accelerate assimilation by transforming their psychology. Freed men would be drawn voluntarily into a modern economic and social order as they came to see their proper self-interest in working for wages. The experience of British emancipation in the West Indies had furthered these hopes, indicating that fears of both insurrection and reversion to 'savagery' were completely unfounded in a context where the metropolitan power exerted control. Indeed, Tocqueville notes a rush among ex-slaves in the British colonies to attend schools, comparing the situation favourably with school attendance in France itself.[61] Africans in the colonies acted exactly as one could expect European workers to act.

The similarity of ex-slaves to European workers had its negative side, in particular a preference for inefficient smallholdings rather than wage labour in sugar refineries.[62] This preference was dangerous because a short-term labour shortage could ruin the sugar industry, thus impoverishing the entire community. Yet Tocqueville did not find this objection fatal to his vision of a new society in the West Indies. He proposed that the state control the labour market for a transitional period; he also entertained the possibility – and his later newspaper articles on the topic made the explicit recommendation – that ex-slaves be forced by the state to remain as wage-workers in the sugar industry by being denied the opportunity to leave the colony or to purchase land for a transitional period, until they could be transformed into workers who would choose (had no choice but) to remain. Tocqueville was at some pains to view these policies as placing freed slaves in a position exactly analogous to European workers, who were similarly 'forced' by the high price of land to remain in industry.

Tocqueville never elaborated his vision of a regenerated society in the French West Indies. His proposal to put a revolution 'in the hands of the government' offered no social blueprints.[63] Rather Tocqueville urged the state to act with energy and vision to force colonial society onto a new evolutionary track that would avoid the disastrous turn to exclusion that had occurred in the United States. Though it is not entirely clear how much he expected from such a revolutionary change of direction, at a minimum it implied the acceptance of social and legal equality, a certain openness on the part of the propertied classes to competitors and workers of all races, and a tolerance of assimilation and intermarriage – hence a society in which *mulâtres*, the scorned outcasts of Beaumont's *Marie*, would become the norm. This vision of state-sponsored reform not only foresaw the 'profound modification of their social state',[64] but also changes in the civic consciousness of ex-masters and ex-slaves under the steady pressure of wise colonial policy.

Conclusion: re-founding fractured societies

I have argued that Tocqueville visualized the legacy of slavery in democracies in terms of a theoretical pair in tension: an American cautionary tale versus a French exercise in statesmanship. He overcomes the paralysis of the French anti-slavery movement in part by displacing its fears on to America, differentiating the French case and rhetorically freeing French statesmen to envision a future for the West Indies that was consistent with an assimilationist notion of democratic universalism.

The fragility of Tocqueville's dream of regenerating colonial societies under the guidance and sponsorship of the French state now appears obvious. And it is Tocqueville himself who reveals its precariousness, for it rests on social processes about which he is elsewhere deeply sceptical. In his writings about democracy in Europe, Tocqueville's hope of establishing freedom rests on successfully overcoming three interdependent and subtly intertwined threats: the isolating absorption of the middle classes in material self-interest, the mistaken passions of *le peuple*, and the emergence of new forms of administrative despotism. Yet when he confronts the legacy of slavery in the colonies, these objects of suspicion become occasions for hope.

Although Tocqueville saw positive affinities between economic and political freedoms in Europe and America, he also dreaded the corrosive effects of interest on civic virtues and the affinities between modern economic 'instincts' and the centralization of power. A key feature of the success of any modern democratic people was its ability to manage these problematic dynamics of self-interest. Tocqueville deplored the apparent inability of the French bourgeoisie to recognize that their long-term self-interest lay in schemes of social cooperation and political inclusion, and he always feared the susceptibility of the European working classes to shortsighted *ressentiment*. Together these failures threatened to deliver France to the clutches of administrative despotism, new forms of tutelary guardianship that sapped the impulse to freedom even as they cloaked themselves in the hypocritical guise of democratic sovereignty. Yet in the slave societies of the West Indies, societies with a deep history of caste exclusion and lawless terror, Tocqueville rests his hope for the viability of a new society on the positive affinities between economic liberalization and free mores. In a society at higher risk than Europe of fracturing along racial and ethnic lines, he projects a future that aligns economic divisions with existing cultural and racial ones.

If the economic self-interest of ex-masters and ex-slaves plays an implausibly large role in Tocqueville's narrative of regeneration in the sugar colonies, so state bureaucracy shows an uncharacteristically positive face. He hoped to attach ex-slaves to the French state by convincing them that their interest lay in temporary subjection to the metropole, that the state – neutral, efficient, and fair – would protect them from social oppression.[65] After a transitional period, ex-slaves and ex-masters would accept even-handed colonial rule, thus preventing their society from being deformed by democratic exclusionary tendencies. Yet Tocqueville himself recognized that *colons* were obstinately attached to their privileges, and that ex-slaves – like European peasants or workers – were apt to adopt an uncompromising and impatient version of democratic equality. It is hard to believe that such a society could be regenerated through the discipline of the administrative state, about whose neutrality and benevolence Tocqueville had few illusions.

One suspects that Tocqueville suppressed his insights about the likely dynamics of interest and power in the French Caribbean because to acknowledge them would be to entertain unthinkable alternatives: the long-term continuance of an immoral despotism that outraged Christian sensibilities, or the humiliating and economically damaging loss of the sugar colonies. Tocqueville touted his plan for a state-sponsored regeneration of formerly slave societies as a model of realistic reform that abandoned oratorical posturing.[66] Paradoxically, however, his proposal to blend ex-masters and ex-slaves into 'one society' under the sponsorship of the metropole appears in retrospect to be more rhetorical than real. While he refuses either to succumb to fatalism or to abandon a just scheme of democratic renewal, these refusals are sustained by selectively blocking the psychological and political insight that makes him such a subtle reader of modern democracy.[67]

Notes

1 Karl Marx, *Eighteenth Brumaire of Louis Bonaparte* (New York: International Publishers, 1969), p. 15.
2 See the recent discussion in James Schleifer, 'Tocqueville's *Democracy in America* Reconsidered', *The Cambridge Companion to Tocqueville*, ed. Cheryl Welch (Cambridge: Cambridge University Press, 2006), p. 123.

3 I assume throughout this essay that there were no significant differences in the views of Tocqueville and Beaumont on race and slavery, and that Beaumont's views in some cases clarify or amplify Tocqueville's. On the agreement between the two, see Benedict Gaston Songy, 'Alexis de Tocqueville and Slavery: Judgments and Predictions', unpublished dissertation, Saint Louis University, 1969, pp. 74–87; Diana Schaub, 'On Slavery: Beaumont's *Marie* and Tocqueville's *Democracy in America*', *The Legal Studies Forum*, 22(4) (1996), pp. 607–8, and Seymour Drescher, 'Tocqueville and Beaumont: A Rationale for Collective Study,' *Tocqueville and Beaumont on Social Reform*, ed. Seymour Drescher (New York: Harper and Row, 1968), appendix.

4 On the *Société de la morale chrétienne*, see Lawrence C. Jennings, *French Anti-slavery: The Movement for the Abolition of Slavery in France 1802–1848* (Cambridge: Cambridge University Press, 2000), pp. 8–23 and Paul Michael Kielstra, *The Politics of Slave Suppression in Britain and France, 1814–48: Diplomacy, Morality, and Economics* (New York: St Martin's Press, 2000), pp. 113–19.

5 Jennings characterizes this politics as a 'typical pattern of promising advances quickly negated by disappointing regressions', *French Anti-slavery*, p. 164.

6 *Ibid.*, pp. 78–82.

7 These persistent features of abolitionist discourse are also evident in the proceedings of the societies, in individual works on abolition, and in a series of parliamentary bills and reports. See, for example, Victor de Broglie's opening speech for the *Société de la morale chrétienne* in 1825, which rejects natural right in favour of appeals to Christian intuitions about moral equality (the 'sun' from which the members drew their light) as the basis of a consensus on philanthropic issues of social reform. 'Discours d'ouverture', *Assemblée générale annuelle de la Société de la morale chrétienne* (15 April 1825), p. 3 and 6.

8 Unpublished until the critical edition by J.R. Derré (Paris: Editions du CNRS, 1977). Rémusat's play represents, according to Dario Roldán, the rather typical philanthropic preoccupation of the liberal milieu in the 1820s 'la préoccupation philanthropique assez typique du milieu libéral des années vingt', *Charles de Rémusat: certitudes et impasses du libéralisme doctrinaire* (Paris: Editions L'Harmattan, 1999), p. 43. Rémusat's article on the slave trade, 'Réflexions et renseignements sur la traité des noirs', *Journal de la Société de la Morale Chrétienne* 3(22) (September 1824), pp. 222–40, expresses similar themes.

9 *L'habitation*, p. 117. See also pp. 66, 67, 74, 75, 78, 82, 91, 94–5.

10 'Rapport sur les travaux de la Société de la morale chrétienne', *Assemblée de la Société de la morale chrétienne* (15 April 1825), p. 3, p. 16.

11 Charles de Rémusat, *Rapport fait au nom de la commission chargée de l'examen de la proposition de M. Passy sur le sort des esclaves dans les colonies françaises, par M. de Rémusat, député de la Haute-Garonne* (Paris: A. Henry, 1838), p. 2.

12 Rémusat, *Rapport*, p. 7.

13 *L'habitation*, p. 111.

14 *Ibid.*, p. 136. Rémusat ends his play with Timur's cry: 'En avant! ... Africains ... Sachez obéir, et vous serez libres.' *Ibid.*, p. 137.

15 Rémusat, *Rapport*, p. 59.

16 'Rapport fait au nom de la commission chargée d'examiner la proposition de M. De Tracy, relative aux esclaves des colonies,' *Oeuvres complètes*, ed. J.D. Mayer (Paris: Gallimard, 1951–)3:i, p. 43 (hereafter cited as OC).

17 'Paris ethnology and the perfectibility of "races",' *Canadian Journal of History* 35(3) (December 2000), p. 454.
18 *Notes on the French Revolution and Napoleon*, ed. François Furet and Françoise Mélonio, trans. Alan S. Kahan (Chicago: University of Chicago Press, 2001), p. 262.
19 *Ibid.*
20 Françoise Mélonio, 'Nations et nationalismes,' *The Tocqueville Review/La Revue Tocqueville* 18(1) (1997), pp. 64–5.
21 *Democracy in America*, trans Arthur Goldhammer (New York: Library of America, 2004), p. 288 (hereafter cited as DAI [for the 1835 *Democracy*] or DAII [for the 1840 *Democracy*]).
22 Furet and Mélonio, *Notes on the French Revolution and Napoleon*, p. 262.
23 DAI, p. 393.
24 For their American interlocutors on slavery, see the careful discussion in Songy, 'Tocqueville and Slavery', pp. 21–38.
25 Beaumont, *Marie or, Slavery in the United States*, trans. Barbara Chapman (Baltimore: The Johns Hopkins University Press, 1999 [1958]), p. 6.
26 DAI, pp. 366, 392, 395, 396, 410.
27 See his 'Translator's note,' in the Library of America DA, p. 876. Tocqueville also uses the language of 'digesting' or 'incorporating' foreigners into the national 'substance'. See, e.g., his pessimistic comments on the likelihood of assimilating immigrants in a letter to Thomas Sedgwick (14 August 1854), OC, 7, p. 159.
28 Tocqueville frequently compares the racial domination of whites over ex-slaves in the U.S. and the West Indies to the former domination of the European nobility, which would never have ceded its privileges without pressure, and was loathe to give up signs of caste exclusivity. See, e.g., 'L'émancipation des esclaves', OC 3(1), p. 80; 'Intervention dans la discussion de la loi sur le régime des esclaves dans les colonies' (30 May 1845), OC, 3(1), pp. 117–18.
29 DAI, p. 405; Tocqueville notes that freed men are already 'disappearing from all the northern states'. DAI, p. 406.
30 DAI, p. 412. For insightful discussions of the psychological link between racism and the anxieties fostered by the democratic condition in the US, see Harry W. Fritz, 'Racism and Democracy in Tocqueville's America,' *The Social Science Journal*, 13(3) (1976), pp. 70–1, Margaret Kohn, 'The Other America: Tocqueville and Beaumont on Race and Slavery', *Polity*, 35(2) (2002), pp. 169–94, and Laura Janara, 'Brothers and others: US Genealogy, Democracy, and Racism', *Political Theory*, 32(6) (2004), pp. 788–93.
31 DAI, p. 412. In a letter from America commenting on race relations in Pennsylvania, Beaumont notes 'it is curious to see what aristocratic pride exists among *these free men* whose government rests on the principle of absolute equality'. Quoted in Songy, 'Tocqueville and Slavery,' p. 32.
32 Beaumont, *Marie*, p. 63.
33 DAI, p. 395, p. 412. See also DAI, ed. Nolla, p. 263, n. f; p. 264, n. n. For Beaumont, see *Marie*, pp. 63 and 74.
34 From an unpublished draft in the Tocqueville Archives at Yale, quoted in James Schleifer, *The Making of Tocqueville's 'Democracy in America'* (Indianapolis: Liberty Fund, 2000), p. 91. This notion is pursued in his 1853 correspondence with Arthur de Gobineau, OC 9, pp. 201–6.

35   According to Tocqueville, repatriation to Africa can never solve the race problem in the new world. DAI, p. 415. This seems to be an answer to Jefferson's *Notes on Virginia*. Tocqueville accepts Jefferson's views that the two races cannot coexist on American soil, but denies that expatriation can solve the difficulty.

36   DAI, p. 409. Cf. Beaumont, *Marie*, pp. 206–12. In his later writings on slavery in the French colonies, Tocqueville repeats the arguments against gradual emancipation.

37   DAI, p. 410.

38   Beaumont, *Marie*, p. 60.

39   DAI, p. 410, cf. p. 416.

40   DAI, p. 413. Tocqueville was highly sceptical about the myth that only blacks could work in hot climates. See Songy, 'Tocqueville and Slavery,' p. 102. For the emergence of a reactive revolutionary consciousness, see Tocqueville's comments on the obvious emergence of black 'outrage at being deprived of nearly all the rights of citizens' (DAI, p. 416), an outrage that will inevitability produce 'future leaders' (DAI, p. 417). Or the alternate text: 'The blacks are a foreign nation that was conquered, and to which one gives a nationality and means of resistance by freeing them, or even enlightening them.' Tocqueville, *De la démocratie en Amérique*, ed. Eduardo Nolla (Paris: J. Vrin, 1990, 2 vols.), I, p. 277, n. j.

41   On Tocqueville's continued interest in the slavery question in the United States, see Songy, 'Tocqueville and Slavery', pp. 125–84; Françoise Mélonio, 'Tocqueville et les malheurs de la démocratie américaine 1831–1859', *Commentaire* 38 (Summer 1987); and Aurelian Craiutu and Jeremy Jennings, 'The Third Democracy: Tocqueville's Views of America after 1840', *American Political Science Review*, 98 (3) (August 2004), pp. 401–4.

42   DAI, ed. Nolla, p. 273 n. a.

43   For discussions of the pessimism inherent in the dramatic structure of *Marie*, see Schaub, 'On Slavery', and Kohn, 'The Other America'.

44   DAI, p. 417.

45   DAI, p. 392.

46   DAI, p. 411.

47   DAI, p. 411: 'A despot who managed to reduce both the Americans and their former slaves to the same state of subservience might succeed in mixing them … .' For the contrast of Protestant to Catholic churches, see Beaumont, *Marie*, pp. 75–9 and 126.

48   DAI, p. 412.

49   Tocqueville describes a society absorptive enough to assimilate other European peoples, while undergoing some change itself. 'As Americans mingle, they assimilate. Differences created by climate, origin, and institutions diminish. Everyone comes closer and closer to a common type. … This constant emigration from North to South significantly favors the fusion of all provincial characters into one national character' (DAI, p. 444).

50   'Intervention dans la discussion de la loi sur le régime des esclaves dans les colonies' (30 May 1845), OC 3:i, p. 114.

51   'Intervention ' (1845), OC 3:i, p. 114.

52   He professes relief that he does not have to refute the 'false and horrible doctrines' justifying slavery, since Europe as a whole has long rejected them. See 'Rapport … sur les esclaves', OC 3:i, p. 42, and also pp. 36, 48, 56.

53 Impatience with anti-slavery breast-beating can be seen in the letters accompanying copies of the report that he sent to friends. See, for example, his letter to Royer-Collard (21 October 1839) OC 11, pp. 87–8.

54 'Dieu ne l'empêche point', 'Seconde lettre sur l'Algérie (22 August 1837)' OC 3:i, p. 153. The translation is from *Writings on Empire and Slavery*, ed. and trans. Jennifer Pitts (Baltimore, Maryland: The Johns Hopkins University Press, 2001), p. 26. In contrast, Tocqueville says that racial antipathy has settled so deeply into American *moeurs* that 'only God can obliterate its trace'. DAI, pp. 341–2.

55 OC 3:i, pp. 75–7.

56 'Rapport ... sur les esclaves', OC 3:i, pp. 57, 48, 45.

57 *Ibid.*, pp. 64–6.

58 'Rapport ... sur les esclaves', OC 3:i, pp. 73 and 59.

59 See his contrast of the English and French as colonizers in 'Fortnight in the Wilderness', George Wilson Pierson, *Tocqueville in America* (Baltimore: Johns Hopkins University Press, 1996), pp. 272–3 and also DAI, p. 381. See also Beaumont, *Marie*, p. 55.

60 Arguments that emancipation is necessary to keep the colonies, and that vibrant vital colonies are necessary to France's economic and diplomatic power and thus her 'greatness', are even more prominent in the 1843 articles printed in *Le Siècle* ('L'émancipation', OC 3[1], 84) and his 1845 parliamentary speech ('Intervention', OC 3:[I], p. 124).

61 'L'émancipation', OC 3(I), p. 94.

62 'Rapport ... sur les esclaves', OC 3(i), pp. 69–71.

63 'Intervention' (1845), OC 3(i), p. 115.

64 'L'émancipation', OC 3(i), p. 84.

65 Tocqueville approvingly notes that former slaves in the English colonies allegedly conceived an attachment for the home country [that was] fervent and one could almost say fanatical', 'L'émancipation', OC 3(i), p. 83.

66 'I confess that I have taken great care to avoid all useless ranting.' Tocqueville to Francisque Corcelles (14 November 1839), in *Lettres choisies, Souvenirs: 1814–1859*, ed. Françoise Mélonio and Laurence Guellec (Paris: Gallimard, 2003), p. 453.

67 An earlier and somewhat different version of this essay appeared in *The Tocqueville Review/La Revue Tocqueville*, 27(2) (2006).

4
Reading Tocqueville: Diachrony, Synchrony and New Perspectives
Jean-Louis Benoît

Introduction

Over the past 170 years, readings of Tocqueville have varied greatly across continents, countries and generations. While he was still alive, his works belonged to political science and history. Since his death, they have also spilled over into sociology, philosophy, administrative and constitutional law, and even literary analysis.[1] In addition, his political career has become an object of veritable interest to us.

Today, the Tocquevillian corpus is almost complete, including – apart from the *Oeuvres complètes*[2] – remarkably good critical editions that have considerably modified our knowledge of his works as a whole, opening new perspectives and raising the level and precision of research at the very moment when a plethora of new approaches to his works are coming to light. Though often relevant, these new readings are sometimes partial (in both senses of the word), rigorous analysis giving way to an ideology that strays from the true path of his thinking.

Raymond Aron and the rediscovery of Tocqueville

We have Raymond Aron to thank for rediscovering Tocqueville and bringing him back into the limelight in France. Aron reread Tocqueville's works as the volumes of the *Oeuvres complètes*[3] came out, but his first important study (a decisive step that opened the way to a renewed reading of Tocqueville in France) was only published in his *Les étapes de la pensée sociologique* from 1967 – in which Tocqueville occupies 50 pages against Marx's 80.[4] Twelve years later, he reviewed the critical and ideological development of Tocqueville's rediscovery in his first article for the *The Tocqueville Review/La Revue Tocqueville*, 'Tocqueville retrouvé', published in its first issue.[5] It should be noted that the 'rediscoverers' of Tocqueville in France were mostly intellectuals with a good knowledge of Marxism, some of whom were even Marxists themselves or proponents of a post-Marxist critique: Jacob Peter Mayer, Raymond Aron,[6] François Furet, Claude Lefort and Marcel Gauchet – a disciple of Lefort; and perhaps we should also add Albert Soboul and Georges Lefebvre, towards whom Furet was (in my opinion) quite unfair.[7]

The rediscovery of Tocqueville in the 1950s was closely linked to the historical, ideological and political conjunction of the times: after Yalta, the two superpowers were confronting each other in the Cold War. In this light, the last page of the first *Démocratie* looks something like an evangelical prophecy: '[The] points of departure [of the Russians and the Americans] are different, their ways diverse. Yet each seems called by a secret design of Providence some day to sway the destinies of half the globe.'[8]

At the end of the war, the opposition between two models – one of which seemed to be a model of liberty, the other, of oppression – was extremely applicable to a moment in time when the United States seemed to be the paradigm of development and success in contrast with the then recent fall of European democracies. It was further a moment when the Communist Party had considerable influence in French politics, and Marxism seemed to be the counter-model favoured by the French intelligentsia in contrast to the economic liberalism epitomized by American capitalism. Having just published *L'opium des intellectuels* and outlined a theory on industrial societies, Aron discovered Tocqueville's writings at the very moment when he was involved in a difficult ideological battle: almost all of the intelligentsia was smitten with Marxism, inventing *imaginary Marxisms* for itself. Aron used *De la démocratie en Amérique* as a textual weapon: what better ally for an ex-left-wing intellectual with a good knowledge of Marxism, and who, knowing what was at stake, also knew that he could not count on any valuable ideological support from the right or the centre? It was thus necessary to reconstruct a coherent conception of the political, to give new strength and vigour to liberalism, in order to offer an alternative to both Marxism and a non-communist left, which was also short of an ideology, ideas and a programme. Henceforth, Raymond Aron's subsequent path would be at least partly inspired by his readings of *De la démocratie en Amérique* and *L'Ancien Régime et la Révolution*.

Les étapes de la pensée sociologique (1967) and 'Tocqueville retrouvé' (1979) are works of a different nature. The first is drawn from a sociology professor's lecture course analyzing the fundamental principles of important works by sociology's founders – Montesquieu, Comte, Marx, Tocqueville – and by sociologists from the turn of the century – Durkheim, Pareto, Max Weber. The second is much more explicitly ideological in nature.

The 1967 text is the first important analysis of Tocqueville's thought in France in the second half of the twentieth century, a historically dated reference work. In Aron's view, Tocqueville's works are those of a sociologist whose method remains imperfect and unfinished (while Raymond Boudon today considers Tocqueville to be one of, if not *the* most important sociologist, arguing convincingly for the rigorousness of his methods[9]).

Aron sees Tocqueville as a comparative sociologist – in line with Montesquieu – whose style and practice do not belong to a 'classical' and accomplished sociology, for he judges the object of his study, and thus lacks scientific objectivity. Tocqueville also belongs to the tradition of political philosophy, like Aron himself, who brings to light the similarities and differences between Tocqueville and Marx in a comparative approach.[10] Both address the historical period and process leading from 1789 to 1851 in terms of social classes, but Aron claims (too quickly and in part erroneously) that, unlike Marx, Tocqueville did not grasp the importance of the industrial revolution and the strong influence it would have upon social life in the second half of the nineteenth century. On the other hand, he considers Tocqueville's approach more suitable than Marx's for analyzing the state of countries in Europe during the second half of the twentieth century, as well as for understanding the Russian Revolution, which does not follow a Marxist logic.

Three things should be specified before finishing with this point. First, Aron's analysis is unbalanced in that he draws a straight lineage between Montesquieu and Tocqueville and goes no further – this is both too much and too little. For Aron, like for the French right wing, liberalism is an absolute political and economic whole, without nuances. Somewhat in contradiction with the preceding claims, he maintains that Tocqueville has no 'economic culture'[11] – which is for the most part inaccurate. Secondly, Aron's *pro domo* usage of Tocqueville's works to defend his own conception of liberalism is still problematic today, just like his use of a limited *corpus* as president (from 1979 to 1983) of the editorial board for the *Oeuvres complètes*.[12]

Third, it is curious to note that, like its nineteenth-century century readers, Aron is thrown off by the second *Démocratie*; he does not see that Tocqueville has followed a method of hypothesis and deduction. And he does not really understand Tocqueville's *modus operandi*, nor can he mentally envisage what is, for him, an adventurous enterprise. In a way, Tocqueville remains an *homme d'opinion* for Aron, to the extent that he passes over Tocqueville's remarkable analyses and misses their scope. For instance, though Tocqueville devotes five chapters to war and gives an in-depth analysis of the process that makes armies extremely dangerous for democracies, Aron considers this judgement to be the result of a gross generalization. Aron's opinion is even more surprising if we take into consideration that France was just emerging from the Colonial Wars and that – from 1846, the days of the almost seditious general Bugeaud in Algeria, until the putsch of 1961 – the army has had considerable influence upon, and had played a very questionable role in, French politics (even if it goes without saying that responsibility also lay to a great extent with the political powers themselves). On this point, let me add in closing that Aron published a very extensive book of 800 pages in 1962, *Paix et guerre entre les nations*, without one single mention of the many pages Tocqueville has written on armies and war.[13]

Gauchet and Tocqueville: a polemical interpretation

Marcel Gauchet's reading of Tocqueville's works in 'Tocqueville l'Amérique et nous', which was published in *Libre* in 1980, is rather polemical in nature. He begins by throwing a few barbs, towards Aron's disciples, to be sure, but also towards others it seems:

> There is a cutting Tocqueville, to be delivered from his pale and lukewarm 'liberal' flatterers, even a polemical Tocqueville, to be contrasted to our mediocre professors in subversion and other contemporaries certified in a subject about which they understand nothing![14]

I leave aside on purpose here the end of text, which has a rather typical structure, similar to other approaches of that time, in contrast to the first half of the text, where Gauchet distinguishes himself from previous readings in three ways. First, Gauchet inverts the precedence Tocqueville gives to American democracy over European democracy. Second, he reintegrates totalitarianism and anti-democracy as authentically integrated moments of the democratic process (where conflict has priority over consensus). Third, Gauchet is highly critical of Tocqueville's blindness with respect to religion.

For Tocqueville, American democracy constitutes a primordial and novel epistemological and heuristic model for reflecting upon, and developing, analyses about the future of European democracies and the forms they may take on. But in Gauchet's view, by starting with America, Tocqueville had failed to go to the essence:

> He was no longer able to discern the inexorable gestation of political novelty in that which the example of America led him to consider, instead, as the normal course of modernity. For this is what characterizes the historical experience that the old continent forged and at long last imposed upon itself, through the very processes that Tocqueville, given his point of reference, judged from the outset to be crucial impediments to the real manifestation of democracy.[15]

At the end of his article, Gauchet takes up this same idea again in his very last line, thus coming full circle: 'And what if Europe were in some sense the future of America?'[16]

Materially speaking, then, this approach constitutes the alpha and omega of Gauchet's reading, even though he is fully aware of Tocqueville's position that the American model could not be adapted to Europe, and of his authoritative demonstration that the emergence of democracy on our continent had been the fruit of a long gestation period.[17] It should also be noted that, since the publication of Gauchet's text, Europe has hardly served as a model for America. Much to the contrary, the distance between the United States and Europe has only grown in the past quarter-century. This fact led Gauchet to update his position by adding a 20-page postface to his article in 2005, 'La dérive des continents'.[18]

I also find Gauchet's second criticism problematic. On the Revolution, he recalls the 'paradoxical'[19] analysis of Tocqueville, for whom – behind the jumps and starts of an endless and always renewed revolution – a democratic system likely to privilege conformism and apathy was being put into place:

> What I fear most for generations to come is not revolutions. ... I am afraid [the new societies] will end up all too invariably attached to the same institutions, the same prejudices, and the same mores, ... that man will exhaust his energy in petty, solitary, and sterile changes, and that humanity, though constantly on the move, will cease to advance.[20]

Despite the absence of ambiguity in these lines, Gauchet wants to substitute confrontation (including confrontation that leads to, or carries the risk of leading towards, totalitarian tendencies within the democratic process itself) for the Tocquevillian consensus that purportedly arises out of 'democratic society's equation with itself'. This 'consensual' conception is supposedly a blind spot in Tocqueville's vision, obscured by the veil of American life. And Gauchet adds: 'we need to reverse Tocqueville's terms and take what he attributed to the after-effects of the revolutionary "accident" as traits of democracy'.[21]

Democracy came into being against the backdrop of the conservative and reactionary forces that opposed it, so much so that 'the possibility of totalitarianism is etched into democracies – as they have developed on the Old Continent – from their very birth'.[22] These oppositions to the establishment of the democratic process are part and parcel of the process itself, claims Gauchet. While his analysis may be true and is certainly of interest, it calls for reconsideration, for Tocqueville's works are much less distant from Gauchet's position than the latter would have us believe. Contrary to common opinion, Tocqueville's vision was not limited to the danger of a 'soft' despotism; he also established how the general will could err and lead the state and the people considerably far off course – this was well understood by Hannah Arendt. In the introduction to the first *Démocratie*, Tocqueville shows how democracy arose in Europe at the end of long historical process, one that was (and remains) a struggle between adversaries battling *nolens volens* for the same cause – be it the very cause to which they were opposed.

Gauchet's last major criticism of Tocqueville (in 1980) has to do with religion, with the relation between the religious and the political. He enters into a strange dialogue with Tocqueville, across time, where their two points of view seem to belong to two different 'orders' (in the Pascalian sense of the word). We are confronted with what seems to be a dialogue at cross-purposes.

Tocqueville is agnostic in the strong sense of the term, but he regrets having lost his faith and admires the message of the Gospel. He is convinced that both the individual and society live better with faith, with communal beliefs, than without. Moreover, he thinks the rise of democracy is accompanied by an increase in the material goods accessible to man, who thus develops, along with society as a whole, a kind of base materialism that neither elevates the individual, nor society. Religion, however, carries with it a more or less rich conception of transcendence, which is in any case far superior to the naturally reductive tendencies of materialism. Tocqueville does not claim to have a complete understanding of the faith of American citizens, yet he is closer here to Gauchet than Gauchet himself thinks. Tocqueville believes that their faith is derivative in nature, mostly Protestant and capitalist, and arises out of the rightly understood self-interest of the first – poorer – moment in Pascal's wager.[23] Americans are religious by choice, out of self-interest:

> People [in the United States] follow a religion the way our fathers took a medicine in the month of May – if it does not do any good, people seem to say, at least it cannot do any harm, and, besides, it is proper to conform to the general rule.[24]

This is a somewhat trivial way (it should be admitted) of reminding us that religion is useful to both the individual and society, that it plays a role in social control and equilibrium. At the same time, however, Tocqueville is a strong proponent of the separation of religion and politics. This separation is what allowed religion to become the greatest political force (in the strong sense of the term) in Jefferson's America, precisely because it did not engage in politics.

For Gauchet, on the other hand, at this stage of his intellectual career, religion is the vestige of an archaic political form from which democracy has the task of liberating us in the name of a militant secularism (*laïcisme*) and atheism. 'Do not come [...] and preach to us about the return of some mysterious "political spirituality" or any other miserable drugstore "monotheism" which would apparently constitute an indispensable defence against the totalitarian perils embedded in social atheism.'[25]

Unable to face the truth of his existential situation without the ideological support of a religion that hands out certainties, the malaise of democratic man opens the way for totalitarianism as a new kind of certainty. Totalitarianism, with its own brand of ideology, is thus deeply linked to a democratic structure (against which it is reacting) that gives it free rein in that it comes to fill a void. Totalitarianism in itself is not a religion, but it has a tendency to reestablish the same kind of communal cohesion as was ensured by religions. Moreover, its increasing power is: 'strictly correlated to the decline of transcendence, ... it marks the coming to an end of modernity'.[26]

At this stage in Gauchet's thought, totalitarianism thus seems to be a necessary step in letting go of religion, a kind of substitute drug that allows us to hope we may eventually free ourselves of dependence on the opium of the people: totalitarianism is to religion what methadone is to opium ... or perhaps, the opposite. He then makes the following peremptory claim, that 'it is certainly not by returning to religion that we will defend ourselves effectively against totalitarianism, but rather by getting rid of it once and for all. Totalitarianism does not arise out of a lack of religion, but because its eradication has been insufficient.'[27] The imperative is categorical: *religio delenda est*. It is 1980, and *The Gulag Archipelago*, with its denunciation of Soviet totalitarianism, has already been available in France for more than six years!

'Tocqueville, l'Amérique et nous' – the founding text of Gauchet's analysis, of his reading of Tocqueville – constitutes an essential step in his investigation. It is here that he puts forward the central theme of the 'disenchantment of the world'.[28] In pre-democratic times, religions offered human beings an enchanted and flawless world, a system that could explain everything. Totalitarianism then came to fill the ideological and existential breach introduced into the religious by democracy. It is now the task of humanity to move beyond totalitarianism, not by returning to the religious, but by learning to bear the vision of a disenchanted world.

In his subsequent reflections, Gauchet comes to think of religion and the religious in a different way. If I understand him well, it is no longer important whether or not one is a believer:

None of us, insofar as we are citizens, can any longer conceive of ourselves as commanded from above. The city of man is the work of man. ... In a word, we have become metaphysically democratic.[29]

The other world is placed at the service of this world. ... The detour through transcendence is justified by the results obtained in immanence. ... A Copernican revolution of religious consciousness is at work. ... Belief has its origin in us, and returns to us – but this is all the more reason for believing, perhaps the best reason of all.[30]

In this way, it seems to me that Gauchet brings about his own Copernican revolution and returns to a Tocquevillian position. In his *L'Ancien Régime et la Révolution*, Tocqueville had established how the French Revolution proceeded 'like a religious revolution' in order to compensate for the disenchantment of the world characteristic of secularization. As such, this 'political' revolution had sought to be universal:

It inspired conversions and generated propaganda. Thus, in the end, it took on that appearance of a religious revolution ... . Or rather, it itself became a new kind of religion, it is true, without God, without ritual, and without a life after death.[31]

Charles Taylor: drawing lessons from Tocqueville

Many North American scholars take a more pragmatic approach to Tocqueville's works – one that is more immediately applicable to present-day society – than the one we have just discussed. In what follows, I propose to examine some of the main characteristics of the influence of Tocqueville on the works of Charles Taylor and Michael Walzer.

In 1995, at a conference on his works at the Centre Culturel International de Cerisy, Charles Taylor explained the influence of Tocqueville on his thought in an interview with Philippe Lara:

> Many things pushed me towards Tocqueville, [who was] a general point of cultural reference that did not penetrate into the narrow specializations of university departments. Analytic philosophy was unaware of politics and history; political 'scientists' were uninterested in Tocqueville's distinctive mixture of philosophy, the study of social values and mores, history and social analysis. ... It is through an academic revolution that people like Michael Mann and Weber, or Furet and Tocqueville have reestablished this middle-ground between history, politics and philosophy.[32]

Taylor does indeed draw on Tocqueville for various approaches that are relatively general in nature, just as likely to be related to the political as to the social sphere, history, freedom or values. These references to Tocqueville are surprisingly frequent – at times explicit, at others implicit, and even methodological.[33] From the outset, Taylor's main concerns are situated in a Tocquevillian framework. For Tocqueville, the main factors that put liberty into question were the obsession with egalitarianism, far-reaching centralization and the excessive weight of bureaucracy. Taylor rightly claims that, since then, the weight of the state, centralization and bureaucracy have only increased. Individuals are blinder than ever with respect to the reality of their situation; turned into mere instruments by the atomic perspective, they support policies that alienate them.

The consequences can be felt on a political level by the almost exclusive predominance of material values – this had surprised and somewhat shocked Tocqueville during his travels in the United States. As Taylor points out, however (referring this time to a passage from *L'Ancien Régime et la Révolution*), 25 years after his trip to America, Tocqueville came to consider the overvaluing of money as a characteristic not only of the Unites States, but as specific to democratic society itself.

Money has acquired an astonishing mobility, ceaselessly changing hands, transforming the status of individuals, raising or lowering families, and at the same time becoming the chief means by which to distinguish between people. ... The desire to enrich oneself at any price, the preference for business, the love of profit, the search for material pleasure and comfort are therefore the most widespread desires. These desires spread easily among all classes, even among those previously most distant from them, and if nothing stops them they soon succeed in demoralizing and degrading the entire nation.[34]

The values and points of reference of modern society are replaced by 'small and vulgar pleasures', writes Taylor,[35] denouncing, like Tocqueville, the materialism of consumer society, which takes on frightening proportions with the fetishization of goods. He further brings out the specific failings of our instrumental and atomized societies, which 'sap the will to maintain this freedom and at the same time undermine the local foci of self-rule on which freedom crucially depends'.[36]

In 1835, after emphasizing how the weakness of the isolated individual in the face of the all-powerful and centralized state was one of the gravest dangers for the *homo democraticus*, Tocqueville provided the necessary – or at least sufficient – remedies put in place in American democracy: active citizenship, freedom of the press, the importance of associations. He further added that the utilitarianism of American citizens, their self-interest rightly understood, allowed them to fight against individualism through free institutions.[37] A hundred and fifty years later, the situation has become worse, for the evolution and fragmentation of modern society leaves us with even fewer opportunities to act upon the most important ills, especially the expansion of the 'soft' despotism so rightly feared by Tocqueville. Even so, his analyses offer a good starting point from which to understand what is happening in the world and how to act upon it. According to Taylor, Tocqueville perceived with much acumen the nature of the ills that afflict modern society. He understood the issues at play in democracy and proposed an epistemological model that is still valid today. Only a social and political approach can help us to analyse how contemporary society both works and fails to work.[38]

Taylor reminds us how individualism, for Tocqueville, naturally leads towards a 'soft despotism' in democracy that can only be counterbalanced (at least in part) by active citizenship and associative practices. In this, Taylor follows 'contemporary thinkers [who] have seen Tocqueville's work as prophetic'.[39] He thus borrows several solutions from Tocqueville, through what he calls 'an alternative of liberalism of Tocquevillian provenance' in 'Modes of Civil Society': 'Tocqueville reformulates the ideals of republican freedom in a context of fragmented, decentralized power, whose formula derives from Montesquieu's "corps intermédiaires." '[40]

It is the task of associations – "the 'mother science' of democracy" according to Tocqueville[41] – to become concrete intermediary bodies. Taylor distinguishes between increasing possible levels of association in civil societies, from free associations that are independent of the state to associations capable of having a significant influence on the course of politics. He thus goes further than Tocqueville, judging that the political sphere is unable to deal with the real problems of the planet's future; it is up to associations then, or to parties that function like associations (the Green Party), to take up the challenge.

Otherwise, Taylor considers that we can take up and adapt the solutions recommended by Tocqueville: 'There is an important set of conditions of the continuing health of self-governing societies, well explored by Tocqueville. These include a strong identification of the citizens with their public institutions and political way of life.'[42] But, as underlined by Jean-Marc Ferry and Justine Lacroix, Taylor further thinks that the real danger for present-day societies is fragmentation:

> The danger is not actual despotic control but fragmentation – that is, a people increasingly less capable of forming a common purpose and carrying it out. Fragmentation arises when people come to see themselves more and more atomistically, otherwise put, as less and less bound to their fellow citizens in common projects and allegiances.[43]

In a way, fragmentation is the death of politics.

Tocquevillian influences in the work of Michael Walzer

Tocqueville's writings have had a lesser influence on the works of Michael Walzer than on those of Taylor, both on a quantitative and qualitative level. Walzer draws on a more limited Tocquevillian *corpus*,[44] and his references are rarely explicit: only four in Chapter 11 of *Spheres of Justice*, which addresses the theme of recognition and refers to Chapter XVIII from the third part of the second *Démocratie* ('On honour in the United States and in democratic societies'). His interpretation of the works he does consider follows an approach characteristic of those for whom an aristocrat thinking on democracy naturally awakens suspicion. Though Tocqueville took particular care in writing his chapter on honour – consulting the head of the archives, calling upon the testimony and memories of his father on the end of the Old Regime, and distinguishing carefully between different 'orders' and epochs – Walzer, much to the contrary, generalizes, thus distorting the perspective of the initial text. For instance, in a text that deals neither with serfs or slaves in the aristocracies evoked by Tocqueville, Walzer writes: 'Tocqueville certainly misdescribes the position of slaves in all the slave-holding aristocracies; he is probably wrong about serfs and servants, who have in any case no very ample stage of their own ... .'[45] As concerns the question of domestic servants, it is addressed previously in Chapter 5 ('How democracy modifies relations between servant and master'), wherein Tocqueville establishes learned distinctions between the different kinds of servants under the Old Regime, from the most respectable ones to mere lackeys. He then gives a particularly subtle analysis of the relationships between masters and servants from 1835–40 in the United States, England and France. This text is historically dated, however, and can only be understood from the standpoint of societies where domestic servants still had an important role to play – for example, in the France of 1914. It is obviously not applicable to our own times or society, and this renders Walzer's generalizations questionable in that they somewhat distort the initial text.

Yet, Walzer's reading does bring us back to Tocqueville insofar as it evokes some Tocquevillian themes and follows some similar, if somewhat altered, approaches: citizenship, social mobility, the relationship between equality and freedom, the importance and role of associations.

On citizenship, in the last pages of *Pluralisme et démocratie*, Walzer argues in response to Chantal Mouffe that the equilibrium between the state and its citizens, the harmonious functioning of society, requires the presence of citizens who are vigilant, active and involved in civil society: these are the very virtues admired by Tocqueville in the American society of 1831.[46]

In *De la démocratie*, Tocqueville shows how the constant agitation – disquiet – of American society comes from the very nature of a democratic society where situations are never established, nor definitive, unlike in caste-based societies: 'Mobility is the mark of a free society whose members are autonomous men and women: they circulate amongst numerous groups and associations, crossing ethnic, religious, and ideological borders.'[47] Walzer, however, insists on the necessity of compensating for the four spheres of mobility he has evoked with a kind of stability that allows individuals as citizens to acquire a form of existential certainty. This does not put into question Tocqueville's analysis, but adapts it to the new characteristics of a society that has changed over a century and a half.[48]

The main thing being to guarantee fundamental liberties, Walzer takes up Tocqueville's approach to the relation between liberty and equality[49] and reaffirms the liberal credo of Tocquevillian democracy:

> We would like to create a society where men and women are free from the domination of the well-born, the rich, and the powerful. This does not mean they all have to be absolutely equal in status, richness and power. Such a simplistic equality is the bad utopia of the old left.[50]

And he adds that this Utopia is what led to tyranny, to the crimes of the twentieth century, against which Tocqueville warned us by anticipating the potential of the general will to stray from the paths of freedom.

Finally, Walzer reconsiders the important place of civil society and associations – a major theme in Tocqueville's analysis, which gives associations an essential role in protecting democracy, sees in their smooth operation a testimony to democratic health, and understands them as a counter-power ensuring the existence of citizens reunited to defend a cause against the all-powerful state. Walzer's position on this point is much less radical than Robert Putnam's,[51] who establishes a direct link between the decline of a sense of political citizenship and of responsibility in civil society. Weak involvement in associations marks the decline of American political society. In a society where the simplest associations are disappearing or losing their authenticity, individualism has overcome politics. This is, according to Putnam, the sign of a society that has lost its main points of reference, its initial virtue.[52]

Walzer does not go as far as Putnam. He approaches the problem from the opposite end. The ideological weight of societies remains considerable in American political life. As he argues in *The Civil Society Argument*, however, a whole portion of existing societies are nothing more than ghosts, fossil societies in which active and concrete participation in non-profit associations has given way to artificial associations without any true place for citizens and whose founding president's sole aim is to obtain credit or financing.[53]

In short, it is clear that a part of Tocqueville's works and some of his themes are present in Walzer's writings. However, it also seems important to underline how different these two thinkers are, in the end, in their perspectives on the relation between philosophy and politics (at least, in my view). Walzer wants to establish a political pragmatics, a practical political philosophy. Recalling Plato's myth of the cave, he emphasizes that the philosopher's task is to remain in the cave with others and search for solutions to the problems of the moment. Tocqueville's path is fundamentally different and, in my view, more authentically Platonic. He leaves the cave and its shadows of reality: his trip to the United States is a kind of initiation, a verification, modification and adjustment of his original intuitions. He then ascends towards the world of ideas by building a model of hypothesis and deduction – the model of the second *Démocratie* – in which, beginning from the essence of modern democracy, he deduces how it has concretely been put into practice, the paths open to it, its possible defects and perverse effects and the possible remedies, which do not, however, allow us to move beyond a fundamental uncertainty. Only at the end of his search does Tocqueville attempt to leave the realm of ideas and enter into the political world in a more proper sense. The two realms are distinct for him. And he finds the mixing of genres to be always unsatisfactory.

A final observation (perhaps already made by others) before concluding: though Taylor and Walzer both belong to what is called the North American brand of neo-Tocquevillianism,[34] their respective links to Tocqueville are quantitatively and qualitatively different. While a major part of Taylor's work follows a Tocquevillian route that is constantly present, whether explicitly or implicitly, Walzer, on the other hand, only makes use of scattered fragments, themes, or 'islets' from Tocqueville's thought, which arise more properly out of a kind of cultural background than out of a real basis or foundation in his own reflections.

Conclusion

My aim in the preceding analyses was not to give an exhaustive account of how the different readings of Tocqueville in France and the United States have evolved, both in their diachronic and synchronic dimensions. In conclusion, however, it seems important to at least give a schematic account of these dimensions in order to put them into perspective.

Since 1840, Tocqueville has been read continuously in the United States, these readings forming a kind of spiral where different aspects are successively brought to the fore: first, an analysis of the national political model, followed by a deepening of the democratic model as an ideal, a reflection upon morality and values, and their application in an attempt to solve contemporary problems.[55] Across the Atlantic, Tocqueville is almost considered today to be one of the founding fathers. It is impossible to engage in political discourse or speak about American political life without some reference to *De la démocratie en Amérique*, be it in reflections on values and the role of associations, or in presidential candidates' professions of faith (whether genuine or not, relevant or not) – all of which can be situated within a Tocquevillian perspective.

Conversely, in France, the reading of Tocqueville is related to fashions.[56] He disappeared almost entirely from the intellectual scene for almost a century (from the 1870s onward) only to truly reappear with Aron's reading from the 1960s. This reading was of political importance mainly from 1960–80, and we can follow its course in Serge Audier's excellent account: political analysts and thinkers like Manent, Casanova, Lefort, Gauchet and the analysts of Sciences Po, were all influenced in their readings by Raymond Aron's vision, whether they were critical of it or not. But this historically dated reading had some perverse effects. To begin with, it brought about a general rejection by the anti-liberals of a caricature of Tocqueville's thought, rather than of his thought itself. It led, moreover, to a kind of sclerosis among a number of Aronians, who have not moved beyond repetitive analyses based on an unchanging and limited *corpus*, producing almost no major works or papers in the past 20 years, barring a few exceptions.[57] Evidence for this can be found in the constant recurrence of questions like, 'Can one still be a Tocquevillian?'[58] and the responses they bring about: 'Farewell to Tocqueville'![59]

Yet, for the past 12 years or so, many researchers at the EHESS (the Ecole des Hautes Etudes en Sciences Sociales in Paris) and in a few universities are carrying out in-depth analyses of the Tocquevillian *corpus* as a whole, discovering new questions and revealing a much more complex Tocqueville – political thinker, historian and committed politician – than is to be found in his liberal proponents or his past and present anti-liberal detractors.

On this level, the methods of present-day researchers in the States and in Europe (not only in France) are comparable – at times identical, and at others complementary. They draw on the entirety of Tocqueville's works and address the various spheres touched upon by the problems and questions he raises. This can be seen in the conferences and bicentenaries where they have presented some of their research themes.[60]

Notes

1 For the bicentenary of Tocqueville's birth, *De la démocratie en Amérique* was added to the programme of the examination for the degree in literature in France.

2 The publication of Tocqueville's *Oeuvres complètes* begun by Gallimard in 1951 – twenty-nine volumes of which are already in circulation – will soon be completed with the upcoming publication of tome XVII's three volumes. Hereafter, these works will be referred to in this paper with the abbreviation OC, followed by the tome (in Roman numerals), and when necessary the volume (in Arabic numerals). (Translator's note: all quotations from *De la démocratie en Amérique* are from Alexis de Tocqueville, *Democracy in America*, trans. Arthur Goldhammer [New York: Library of America, 2004], hereafter referred to as DA in the footnotes.)

3 The two volumes of *De la démocratie en Amérique*, from 1835 and 1840, were also the first to be published in Gallimard's OC in 1951 (OC, I, 1 & 2).

4 Raymond Aron, *Les étapes de la pensée sociologique* (Paris: Gallimard, 1967). In this same book, Aron also devotes 30 pages or so to 'Comte, Tocqueville et Marx et la révolution de 48'.

5 *The Tocqueville Review/La Revue Tocqueville*, 1(1) (1979), pp. 8–23; reprinted in 26(1) (2005), pp. 25–46.

6 See Raymond Aron's article, 'De l'existence historique', published in *Cahiers de philosophie politique et juridique de l'Université de Caen*, 15 (1989) pp. 147–62.

7 Hence, Aron writes: 'Furet's elevation of *L'Ancien Régime et la Révolution* seems all the higher in contrast to his depreciation of academic historiographies of the Revolution from Aulard to Soboul.' Nonetheless, the preface to *L'Ancien Régime*, written by Lefebvre, remains an interesting piece on more than one level. As for Soboul, it is worth looking at his extended eulogy of Tocqueville's philosophy of history in his *Encyclopaedia Universalis* article on the French Revolution. For him, '*L'Ancien Régime et la Révolution* is impressive because of its intelligence and awareness. ... as a model of rationality ...' (*Encyclopaedia Universalis*, vol. XIV, 6 th ed, 1975, p. 218).

8 OC, 1:i, p. 431.

9 In *Tocqueville aujourd'hui* (Paris: Odile Jacob, 2005).

10 This explains why, despite chronology, Aron addresses Tocqueville after Marx in *Les étapes de la pensée sociologique*.

11 In 'Tocqueville retrouvé', *The Tocqueville Review/La Revue Tocqueville*, 26(1) (2005), p. 32. On this subject, see: J.L. Benoît and E. Keslassy, *Alexis de Tocqueville, textes économiques, anthologie critique* (Paris: Pocket-Agora, 2005).

12 Aron also very briefly mentions the *Souvenirs*, but he only refers to five – at most – of the 17 volumes already published by 1979.

13 Raymond Aron, *Paix et guerre entre les nations* (Paris: Calmann-Lévy, 1962).

14 Marcel Gauchet, 'Tocqueville, l'Amérique et nous', *Libre*, 7 (1980), pp. 83–4.

15 *Ibid.*, pp. 44–5.

16 *Ibid.*, p. 120. '*Et si l'Europe était en quelque manière l'avenir de l'Amérique?*'

17 In Europe, this period of gestation had begun 'seven hundred years earlier' and came to an end with a painful birth!

18 In November 2005, Gauchet's article was published again in *La condition politique* (Paris: Gallimard, 2005). In the postface, he writes: 'The question is whether the discrediting [*mise à mal*] of this credo [the thesis put forward in 1980] and the distance that has grown since then between the two worlds puts into question the basic diagnosis. I don't think it does' (p. 387). I have to admit, I am not fully convinced by this justification, or by the rigorousness of his argument.

19 I use this term because it seems most appropriate insofar as, at the time, Tocqueville's analysis was contrary to the ideological 'doxa' about the history of the French Revolution.

20 Second *Démocratie*, 3.e, Ch. 21 (OC, II, 1, p. 269).

21 'Tocqueville, l'Amérique et nous', p. 61.

22 *Ibid.* This explains how European democracies moved towards fascism or communism precisely in countries where the state structure was weak or recent (Italy, Germany), or in Tsarist Russia, where the old imperial model continued to exist.

23 'Cette pensée qui ne me paraît pas bien digne de la grande âme de Pascal résume parfaitement l'état des âmes dans [ce] pays', writes Tocqueville, not having taken into account the strategic aspect of Pascal's wager, which first tries to unsettle the libertine through a relatively simple calculation of probabilities (*De la démocratie en Amérique*, ed. Eduardo Nolla [Paris: J. Vrin, 1990], 2 vols, I, p. 117, n. d).

24 Letter to Louis de Kergorlay, 29 June 1831, *Selected Letters on Politics and Pociety*, p. 49.

25 'Tocqueville, l'Amérique et nous', pp. 72–3.

26 *Ibid.*, p. 70: 'strictement correlative du déclin de la transcendance, ... il signe l'achèvement de la modernité'.

27 *Ibid.*, p. 73.

28 This expression from Schiller was taken up again by Weber, before Marcel Gauchet made it his own.

29 Marcel Gauchet, *La religion dans la démocratie* (Paris: Gallimard/Le débat, 1998), p. 8.

30 *Ibid.*, pp. 108–10.

31 *L'Ancien Régime et la Révolution*, L. I, Ch. 3 (OC, II, 1, p. 86). (Translator's note: all quotations are from Alexis de Tocqueville, *The Old Regime and the Revolution*, trans. Alan S. Kahan, ed. François Furet and Françoise Mélonio [Chicago: University of Chicago Press, 1998], p. 101, hereafter referred to as ORR in the footnotes.).

32 *Charles Taylor et l'interprétation de l'identité moderne, Entretien avec Philippe de Lara* (Paris: Cerf, 1998), pp. 352–3.

33 Charles Taylor, 'The Politics of the Steady State', in Beyond Industrial Growth, ed. Abraham Rotstein (Toronto : University of Toronto Press, 1976) pp. 47-70, which Taylor considers particularly important from this point of view, as he underlines on note 14 of page 592 in *Sources of the Self* (Cambridge, MA: Harvard University Press, 1989).

34 *L'Ancien Régime et la Révolution*, avant-propos (OC, II, 1, p. 74), ORR, p. 87.

35 In Charles Taylor, 'Modes of Civil Society', *Public Culture*, 3 (1990), p. 111. Here, Taylor is taking up an expression already used by Tocqueville.

36 *The Sources of the Self*, p. 502.

37 Seconde *Démocratie*, ii, Ch. IV and VIII.

38 Charles Taylor, *The Ethics of Authenticity* (Cambridge, MA: Harvard University Press, 1992), p. 4.
39 *Ibid.*, p. 1.
40 Taylor, 'Modes of Civil Society'. In fact, Tocqueville is repeating here the idea of the great importance of intermediary bodies to be found both in Malesherbes, his great-grandfather, and Montesquieu, in *L'esprit des lois*.
41 Tocqueville's position here is diametrically opposed to Rousseau's, who denounces all associations of citizens as rupturing the special political tie between the citizen and the sovereign. Tocqueville believes that the citizen has no power in the face of a tutelary and despotic state; only associations are effective in guaranteeing the rights of citizens when they unite to defend a common cause.
42 *The Sources of the Self*, p. 505.
43 *The Ethics of Authenticity*, pp. 112–13.
44 Robert Laffont's edition of the Tocquevillian *corpus* (Paris: Collection Bouquins, 1986), which is limited to the main works and ignores his letters, travel notes and speeches. My own position here is based upon my readings of: *Just and Unjust Wars* (New York: Basic Books, 1977); *Spheres of Justice* (New York: Basic Books, 1983); *Thick and Thin: Moral Argument at Home and Abroad* (Notre Dame/Indiana: Notre Dame Press, 1994); *Pluralisme et démocracie* (Paris: Esprit/Seuil, 1997); *Arguing about War* (New Haven: Yale University Press, 2004); 'Un empire américain', *Raison publique*, 3 (2004); 'The Civil Society Argument', published in Chantal Mouffe's *Dimensions of Radical Democracy* (London: Verso, 1992); and the articles published in *Dissent* magazine from 2001 to 2005 (which can be accessed on the internet). I also referred to Justine Lacroix's book, *Michael Walzer, Le pluralisme et l'universel* (Paris: Michalon/Le bien commun, 2001), and to *La pensée politique contemporaine*, which she published with Jean-Marc Ferry (Brussels: Bruylant, 2000).
45 *Spheres of Justice*, p. 250.
46 *Pluralisme et démocratie*, p. 211.
47 *Ibid.*, p. 153.
48 Robert Dahl gave an excellent paper on this theme at the Bicentennial Conference at Yale: 'Political equality, then and now', Conference on Alexis de Tocqueville, Yale University, 2005, published in *The Tocqueville Review/La Revue Tocqueville*, 37(2) (2006), pp. 461–78.
49 As we know, in Tocqueville's view, the primary risk in democracy of going astray naturally comes from the immoderate taste of citizens for equality to the detriment of freedom.
50 *Pluralisme et démocratie*, p. 153.
51 In *Bowling Alone: The Collapse and Revival of American Community* (New York: Simon and Schuster, 2000), Putnam considers 'bowling alone' to be characteristic of the loss of values and of a sense of community – proof, in his view, that American society in its original form is truly dead.
52 In *The Tocqueville Review/La Revue Tocqueville*, 21(1) (2000), p. 166, Maxime Parodi criticizes Putnam's view: 'The withdrawal of civism feared by Tocqueville is far from being confirmed ...'. The problem, however, is that this claim is made without proof to support it, while Putnam provides us with numerous concrete examples and statistical data.

53 Published by Mouffe in *Dimensions of Radical Democracy*, pp. 89–107.
54 This trend can be tied to thinkers like Putnam, Edwards and Foley, as well as many others. It is further worth reading: Bob Edward and Michael W. Foley, 'Civil Society and Social Capital: A Primer', in *Beyond Tocqueville: Civil Society and the Social Capital Debate in Comparative Perspective*, ed. Bob Edward, Michael W. Foley and Mario Dani (Hanover, NH: University Press of New England, 2001); and Johann N. Neem, 'Squaring the Circle', *The Tocqueville Review/La Revue Tocqueville*, 27(1) (2006), pp. 99–121.
55 These remarks were made by James Schleifer in his paper given at the St Lô conference in 1990, 'La réception de l'oeuvre de Tocqueville aux Etats-Unis', which was unfortunately never published. Seymour Drescher completed this analysis in his article, 'L'Amérique vue par les tocquevilliens', *Raisons politiques*, 1 (February 2001), pp. 62–76.
56 Françoise Mélonio, *Tocqueville et les Français* (Paris: Aubier, 1993), p. 11.
57 For instance, the numerous, interesting and original articles written by Lucien Jaume in this time period: 'Tocqueville et le problème du pouvoir exécutif en 1848', *Revue française de science politique*, 41(6) (1991), pp. 739–55; 'Tocqueville: un utilitarismo temperato', *Contemporanea*, 2(1) (1999), pp. 119–25; 'Problèmes du libéralisme. De Mme de Staël à Tocqueville', *Droits*, 30 (January 2000), pp. 151–62; 'Tocqueville et la perspective libérale sur le jury', in *La cour d'assises. Bilan d'un héritage démocratique. Association française pour l'histoire de la Justice* (Paris: La Documentation Française, 2001), pp. 111–24; 'Tocqueville dans le débat entre le droit de l'Etat et le droit de la société', *La pensée juridique d'Alexis de Tocqueville*, ed. Manuel Carius, Charles Coutel and Tanguy Le Marc'hadour (Arras: Artois Presse Université, 2005), pp. 27–39; 'Tocqueville face au thème de la "nouvelle aristocratie". La difficile naissance des partis en France', *Revue française de science politique*, 56(6) (2006), pp. 969–83.
58 A question asked by Nicolas Weill in *Le Monde* (25 May 2005) and raised again by Daniel Bensaïd on France Culture in December 2006.
59 In *Le Monde* (27 July 2005), where it becomes clear that André Fontaine's reading of Tocqueville stops at the last page of the first *Démocratie*, in an approach that dates back to the 1970s.
60 See for instance *The Tocqueville Review/La Revue Tocqueville*, 27(2) (2006), where the papers given by various researchers at the double conference of Cerisy/Yale in 2005 are published.

5
The Return of Tocqueville in Contemporary Political Thought: Individualism, Associationism, Republicanism

Serge Audier

Introduction

The aim of this article is to draw a comparison between French and Anglo-American readings of the thought of Tocqueville, in hope of revealing some of the intellectual and philosophical, but also cultural and civilizational differences that separate France from the United States and Canada.[1] Such a comparison is all the more interesting in the wake of Tocqueville's well-known 'renaissance' over the past few decades on both sides of the Atlantic. He has inspired some of the United States and Canada's most famous political philosophers, such as Michael Sandel, Benjamin Barber, Charles Taylor, James S. Fishkin and Bruce Ackerman; and he has equally been a guiding light for French thinkers like Claude Lefort, François Furet, Marcel Gauchet and many others. In this, we find a meeting point with few equivalents, and this is certainly due, in part, to the singularity of Tocqueville's itinerary and comparative method. However, behind this apparent international consensus on the importance of Tocqueville in thinking democracy today, profoundly different presuppositions and conclusions lie hidden. In fact, I would like to show that Anglo-American readings of Tocqueville can generally be distinguished from French interpretations according to two inseparable themes: republican 'virtue' and civic participation on a local and associative level. Though these dimensions of his works have not been completely overlooked by French thinkers, other themes have received more attention – particularly, contemporary individualism, for reasons that will have to be clarified. Further, in order to draw a fruitful comparison that avoids caricatural opposition, we will have to divest ourselves of certain, still prevalent, commonplaces about the meaning of Tocqueville's return in France.

The limits of Aron's reconstruction

The rediscovery of Tocqueville in France is much more complex than is commonly thought, and cannot be reduced to a trend or a substitute ideology for a fallen Marxism. To be sure, a relative consensus about the importance of Tocqueville arose around the 1970s, but the reasons that led many authors to his works differ. This great diversity is rarely mentioned – as if these French readings constituted a more or less homogeneous block devoted to celebrating the return of liberalism after its long eclipse by the hegemony of Marxism. And generally speaking, even less so is the complex path that led from the rediscovery of Tocqueville to his present acclaim in France. According to current opinion, Tocqueville's works were completely forgotten by the end of the nineteenth century, and were only rediscovered in the 1950s by Aron. I think it is time we put this interpretation back into question as perhaps only a myth – or at least, an extreme oversimplification – that has been maintained for decades, to the point that it now passes for a verified truth.

While Aron played down his own role in the return of Tocqueville, he did not suggest any other serious options. His article from the end of the 1970s, 'Tocqueville retrouvé',[2] is instructive with respect to his own itinerary, but it overshadows other interpretations from the interwar period. Aron gives three reasons for the return of Tocqueville in France. The first concerns changes in French sociology, particularly, the crisis of the positivist school – as long as Comte and Durkheim remained the main points of reference, Tocqueville would not count among sociology's founding fathers. The second reason has to do with the evolution of contemporary societies since the 1950s. During this period of economic prosperity – the '30 Glorious Years', which seemed to be marked by a partial social equalization and improved living conditions for the poorest classes – the Marxist prophecy of the impending self-destruction of capitalism, already long undermined by Bernstein's revisionism, lost all credibility. Yet, the analyses made in *De la démocratie en Amérique*, focused as they were on egalitarianism, seemed more than ever relevant to the times. The third reason for Tocqueville's return is the fact that he conceptualized in advance what would become the main alternative of the twentieth century, namely, the choice between democracy and totalitarianism. In this sense, the rediscovery of Tocqueville seems to coincide with the rebirth of *political* liberalism. Indeed, as an exemplary proponent of the primacy of the political, Tocqueville showed that, while all modern societies tend towards social egalitarianism, it is up to these societies themselves whether they become politically free or despotic.

As I have tried to show elsewhere,[3] however, this explanation of Tocqueville's return in France overshadows a group of readings from the beginning of the twentieth century that put forward an interpretation far different from Aron's liberal approach – for instance, Antoine Rédier's almost entirely forgotten book from 1925, *Comme disait Monsieur de Tocqueville*. This particular case can be easily explained, since Rédier was a follower of *Action Française* and gave an explicitly biased reading of Tocqueville underpinned by a hatred of democracy. Nonetheless, this bias allowed him to see Tocqueville in a new light: though often presented as a 'liberal' in a rather ordinary sense – for example, in the reading of Eugène d'Eichthal[4] – Rédier wanted to prove that Tocqueville was in fact what he called 'a liberal of a new kind'. Among other things, this brought to the fore profound differences between Constant and Tocqueville, the latter placing far more importance on civic participation than the former. The fact that Rédier's reading of Tocqueville was fundamentally flawed on several levels should not lead us to overlook his contribution in this respect.

Further, his innovative reading was not without influence, as we can see from Jacob Peter Mayer's forgotten interpretation of it. For it is in reference to Rédier's book – to which he pays homage – that Mayer imposes his own image of a Tocqueville very different from the common liberal reading. As is evinced in the title of his book from 1939, *Prophet of the Mass Age*,[5] Mayer found in Tocqueville a lucid critic of modern pathologies, that is, of a levelling egalitarianism, conformism and civic apathy that favoured a new despotism. Even in the 1960s, Mayer continued with this type of reading, elevating Tocqueville to a prophet of massification, in parallel with his own specialized work on modern or mass media. In addition, as early as the 1930s, a radical denunciation of the technicizing of the modern world and state arose alongside the Tocquevillian critique of modernity. This trend followed closely in the footsteps of personalism and was a precursor to an ecological politics inspired by Tocqueville and embodied in the thought of Jacques Ellul and Bernard Charbonneau.[6]

Against the common tendency to reduce the meaning of Tocqueville's return in France to a simple return of liberalism – reduction that we find, it should be noted, in contemporary specialists and non-specialists alike – it is important to recall the early twentieth-century tendency in France to interpret Tocqueville within the framework of a *critique of modernity*. This trend was passed over in silence by Aron, a silence that played a decisive role in the reception of Tocqueville after the Second World War. In fact, as we have seen, Aron's interpretation totally overshadowed Mayer's. Thus, it has become common in France to characterize Tocqueville as a liberal thinker in exactly the same sense as Constant – whose own thought has also been grossly oversimplified up until the present day.[7]

The spreading of this common and complacent reading has further come to blur the finesse of both Aron's reading of Tocqueville and his thought in general, blatantly reducing these to a defence of liberalism and a plea against totalitarianism. Aron was in no way ignorant of the crucial importance given to political liberty by Tocqueville. In fact, he underlined its supreme value for Tocqueville. Neither did he neglect Tocqueville's concrete analyses of municipal and associative liberty. Much to the contrary of what can be read almost everywhere, all of these dimensions are already present in Aron's reading, not only for *philological*, but for *normative* reasons. This becomes clear if we recall that Aron, far from being content with a minimal democracy, placed great importance on civism and participation ... but perhaps this has been forgotten. Let me add in passing that Aron went far beyond a summary opposition of Tocqueville and Marx by noting the relevance of Tocqueville's analyses to pauperism. It is true, however, that Aron did not place enough emphasis on Tocqueville's development of civic participation, and that he sought to present Tocqueville as a theorist of liberal democracy rather than as a philosopher in the European republican tradition.

Claude Lefort and the contradictions of democratic societies

After Aron, it is significant that one of the major interpretations of Tocqueville in the 1970s was philosopher Claude Lefort's, whose own research also centred around the questions of totalitarianism and democracy.[8] Similarly to Aron, Tocqueville's thought is particularly important for Lefort in the context of communist totalitarianism. Though Lefort stops short of calling Tocqueville a prophet of totalitarianism, he nonetheless claims that his thought provides us with a key for unlocking its meaning.

Lefort refuses to present Tocqueville as a paradigm of liberalism. His point is rather to show that, if Tocqueville is indeed a liberal, he is a liberal in an entirely *singular* sense. Thus, Tocqueville's return cannot legitimately be said to coincide with the rebirth of classical liberalism. Yet, neither does this mean that Lefort follows Rédier's anti-modern reading: he never approaches Tocqueville from a traditionalist standpoint. Nor does he present Tocqueville as a child of republicanism, as does the American author Roger Boesche, for instance, in *The Strange Liberalism of Alexis de Tocqueville.*[9] Unlike Boesche, Lefort does not associate Tocqueville to various heterogeneous trends – liberal, republican, or traditionalist; rather, he tries to recapture the singularity of Tocqueville's enquiry into the development of liberty in modern societies.

Tocqueville's thought is thus valuable to Lefort because, in considering democracy not only as an institutional tool, but as a *type of political society*, it brings to the fore the contradictions at work on all levels of democracy. Tocqueville shows how, through a kind of reversal, some of the apparently most promising democratic phenomena lead to their complete opposites. In the end, the promotion of the individual reverts into anonymity, the advocating of diversity turns into homogeneity and, on a more general level, freedom gives way to servitude. Like Aron, however, Lefort does not entirely agree with Tocqueville's analysis. Rather, he argues that Tocqueville's understanding remains *unilateral* in exploring the reversal leading from freedom to servitude. On this point, a critique of Tocqueville would thus be necessary. It seems we should not only look at the counterpart that results from each phenomena turning into its contrary – that is, from freedom comes servitude – but also (and especially) at what Lefort calls 'the counterpart of the counterpart'.[10] In other words, we should look at how the democratic individual can find resources within this new servitude for escaping it. Much to the contrary of pessimistic readings of modernity, no fixed dialectic can illuminate the contradictions at work in democratic societies for Lefort.

One should not be misled, then, by Lefort's return to Tocqueville. He claims that, despite its fecundity, Tocqueville's thought can only partially explain the changes brought about by the democratic revolution. Centred upon the egalitarian process, it does not show clearly enough the essential difference between society under the Old Regime – founded upon the principle of monarchy – and post-revolutionary society – inseparable from a new conception of power. This is what is at stake in the comparison Lefort suggests between Tocqueville and Michelet. According to Lefort, Michelet's analysis is particularly useful in helping us to explain the transformations brought about by the fall of the monarchy, for he gives a crucial role to the symbolic function of power in the forming of social relations.

This critique clarifies why Lefort refuses to explain the genesis of total-itarianism only in terms of Tocqueville's prophecy of a tutelary state. In fact, Lefort never presents Tocqueville as a true *prophet of totalitarianism* (and neither does Aron, for that matter). He does, however, discover in Tocqueville's thought elements that allow us to understand what it is exactly about democratic societies that makes the birth of totalitarian-ism *possible*. In this way, Lefort points out the limits of analyses that sometimes draw on Tocqueville to speak of 'totalitarian democracy', as if totalitarianism were the natural end of democracy, and not its reversal. This is the case, for example, with Talmon's famous book, *The Origins of Totalitarian Democracy*.

Louis Dumont and his legacy: neo-Tocquevillian individualism

In ending this by no means exhaustive survey, it should be empha-sized that Tocqueville's return in France is not limited to the interpre-tations of Aron and Lefort. Other authors, such as Louis Dumont, have also played a central role.[11] In focusing his reading of Tocqueville on *individualism*, Dumont can even be seen as the founder of a trend called 'neo-Tocquevillian individualism', which covers the different interpretations of thinkers as diverse as François Furet, Marcel Gauchet and Gilles Lipovetsky. For these thinkers, Tocqueville is essential in that he provides the key for grasping modernity as a process of emancipation for the individual from the various forms of dependence at work in traditional societies. These readings can of course be differentiated from one another, but they can be further clarified by approaching them according to a certain logic. For instance, it is possible to reconstruct the history of French neo-Tocquevillianism in the following way: while Dumont is suspicious of the individualistic tendencies of modernity, the neo-Tocquevillians – though influenced by Dumont – relativize this suspicion regarding the theoretical relevance and practical viability of individualism in their own reading of Tocqueville.[12]

To understand the particularity of the path opened up by Dumont in France, we have to go back to the authors that inspired his analysis – first and foremost, the sociology of Célestin Bouglé, too often classified as a follower of Durkheim, but also a student of Henry Michel (himself a disciple of the great republican thinker, Charles Renouvier). In *Les idées égalitaires* from 1899, Bouglé argues that modernity is characterized by an equalization process leading to the rise of the individual. Basing himself on Tocqueville's predictions of an unavoidable movement towards equality, Bouglé shows that human beings in modern society, no longer defined by groups of belonging, gradually come to understand themselves as unique beings. Moreover, though Dumont recognized his debt with respect to Bouglé, he was more discrete about the nevertheless decisive influence of René Guénon, an ultra-conservative Indianist who was extremely hostile to Western individualism. Though Dumont is neither entirely nor explicitly an anti-modernist, like Guénon before him, he repeatedly underlines the limits of what he significantly calls an individualistic 'ideology' that reduces society as a whole to an association of independent individuals, as opposed to 'holistic' societies that subordinate the individual to the whole. Tocqueville's analyses are exemplary for Dumont on this point: they show that 'individualism' – which should not be reduced to the 'egoism' characterizing more or less all societies – is the defining characteristic of Western modernity. According to Dumont, Tocqueville has perfectly illustrated the dangerous and illusory nature of this individualism, be it with respect to gender differences or, more importantly, the crucial question of religion. Still untouched by what would become the French model of secularism (*laïcité*) and steeped in his American experience, Tocqueville argued for a necessary complementarity between a complete freedom of action for individuals in the earthly sphere and a corresponding submission in the heavenly sphere. Unfortunately, in Dumont's view, this *system of complementarity* was abandoned by European societies. This has led to modern hubris and, consequently, to the worst catastrophes of the twentieth century, including Nazism.

It is useful to draw a contrast here with the claims made by Lipovetsky twenty years later. Following Tocqueville as well as Dumont to a certain extent, in *L'ère du vide*[13] and other works, Lipovetsky maintains that since the 1960s the West has been in the throws of a 'second individualist revolution' characterized by the predominance of a quest for personal self-realization and well-being. Referring frequently to Tocqueville, he underlines that the primacy of individualism leads to the weakening of public life and, in the end, to an unavoidable deserting of civic life. But this is not a condemnation in his eyes: for Lipovetsky, individualism is not subjected to the restrictions imposed upon it by Dumont, and its practical effects seem 'generally positive'.

French and American similarities: a sociology of the individual

One might object that these French neo-Tocquevillian readings ignore certain dimensions of Tocqueville's works that have received much attention in other countries. This is particularly the case with *civic participation*, of central importance in the United States since Hannah Arendt, but also in Italy through the works of Costanzo Cipolla. This dimension has been partially eclipsed in France because of the accent placed on the question of the individual. Before exploring this difference, however, I would like to briefly consider a few points of similarity between France and the United Stated with respect to contemporary individualism.

Though we saw that Mayer's interpretation of Tocqueville ended up having very little influence in France – eclipsed as it was by the prevalence of Aron's reading – its influence in the United States was remarkably stronger. This came about through the works of sociologist David Riesman, who was inspired by both Mayer (a personal acquaintance) and the Frankfurt School psychoanalyst Erich Fromm (his analyst) to construct what might be called a 'Tocquevillian' grid of interpretation for the changes at work in American society. In his magnum opus from 1950, *The Lonely Crowd*, wherein many chapters open with quotes from Tocqueville,[14] Riesman lists three character-types related to three types of society: *tradition-directed*, *inner-directed* and *other-directed* characters. *Other-directed* individuals depend on the approval of others: their behaviour is determined by those close to them and by mass media. In this respect, Tocqueville was not an entirely infallible guide for Riesman, for the conformism Tocqueville found at work in his own times did not completely coincide with the situation in Riesman's day. Nonetheless, Riesman found in Tocqueville abundant food for thought. Similarly to Dumont in France – though upon a different basis – Riesman thus opened up a field of investigation around Tocqueville. This can be particularly seen in sociologist Richard Sennett's work from 1977, *The Fall of Public Man*, which also opens with a quote from Tocqueville, in this case, on civic apathy and individualism.[15] Sennett argues that we need to turn Riesman's typology on its head. He thinks Riesman is mistaken in claiming that the West is moving from *inner-directedness* to *other-directedness*. In fact, an entirely different process than the one leading to mass conformism is at work: the change is rather one from an *other-directed* to an *inner-directed* society. This transformation – which can be defined as a movement from 'conformism' to 'subjectivism' – finds its strongest and, for Sennett, most dramatic expression in a confusing of the public and the private spheres. From the 1970s onwards, Sennett argues, individuals have developed a tendency to treat issues related to impersonal codes in terms of personal feelings. In this way, a tyranny of intimacy is destroying public life, just as Tocqueville foretold in his darkest prophecies.

As we have seen, then, Tocqueville inspires a whole branch of American sociology in its description of contemporary individualism. The critical dimension of this American reading explains why it has come to be called 'neo-conservative'.[16] Despite its at times highly critical approach to modernity, however, its underlying paradigm differs from the French readings. In my interpretation, while the path opened up by Dumont follows in the footsteps of René Guénon's traditionalist language, a sociologist like Sennett speaks to us from an entirely different standpoint. One could characterize this standpoint as 'republican', since Sennett's difficulty with individualism is that it leads to the downfall of the *res publica*. This brings us to a central theme in the American readings of Tocqueville, in large part already anticipated, as I have argued above, in Arendt's interpretation: the theme of *civic and associative participation*.

Tocqueville and communitarianism: Sandel's reading

Let us now turn to a first difference: while Tocqueville was mostly received in the French public sphere as a 'liberal', in the United States he was more often heralded as a precursor to a philosophical trend more or less hostile to liberalism, namely, communitarianism. As we all know, this trend is far from homogeneous: we have only to think of Charles Taylor and Michael Walzer's differing relations to 'liberalism'. It remains that many of these authors have found in Tocqueville an essential point of reference for moving beyond liberalism. It would bring us too far to examine in detail here the differences between these readings, which is why I have chosen to focus primarily on Sandel's reading.

Sandel sees an alternative to liberalism in a certain kind of republicanism. The critique he formulates in *Liberalism and the Limits of Justice* is aimed at modern liberals such as Locke and Mill, and contemporary ones such as Rawls. Incidentally, Mill was a friend and admirer of Tocqueville and has often been compared to him. According to Sandel, however, Mill is a 'liberal', while Tocqueville should be approached *outside* liberalism. To clarify the reasons behind this choice, let us briefly recall the communitarian objections to liberalism. To begin with, liberalism purportedly promotes a false conception of an 'unencumbered', 'Kantian' self: this 'self' can be thought and defined independently of any social or cultural context. The idea of the 'right' having priority over the 'good' would equally be false: liberals purportedly believe in the possibility of neutral procedures that would regulate the coexistence of individuals with different values.

In *Democracy's Discontent*,[17] Sandel argues that the original form of American republicanism is the exact opposite of this so-called 'Kantian liberalism' and thus offers a solution to the two threats that hang over public life: the citizens' loss of control over their own lives and the destruction of different communities. Sandel even calls for a return to Aristotle, who – contrary to modern liberals – defined politics as a search for the 'best constitution' and saw citizens as 'political animals' that brought their humanity to full fruition by participating in the life of the city-state. Indeed, are 'citizens' not defined by their capacity to alternately govern and be governed in the *Politica*? Yet, in his attempt to revitalize the spirit of American republicanism, Sandel prefers to explore the present-day importance of Tocqueville. He attempts to demonstrate the depth of Tocqueville's praise of communal institutions as 'schools of liberty', which capture, according to Sandel, the spirit of the American Republic: the relation between the individual and the state was not direct at the time, but rather 'mediated by decentralized forms of political association and participation'.[18] In this way, Sandel distinguishes the republicanism of Tocqueville from Rousseau. In *Le contrat social*, a determining role was given to the absolute unity of the political body and even to constraint. On this level, Rousseau does not have much to offer to communitarians, who insist instead on the necessary dissemination of places for civic participation.

Sandel's choice of Tocqueville over Rousseau also reveals his position on the possible future of civic commitment in the age of globalization. On a global scale, he thinks that American patriotism can no longer be primarily directed towards the nation-state. Yet, he is skeptical about cosmopolitan citizenship theories, for he feels they underestimate our need to identify with particular communities. The proper response to globalization is thus not in a cosmopolitan, but a dispersed citizenship. It is Tocqueville's associationism, then, that opens a way back towards the ideal of self-government in the age of globalization.

All things considered, however, I think Sandel gives a questionable reading of Tocqueville: while he rightly emphasizes the importance of participation, he neglects the liberal dimension of Tocqueville's thought. This can be seen in the fact that, like other communitarians, he only gives a secondary place to law, which in fact played an important role for Tocqueville in maintaining liberty.

Civic tradition and social capital: Putnam's neo-Tocquevillian sociology

Sandel's radical questioning of the role of the nation-state brings to the fore tangible differences with a whole sphere of French thought. Another difference is to be found in the use of the expression 'neo-Tocquevillian'. In France, following Dumont, we have seen that this term designates a trend characterizing modernity as a process that emancipates the individual from tradition. In the United States, 'neo-Tocquevillianismism' stands instead for a political sociology describing the crucial role of associative relations in fostering a common life based in mutual trust. Robert Putnam's research on social capital falls within this purview – and he draws on Tocqueville as early as his works on civic life in Italy.

The aim of his book, *Making Democracy Work*,[19] is to show that the general success of Italy's different regions can be correlated to the density of civic relations established through municipal life and free associations. Putnam already presents Tocqueville's thought as the framework for his research here. *De la démocratie en Amérique*, for instance, would demonstrate the relation between societal habits and politics: civic associations reinforce the 'habits of the heart' indispensable to democratic life. Moreover, in line with some other American interpretations – in particular, Roger Boesche's – Putnam almost goes so far as to claim that Tocqueville is the heir of Renaissance republicanism. Putting forward the concept of 'civic community', he stresses (following John Pocock)[20] that the success of free institutions in the Florentine tradition depended upon 'civic virtues'. But this concept was overshadowed by liberalism from Hobbes and Locke onwards according to Putnam and Pocock. In returning to republicanism, Tocqueville shows that only an active participation in civic associations can guarantee an authentic citizenship built upon a sense of cooperation, solidarity and mutual social responsibility. Empirical research would corroborate the fact that associative commitment creates habits of cooperation and responsibility sharing in individuals: even participation in bird-watching groups would develop a sense of self-discipline and collective responsibility.

Yet another Tocquevillian discovery is the role of local media in civic life. Here also, research would confirm that an active local press indicates a higher level of civic consciousness and an optimal capacity for communal harmony and problem-solving. A personal and daily knowledge of local issues is a necessary condition for citizens to be able to address these issues together. Confirming Tocqueville's hypotheses, it has been found that in regions with a very vibrant associative life, like Emilia-Romagna, citizens follow local public debates closely and are highly involved in projects aiming at communal well-being. Conversely, in regions with less associative involvement, like Calabria, clientelism and corruption are the order of the day and inhibit development.

Putnam draws on Tocqueville to the greatest extent, however, in his research on the United States,[21] referring to him as the 'patron saint' of both communitarians and social capital sociologists. By 'social capital' Putnam means the formal and informal networks that bind human beings together in relations of cooperation based on mutual trust. It seems that Tocqueville put his finger on the nerve of American civic culture, namely: the *associationism* that brings individuals together in the most diverse communities through objectives that vary from peer tutoring at school to musical groups. Tocqueville also grasped the role of religious communities in making civic education concrete. His genius finally lies in having understood what Putnam calls the generalized norm of reciprocity with his theory of 'self-interest rightly understood': individuals in American society are more likely to get involved in common causes if they expect profitable returns for themselves at some point.

Far from restricting Tocqueville to an idealized nineteenth-century era, Putnam thinks that his vision has been accomplished in the twentieth century – up until the 1960s at least, when Americans devoted much of their time to associative life. But from the 1970s onwards – a time characterized by a fall in associative participation – the United States has moved away from the Tocquevillian picture. There are many reasons for this: changes in work patterns, lengthy commutes, the crisis of the family, the increasing weight of media, etc. Yet, in drawing his analysis to a close, Putnam takes up a somewhat Tocquevillian perspective by calling American citizens to prepare the way for a revitalization of associative life, rather than deploring the current situation. This would imply: a renewal of active civic education; the implementing of commuting conditions and work schedules that allow enough time for involvement in associations; a great religious reawakening (though Putnam warns against its dangers in claiming that it must be pluralistic and tolerant); new forms of electronic communication (internet, rather than the isolated television); an increase in communal festivities; and, finally, a greater commitment by all to traditional political life (elections, etc.).

Tocqueville and 'strong democracy'

Let us now turn to a third kind of reading of Tocqueville, which contrasts with both the communitarian and French readings: Benjamin Barber's approach in his defence of a 'strong democracy' essentially consisting in the revitalization of civil society – an idea he first wrote about in 1984, but has continued to develop up until the present day. Barber is not unaware of the confusion surrounding the concept of civil society. First conceived by Locke and Hegel specialists, it has since been so widely used and misused in the public sphere that, in Barber's own words, it is little more than a 'chic slogan'.[22] This is why he has established a typology of the different conceptions of 'civil society'. The first is a dogmatic 'liberal' conception elaborated in a framework promoting a free market economy: it reduces civil society to a private realm characterized by purely contractual relations between individuals. Opposing the state to almost everything else – and, as such, confuting economic and civic associations – liberals argue for a radical opposition between the public and private spheres. One might add that these liberals, following in the footsteps of Friedrich Hayek, draw Tocqueville into their cause by referring to his prophecy of a tutelary state that crushes all social and economic life. In its second, communitarian conception, civil society becomes synonymous with community, with all the ambiguities that ensue if this is understood as legitimizing all types of closed community. Communitarianism of this kind can be harmful to the ideals of public space and democracy. This is why it is necessary to adopt one last perspective: a strongly democratic one where civil society becomes a key for rehabilitating republicanism – a specifically modern republicanism, it should be noted, for Barber rejects 'the republican nostalgia of such commentators as Hannah Arendt or Leo Strauss'.[23] His defence of a 'strong democracy', that is, of active and continuous citizen participation in civil society, is instead inspired by John Dewey, the great theorist of associationist democracy. But he also refers to Tocqueville to emphasize that a free political community depends on a civil society that is not stagnant:

> Alexis de Tocqueville praised the *local* character of American liberty and he thought that democracy could only be upheld through vigorous civil activity on a municipal level following a model inspired by President Jackson's example. He would be hard put to recognize the United States today, where our alternatives have been reduced to either gigantism and a market-driven acquisitiveness (the liberal model) or a parochial sense of identity (the communitarian model).[24]

Tocqueville is no defender of a minimal democracy or of one based on self-interested bargaining, both of which would consist of an electoral competition between the political elite. He is rather the great mind behind civic education, if we mean by this the active participation of all citizens on a local and associative scale. Barber thus reminds us: 'The politically edifying influence of participation has been noted a thousand times since first Rousseau and then Mill and Tocqueville suggested that democracy was best taught by practicing it.'[25] However, as had already been specified by Tocqueville in his theory of 'self-interest rightly understood', associative life does not imply an exceptional altruism or any kind of asceticism that would require individuals to forego their own interests: rather, they are simply brought to an awareness that collaborative associations are the best way to achieve their own ends. And only a tight-knit associative network effectively allows the mutual trust indispensable to the success of communal endeavours to arise between individuals. Compared to other republicans like Rousseau, who distrusted particular groups, Tocqueville's important contribution has been to show how associations are decisive factors in the running of democratic institutions and in public deliberation – they are the only way of settling differences of interest with a view to the common good. For Barber, this Tocquevillian conception is even more worthy of our attention in that it provides the only way to ensure a future for participative democracy in the age of globalization. In *Jihad vs McWorld*,[26] Barber emphasizes the double threat to democratic life of two interrelated phenomena: the unlimited expansion of 'McWorld', that is, of global capitalism and its telecommunication and information networks controlled by a few big multinationals; and the Jihad reaction, that is, all forms of ethnic or religious fundamentalism and particularism. According to Barber, the 'McWorld tyranny' calls for a democratic response based in the development of a civil society with global dimensions. This would be the only way of protecting against the involuntary despotism of the new global capitalism. Here again, Barber refers first and foremost to Tocqueville and his philosophy of civil society to sketch the outline of a global civil society that can neither be reduced to the state nor to a free market framework.

Neo-Tocquevillianism and deliberative democracy

The difficulty with both Putnam and Barber's readings is that they lack realism. Indeed, how can we renew Tocqueville's civism in the face of contemporary economic, social and technological changes that exclude from the outset any simple return to the associative citizenship of 1830? These are the issues facing present-day theorists of deliberative democracy who draw on Tocqueville, such as James S. Fishkin and Bruce Ackerman.[27] Here, we can once again speak of 'neo-Tocquevillianism', but in a very different sense than in France, where we saw the term used to describe the individualist approaches of Dumont, Gauchet, Furet and Lipovetsky. Deliberative democracy stands for a conception of democracy that is not simply reduced to an election model where political elites run for the votes of the electorate. Instead, it implies a *discussion* where citizens present and *debate* their respective viewpoints, by the end of which initial preferences may be set aside in favour of a stance that integrates the views of the various interlocutors. However, this dialogue-based model – in line with Tocqueville's defence of municipal assemblies – is threatened by the increasing influence of opinion polls, where a snapshot of different opinions is given, but no real confrontation arises. Hence, the increasing risk of a political crisis in societies where the government and citizens act according to the so-called 'public opinion' discovered in polls – which is in fact nothing more than a sum of heterogeneous preferences.

In Fishkin's view, the active participation in associations and local assemblies described by Tocqueville is an excellent model for collective deliberation, but only on a local scale. On a broader scale, changes in the *media* have made it necessary to reconsider the concrete aspects of civism. Tocqueville's view on newspapers in *De la démocratie en Amérique* provides us with some insight in this regard: he saw newspapers as linked to specific parties or associations and as thus complementing civic participation.[28] As Fishkin remarks, however, these newspapers were soon replaced by more informative dailies aimed at a wider audience and no longer provided the civic function so admired by Tocqueville. It is in this framework that polls claiming to reflect public opinion arose – though the snapshot of an opinion can never replace its elaboration in an actual dialogue. Hence, the proposition to institute deliberative polls in a Tocquevillian spirit: a panel representing the various opinions polled would be chosen to meet and *actually discuss* a given issue with the support of specialists and impartial documents on the problem under discussion. In Fishkin's experience, these deliberative polls often lead to a change in opinion by the end of the discussion; and they represent the results of an *actual deliberation*. Both Fishkin and Ackerman feel that this invention renews the spirit of Tocqueville's associationism by bringing it into the age of mass media.[29] A neo-Tocquevillian by his own admission, Fiskhin emphasizes that, though

Tocqueville was interested in 'institutions that encourage dialogue between individuals', today, we can no longer focus so strongly on associations. While Ackerman also calls himself a 'neo-Tocquevillian', he claims that his vision is 'less idyllic' than Tocqueville's: 'we can no longer expect civil society to develop on its own' and we thus have an active role to play in its development, in particular, through 'deliberative polls' that reach out to a wide audience on a national scale.[30]

One may certainly be sceptical about deliberative polls,[31] for they might seem unrealistic or incapable of resolving all the problems linked to the actual influence of polls. Nonetheless, they do bear witness to a vibrant Tocquevillian tradition in contemporary American thought. The issues surrounding democratization in Europe might thus find similar sources in Tocqueville for rethinking the ideal of deliberative democracy: a democracy characterized by continuous public debate in a civil society where associations have a role to play, without necessarily being the main interlocutors of political power. In any case, at least in spirit, deliberative democracy hearkens back to two central themes in Tocqueville that remain important today: a warning against the dangers of individualism and a search for means that would promote active citizen participation in a communal approach to political problem-solving. While the first theme has been given in-depth consideration by French neo-Tocquevillians, it is clear that the second has received more attention in contemporary American thought.

Conclusion: A partial parting of ways

Tocqueville's return manifests itself quite differently, then, on each side of the Atlantic, both with respect to its presuppositions and conclusions. More specifically, Anglo-American readers have paid much more attention to association and participation than their French counterparts, both on an interpretative and normative level. Further, it is much more common to interpret Tocqueville in the light of republican ideals in the United States and Canada. Yet, we should not paint too simplistic a picture. It was after all Jean-Claude Lamberti, a French thinker, who brought the significance of Tocqueville to the fore in European republicanism.[32] And it is not unheard of in France to link the ideas of 'civil society' and 'associationism' to Tocqueville, as any reading of Lefort will demonstrate. On the other hand, neither is the 'liberal' Tocqueville, prophet of totalitarianism, a solely French invention: this interpretation is also prevalent in Anglo-American readings – for example, in Talmon or, on an entirely different level, in the neo-liberal interpretations like

Hayek's. The fact remains, however, that the French have tended to underestimate associationism, to say nothing of the religious question, which has often been passed over in silence, though it constitutes an essential dimension of Tocqueville's thought.

It is my contention that this difference can be explained by the history of the two continents, and the philosophical theories that have held sway on each. Doubtless more than any other, French political thought has been constantly troubled by the question of the state and centralization – be it to celebration, amendment, or harsh criticism of the state. This question is central not only to many republican theories, but also to a whole sphere of French liberalism, especially Guizot. I mentioned above that Dumont's interpretation of Tocqueville was partially inspired by Bouglé, a student of Henry Michel, who was himself a disciple of Renouvier. What is remarkable is that Henry Michel had already referred to Tocqueville in his defence of the idea of the state understood as guarantor of individual liberty.[33] Michel even had some affinities with Charles Dupont-White, an economist who developed one of the most fervent French apologies of centralization and who was also a great reader of Guizot. Michel did not share, however, in Dupont-White's distrust of civil society, and it was precisely in Tocqueville's associationism that he attempted to find a theoretical model for thinking about the necessity of mediation between individual and state. Still, the neo-Tocquevillian individualism we saw arising out of Dumont, and which subsequently had a profound effect on the French reception of Tocqueville, found one of its key sources of inspiration in this French thought on the state.

Moreover, the French republican model has arisen out of a specific understanding of the relation between politics and religion – an understanding from which it is inseparable and that we all know is completely different from the American approach. French secularism (*laïcité*), as it has manifested itself since the 1905 law separating church and state, also implies a wholly different understanding of the place of religion in politics than what Tocqueville found and admired in the United States. In this respect, I would argue that Tocqueville's thought remains, until today, more easily assimilated in its coherent totality – that is, including the decisive question of religion – by Anglo-American thinkers than by their French counterparts.

Notes

1 This framework has led me to leave aside here the contribution of British interpretations, despite their richness. The various references of Isaiah Berlin

to Tocqueville would require a whole chapter to themselves. See also, more recently: Larry Siedentop, *Tocqueville* (Oxford: Oxford University Press, 1994).

2   Raymond Aron, 'Tocqueville retrouvé', *The Tocqueville Review/La revue Tocqueville*, 1(1) (1979), pp. 8–23.

3   Serge Audier, *Tocqueville retrouvé* (Paris: Vrin/EHESS, 2004).

4   Eugène d'Eichthal, *Alexis de Tocqueville et la démocratie libérale* (Paris: Calmann-Lévy, 1897).

5   Jacob Peter Mayer, *Prophet of the Mass Age. A Study of Alexis de Tocqueville* (London: J.M. Dent & Sons, 1939). This book has been translated into French by J. Sorin under the title *Alexis de Tocqueville* (Paris: Gallimard, 1948).

6   On this reading, see Audier, *Tocqueville retrouvé*.

7   See Stephen Holmes, *Benjamin Constant and the Making of Modern Liberalism* (New Haven, CT: Yale University, 1984).

8   See especially, 'From Equality to Freedom: Fragments of an Interpretation of *Democracy in America*', in Claude Lefort, *Democracy and Political Theory*, trans. David Macey (Minniapolis: University of Minnesota Press, 1988), pp. 183–209. See also the essays in *Writing. The Political Test*, trans. David Ames Curtis (Durham, NC, and London: Duke University Press, 2000).

9   Roger Boesche, *The Strange Liberalism of Alexis de Tocqueville* (Ithaca: Cornell University Press, 1987). It should be noted that Boesche mentions Rédier's work.

10 Claude Lefort, 'Tocqueville: democracy and the art of writing', in *Writing*, p. 49.

11 Louis Dumont, *Homo Hierarchicus: The Caste System and its Implications*, trans. George Weidenfeld and Nicolson Ltd (Chicago: University of Chicago Press, 1980).

12 We should note, however, some evolution of thought in a few of these thinkers. For instance, in his more recent writings, Marcel Gauchet is increasingly worried about the effects of contemporary individualism. See especially: Marcel Gauchet, *La démocratie contre elle-même* (Paris: Gallimard, 2002) – the title of which refers to a passage from *De la démocratie en Amérique*.

13 Gilles Lipovetsky, *L'ère du vide. Essai sur l'individualisme contemporain* (Paris: Gallimard, 1983).

14 David Riesman, *The Lonely Crowd* (New Haven, CT: Yale University Press, 1952). The French translation – *La foule solitaire* (Paris: Arthaud, 1964) – opens with a preface by Edgar Morin that emphasizes (in a Tocquevillian spirit) how Europeans ought to direct their attention towards the United States.

15 Richard Sennett, *The Fall of Public Man* (New York: Knopf, 1977).

16 Alessandro Ferrara, *Modernity and Authenticity: A Study of the Social and Ethical Thought of Jean-Jacques Rousseau* (Albany, NY: State University of New York Press, 1993).

17 Michael Sandel, *Democracy's Discontent. America in Search of a Public Philosophy* (Cambridge, MA: Harvard University Press, 1996).

18 *Ibid.*, p. 27.

19 Robert D. Putnam, *Making Democracy Work: Civic Tradition in Modern Italy* (Princeton, NJ: Princeton University Press, 1993).

20 John G.A. Pocock, *The Machiavellian Moment. Florentine Political Thought and the Atlantic Republican Tradition* (Princeton, NJ: Princeton University Press,

1975). An in-depth consideration of Pocock's theses on Machiavelli and Republicanism is well worth one's while. On this topic, see Serge Audier, *Machiavel, conflit et liberté* (Paris: Vrin/EHESS, 2005).

21 Robert D. Putnam, *Bowling Alone. The Collapse and Revival of American Community* (New York: Simon and Schuster, 2000). Just like *Making Democracy Work*, this book by Putnam has also caused a great deal of academic controversy that I do not have time to address here.

22 Here, I am quoting from Barber's paper, ' "Moderno repubblicanesimo?" La promessa della società civile', presented in Italian at a conference of the Agnelli Foundation, and to be found in: M.Viroli (ed.), *Libertà politica e virtù civile. Significati e percorsi del repubblicanesimo classico* (Turin: Edizioni Fondazione Giovanni Agnelli, 2004), p. 278.

23 Benjamin Barber, *Strong Democracy: Participatory Politics for a New Age* (Berkeley: University of California Press, 1984), p. 118.

24 Barber, ' "Moderno repubblicanesimo?" ', p. 278.

25 Barber, *Strong Democracy*, p. 235.

26 Benjamin Barber, *Jihad vs McWorld* (New York: New York Times Book, 1995).

27 James Fishkin, *Democracy and Deliberation: New Directions for Democratic Reform* (London: Yale University Press, 1991); *The Voice of the People* (London: Yale University Press, 1995). See also: James Fishkin and Bruce Ackerman, *Deliberation Day* (London: Yale University Press, 2004).

28 Alexis de Tocqueville, *Democracy in America*, trans. Arthur Goldhammer (New York: Library of America, 2004), vol. 2, Part II, Chap. VI.

29 They also propose creating one or several *deliberation days* that would mobilize millions of citizens before elections. Less Tocquevillian is the idea of an internet deliberation: for Tocqueville it is of central importance to civic life that citizens actually meet with each other.

30 See the interviews given by Ackerman and Fishkin at Luiss University in Rome in: *Democrazia deliberativa: cosa è*, ed. G. Bosetti & S. Maffettone (Rome: Luiss University Press, 2004).

31 In his reflections on the appropriate model for democracy in the European Union, while Jean-Marc Ferry argues for a deliberative model, he also emphasizes that deliberative polls may 'disturb the framework of representative democracy', by replacing periodic elections with 'uncontrollable harassment' and demands upon one's time. Jean-Marc Ferry, *L'Europe, L'Amérique et le monde* (Nantes: Editions Pleins Feux, 2005) p. 89.

32 Jean-Claude Lamberti is one of the few thinkers in France to hold this view of Tocqueville: 'His work was the last great theoretical embodiment of civic humanism, whose influence can be seen in the Renaissance and in both the American and French revolutions.' Jean-Claude Lamberti, *Tocqueville and the Two Democracies*, trans. Arthur Goldhammer (Harvard: Harvard University Press, 1989), pp. 187–8.

33 On Michel's contribution, see the special issue of *Corpus* 48 (2005), *Henry Michel: l'individu et l'état*, ed. S. Audier. On Michel and Pillon's readings of Tocqueville, see Audier, 'Les républicains français ont-ils ignoré Tocqueville?', *Respublica*, 40 (January 2004) and 'Tocqueville et la tradition républicaine', *Cahiers de philosophie de l'Université de Caen*, 43 (2007).

6
Democratic Threats and Threats to Democracy

Ringo Ossewaarde

Introduction

In his introduction to *De la démocratie en Amérique*, Alexis de Tocqueville announces that democracy is to be understood as 'a providential fact'.[1] He perceives democracy as being part of an overarching order. This order is not the creation of the human will and imagination, but a providential, given order, which means that humans can only fulfil their given potentialities within and not outside this order.[2] Democracy, being divinely planned, is in accordance with the 'hidden law of Providence',[3] that is, reveals 'God's laws in the conduct of societies'.[4] Indeed, Tocqueville shows traits of a classical, theocentric thinker, with strong Aristotelian and Augustinian or Pascalian inclinations,[5] who sees the field of human activity as being embedded within a greater order or 'a general and constant plan according to which God guides the species'.[6] Democracy, which he understands as a 'state of society in which everyone more or less would take part in public affairs',[7] must be carefully distinguished from aristocracy. Tocqueville interprets aristocracy, a state of society in which not everyone has the right to take part in public affairs, as a human – all too human – creation.[8]

Democracy, being providentially willed from the very beginning, had to allow the passage of various states of society, from tribal society and the Greek *polis* with its slaves to the feudal society with its privileges, before being able to make its entrance. It is not a jubilant Tocqueville who observes democratization in political history, trying to legitimize his democratic taste by bringing in providence. Indeed, it is with great difficulty that he is obliged to conclude, for the sake of justice or natural right, that 'what seems to me decadence is therefore progress in his eyes; what wounds me is agreeable to Him. Equality is perhaps less elevated;

but it is more just, and its justice makes for its greatness and its beauty.'[9] Aristocratic inequality of living conditions is the rule of privilege, landed property and ascribed status (nobility) according to birth and family name. The aristocratic societies of 'childish and ridiculous privileges' were unjust.[10] Aristocracy is unjust, not according to human, democratic or legal criteria, but according to the divine plan: privilege is not part of the providential order.[11] Even though aristocratic societies may excel in philosophy and poetry, and aristocrats may be great in statesmanship, such societies are always unjust.

Knowing Tocqueville's admiration for his compatriot Bossuet, it is easy to recognize a parallel between the statesman's providential understanding of the democratic revolution and the bishop's theory of universal history. Bossuet writes a providential history of Christianity; Tocqueville writes a providential history of democracy. The former attempts to show that the whole of European history points to the advent of the true religion; the latter attempts to show how providence has been guiding humankind towards the more natural form of society.[12] Bossuet stresses that the pagan mind had been unable to develop truthful knowledge of God; Tocqueville observes that the ancient pagans were unable to grasp the fundamental equality between master and slave, man and woman, black and white. The history of Israel, Greece and Rome, the advent of Christ in the Roman Empire and the history of the church are all meaningful events in Tocqueville's history of democracy. Even the greatest philosophers and statesmen of antiquity, from Plato to Cicero, were, despite their enormous political wisdom, incapable of grasping the simplest truths of democracy.[13] In Tocqueville's history of democracy, 'it was necessary that Jesus Christ came to earth to make it understood that all members of the human species are naturally alike and equal'.[14] Christ, not Socrates or Aristotle, is the teacher of democracy.

As Tocqueville sees it, the problem of democracy is that it does not promise liberty for everyone. Instead, it abolishes privileges and creates equal social opportunities or life chances, hence, making room for personal achievement and meritocratic rule. However, though democracy is a providential fact and therefore just in itself, it is still dependent upon human effort for its unravelling. Democratic *culture*, which was still coming into being during Tocqueville's lifetime, was no cause for great joy:

you know that I am not exaggerating the final result of the great democratic revolution that is taking place at this moment in the world; I do not regard it in the same light as the Israelites saw the Promised Land.[15]

Tocqueville saw that the great passion for liberty or self-government was gone in the heart of his contemporaries.[16] *Equality*, as such, does not exclude equality in chains. This is the great threat that becomes real if men are led to serfdom, that is to say when democracy is left, without the statesman's prudence, to its 'blind instincts'.[17] Human leadership towards a democracy of slaves may come from men, from demagogical parties and from populism. But reason and faith show that it is *liberty*, not equality, that is the supreme good. As Tocqueville states:

> I cannot believe that God has pushed two or three million men for several centuries toward equality of conditions in order to have them end in the despotism of Tiberius and Claudius ... Why He is carrying us along this way toward democracy, I do not know; but embarked on a vessel I did not construct, I look for the means to reach the nearest port.[18]

Hence, for Tocqueville, reviving and safeguarding liberty, as it is classically understood, are the real challenges of democracy. These are most difficult tasks for statesmen and citizens, even more difficult than in an aristocracy. Liberty is a classical, not an aristocratic value. It is exercised by citizens, not aristocrats. Yet aristocrats are more experienced in 'the art of being free'. A young democratic people is still in the process of learning how to govern itself as a citizenry. Democracy may well be according to the providential order, but the existence of a democratic culture where freedom and the respect for the equal dignity of each human being prevail depends on civic activity. Providence does not imply human passivity, but is like a lighthouse that is present, even in the middle of nowhere, guiding the human race even when it has strayed far away from its final destination or *telos*. The search for liberty, in the democratic age, implies determining which cultural conditions sustain or violate the natural right to participate in the common good, through civic self-government. This is achieved through a cultural study of 'the sentiments, the ideas, the mores that alone can lead to public prosperity and liberty', as well as of 'the vices and errors', which prevent a democratic people from being free.[19] The struggle for freedom, then, requires a particular kind of democratic culture. This chapter seeks to retrace the meaning of, and threats to, this particular culture of democracy, which Tocqueville envisions.

Democratic cultures

For Tocqueville, the cultural condition is identical to the state of the *moeurs* or mores classically understood, prevailing among a people. The mores, for him, is the equivalent of 'habits' or, in Thomist language, the *habitus*, that is, the general inclinations of heart *and* dispositions of mind. Tocqueville understands 'the expression *moeurs* in the sense that the ancients attached to the word mores'.[20] He writes:

> not only do I apply it to mores properly so-called, which one could call habits of the heart, but to the different notions that men possess, to the various opinions that are current in their midst, and to the sum of ideas of which the habits of the mind are formed.[21]

Thus defined, the cultural condition that Tocqueville investigates, includes both the 'habits of the heart' and the 'habits of the mind' of a group.[22] These are the collective sources of the moral and intellectual virtues – a distinctive repertoire of more or less predictable dispositions that belong to a cultural group of people. For the ancients, this group was the fatherland; for Tocqueville, it is the nation. Hence, it is possible to speak of an American, Dutch or French heart and mind.

Tocqueville observes that, in the nations of Europe, a 'secret force', operating in providential history, has been shaping a democratic *habitus* in the motives that make a people act. In the (democratic) movement from the Old Regime to equality of living conditions, the European peoples did not understand the changes taking place in their hearts and they did not realize that they were playing their part in the structural transformation from the Old Regime into the democratic state of civilization. But they all instinctively felt that new times were coming. Tocqueville points out that, in the movement towards the event of 1789, in the Age of Enlightenment,

> there were few who could understand what caused such deep emotion within their own hearts; but all were moved and all heard the faraway sound as a sign; what is prophesied, people didn't yet know. It was like the voice of John the Baptist crying from the wilderness that new times were coming.[23]

Similarly, in his *Souvenirs*, Tocqueville insists that in the movement towards the February Revolution, great masses of men move for reasons almost as unknown to mortal men as the reasons that regulate the movements of the sea. In both cases the reasons are in a sense hidden and lost in the sheer immensity of the phenomenon.[24]

Tocqueville's cultural enquiry into the habits of the heart and the habits of the mind is ultimately a study of how the democratic revolution, taking place in the heart and the mind, shapes the destiny of nations. Hence, in 1853, Tocqueville, working on his final book, explains in a letter to a critical friend that he is not, in the first place, interested in the question of how the democratic revolution structurally transforms institutions, such as languages, laws, markets, literature, states, or churches.[25] Instead, he wants to penetrate into the core of the democratic culture. He wants to know the dispositions of the mind and inclinations of the heart, which enable such institutions to develop and to be destroyed. Tocqueville constantly searches for the hidden, for the secret motives and dark corners of the heart, which made men act in such ways that democratization of institutions continues. Such a philosophical comprehension of the sources of democratic culture supports statesmen in governing democratic peoples towards a freer, more self-governing, state of being.

The habits that 'make democracy work'

Tocqueville, the to-be statesman, went to America to see how specifically American habits of heart and mind made American democracy work. In his own words, 'providence has put a torch within our reach that our fathers lacked and has permitted us to discern in the destiny of nations first causes that the obscurity of the past concealed from them'.[26] With the help of this new light, Tocqueville was able to determine that it was the Puritan habits of mind, developed throughout Europe's Reformation, which were the source of the American democracy. Politically, the Puritans were exiled from the old world, in particular from England and Holland. Their religious extremism could not be accommodated within Europe's old regime without battle. Religiously, 'in exposing themselves to the inevitable miseries of exile, they wanted to make *an idea* triumph'.[27] That idea is the idea of democracy, the idea of making living conditions equal for all citizens.

Like Plato, Augustine, Aquinas and Pascal, Tocqueville believes that religion and politics, the city of God and the city of man, church and state, heaven and earth, must always be distinguished from each other, as distinct things, but can never be fully separated.[28] The Reformation in the city of man, for him, helped shaping a democratic culture: 'Puritanism was not merely a religious doctrine, but corresponded in many points with the most absolute democratic and republican theories.'[29] Tocqueville points out that, politically and socially, the Puritan habits of mind are typically middle class and yet not bourgeois.[30] Being middle class, the Puritans are not aristocratic but, in contrast with the bourgeoisie, they are pro-democratic *and* constitute a self-governing citizenry. Puritans take equality of status for granted, within their own middle class, and passionately govern their own destiny within their own religio-political association of the township, in which they breathe 'an air of antiquity and a sort of biblical perfume'.[31] Hence, the Puritans have managed to reconcile democratic equality and classical liberty.

Tocqueville perceives the Puritan township as being so much in conformity with natural law that it seems to be a divine gift.[32] It is through this specific township association, combined with the Puritan zeal, that the Puritans are able to make the democratic idea triumph. In the Puritan mind, the democratic idea does not refer to some formal institution, like a parliament or an election system, but is the application of the doctrine of popular sovereignty in all circumstances. In its Puritan, middle-class understanding, popular sovereignty means that 'the people reign over the American political world as God does over the universe'.[33] To make the democratic idea triumph in America means that the doctrine of popular sovereignty comes to inhere in the entire social structure, in all institutions of society – from families to businesses and from schools to armies. For both Tocqueville and the Puritans, democracy means *democratic social structure* in mind and heart. Democracy takes possession of the habits of the mind and heart of a people that is organized as a nation. Without democratic ideas and sentiments ruling a people, nations cannot rule themselves democratically.

Tocqueville is at pains to show that the township in New England is an order that is part of an overarching providential order, and, accordingly, conforms to nature. Though the New England township is typically Puritan, and, as such, the distinctively American seat of democratic citizenship that makes American democracy work, it is not a human construct but shaped by providence. Like the French commune or the German town,[34] the Puritan township follows the natural law that states that each man should be free to use his right to govern himself.[35] The New England township ensures that American liberty, the highest national good, is preserved through democratic citizenship. In other words, within the specifically American historical context, all citizens can take an active part in public affairs and bring the principle of popular sovereignty into effect through township self-government. The

Puritans were prevented from doing so in the old world. Their emigration to America has made them, like the survivors of Troy in Virgil's *Aeneid*, exiles in the American wilderness, forced to establish a new world.[36]

Democracy outside Christendom?

According to Tocqueville, the great contemporary problem of democracy, and perhaps the most important reason to publish the *Démocratie*, is the political problem of 'the organization and the establishment of democracy in Christendom'.[37] Tocqueville does not believe that a democratic social structure in the habits of the mind and heart can exist outside the Christian world. In his view, democracy outside Christendom can only be an empty form, a complex of formal institutions, devoid of democratic spirit.[38] He points out that even the greatest minds of antiquity were incapable of grasping the simplest truths of democracy. Democratic truths, like the truth that all humans are naturally equal, independently of their social and cultural identities (gender, race, class, nation or religion), did not come naturally to the human mind, through Socratic reasoning, but presented themselves as revealed truths in providential history. Tocqueville points out that providential history is the history of democratization, including its battles, reformations, sectarianism, materialism, anthropocentric humanism and individualism, within Christendom.[39] Outside Christendom, democracy does not penetrate into the habits of mind and heart.

India is an illustrative case. Arend Lijphart observes that India must be classified as a democracy because it has government forms such as a cabinet, a legislature, more than one party, an election system, majority rule, a supreme court, several interest groups, a free press and a central bank.[40] For Tocqueville, who always took a keen interest in Indian culture (he initially planned to write a book on India), Lijphart's indicators would have been just empty forms.[41] These forms neither express nor guarantee the democratic habits of mind and heart of a sovereign people, which alone can make democracy work. When political forms are devoid of such democratic substance, then democracy becomes an abstraction, not a concrete, socially structured experience in the daily lives of families, neighbourhoods and communes, or in art, philosophy, industry, language, religion and education. In India, there may be formal democratic institutions, but there appears no democratic social structure in the ideas and sentiments of a sovereign people.

Like the ancients, the Indian mind, it seems, fails to recognize the fundamental equality of dignity of all members of the human species. Tocqueville observes that the Indian habits of the mind and heart are so opposed to equality of status, to washing the dirty feet of the lowly, that the principle of popular sovereignty could only be brought into effect there if the Indian nation would become a part of Christendom. The Indian caste system that ensures that inequality of dignity and fatalism prevail, making democracy an empty word, is part of a complex religion that has no idea of a living, personal God who creates and renews nature out of love for the creatures. As Tocqueville puts it, Hinduism is 'a religion which has enough grip on minds for it has been able to create and maintain a social state so contrary to nature .... The religion has introduced among them so many vicious institutions and evil maxims ... .'[42]

One of the most 'vicious institutions' is obviously the caste system, which cannot be reconciled with democracy. The fundamental inequality of dignity within the caste system is deeply rooted in the Indian habits of the mind and heart, meaning that any 'official' abolition of the caste system does not transform the Indian way of thinking and feeling – does not generate the recognition of the hidden law of providence, let alone its obedience. Even if all Indians are offered equal opportunities and equal treatment by law, their habits of the mind and heart will not change in their political and social relationships. The likely reason for this is that this 'vicious institution' is intimately linked with the 'evil maxim' of reincarnation, of the cycle of birth, death and rebirth, which is firmly rooted in the Indian habits of the mind. The Indian mind and heart are so habituated to *explaining and understanding* the wealth or poverty, health or sickness and the moral dignity or poverty of someone by referring to the karma and cycle of reincarnation of each and everyone, that they are not able to recognize the hidden law of providence.

Indian culture is deeply shaped by the 'evil maxim' of karma and reincarnation, which is communicated to them through the words and deeds of the Hindu gods and goddesses, which in turn legitimates the social laws of the caste system. The idea of karma, reincarnation and the caste system are absolutely opposed to the principle of sovereignty: they impose the conditions of fundamental inequality on social relationships and limit the political liberty to exercise responsibility for oneself and for others. For most Hindus, it would be unjust, and unfavourable to their 'stock' of accumulated merits for the next life, to love someone who does not deserve it or to give something to someone who is perceived as 'spiritually depraved'. Indian habits do not sustain equality of living conditions. The 'evil maxims' make democratic relationships in temporal life impossible; the corrupted hearts reject the equal dignity of each and everyone.

The democratic disease: the revolt of the masses

Though Tocqueville believes that being free, as a citizen, is more difficult in a democracy than being free as a gentleman in an aristocracy, he does not believe that liberty is *naturally* in contradiction with equality of living conditions. Liberty and equality are not opposed to each other when liberty is understood as the natural right to self-government in public affairs and equality as the natural equality of this right. In other words, while liberty and equality can become fierce enemies of each other in the social context, depending on how they are understood, they can find their natural harmony with each other in the equality of liberty. In democratic societies, equality becomes opposed to liberty when the passion for equality is animated by envy and class hatred, and no longer by the belief in the equal dignity of every person – when the class spirit is stronger than the civic spirit. When the hatred of aristocratic privileges and the jealousy of those above oneself can be satiated by a social life in tutelage, then egalitarian barbarism appears preferable to a free life. The desire for freedom implies the desire to become virtuous and, hence, may well imply obedience to teachers or the wise. However, hatred of any sort of hierarchy also means that even the desire to learn is repressed. In such a degenerated state of democratic society, citizens do not govern themselves in townships and communities, but they are governed as, or rather, reduced to, isolated 'individuals', as a crowd, depraved of the public virtues and left to its own devices, outside the polis.[43] Such a democracy without citizens is called a *mass democracy.*[44]

Tocqueville's theme of the mass society is a classical, perhaps aristocratic theme, which goes back to antiquity, to the battle between the patricians and the plebeians, reflecting the fear of slave revolts and the barbarians. Coriolanus, as Plutarch informs us, devoted his public life to the war against the plebeian crowd, which he found vicious, vulgar, mediocre and oppressive. La Bruyère, in his *Caractères*, points at the maniac masses that emulate and venerate the great men of the court of Louis XIV. The crowd, of course, is not a democratic people, but a concentrated mass of isolated individuals, who, Tocqueville points out, are 'so similar that it would have been enough for them to change places to become unrecognizable'.[45] Unlike the people or the citizenry, the masses constitute an enormous concentration of uncontrolled *social* force that becomes embodied in the social and political life, reducing the latter to a battlefield, where the will to power predominates and where each and everyone tries to satiate his or her self-interests. In order to liberate itself from this crowd, a people must organize itself as a citizenry and check and balance, disperse and resist this blind egalitarian power. Only when the people are not governed by mass institutions but constitute a self-governing citizenry, can we speak of a free democracy.[46] A free democracy is a democracy without a crowd – without concentration of social power.

Tocqueville admits that he has an aristocratic fear of the crowd. He does not trust the crowd that, in his view, is deaf to the truth and so easily flattered by the sweet music of demagogues.[47] It is the capricious will of the easily swayed mass, and not reason, which guides the thought and action of the crowd. Uncontrolled blind passions, and not the virtues, or even self-interest rightly understood, are the ones that rule this crowd. In mass democracy, public opinion, a key democratic institution, does not develop freely through the higher faculties of the mind, through history, literature and philosophy, but is provided, ready-made, to the mass through the mass media. It is this crowd that makes itself heard and hence, takes important political decisions, through political parties,[48] opinion polls, mass media, statistics[49] and universal suffrage.[50] In the mass society, political life, with its painful battle of ideas, tastes and values, is not perceived as a democratic end in itself, whereby the citizen is able to govern himself or herself, but is seen as a means, as an administrative power to satisfy its own passions.[51]

While Tocqueville celebrates the township as the seat of American liberty, he nevertheless discovers some features of American mass democracy that constantly threaten to destroy township liberty. In the township, American citizens regulate their own political conduct; yet, Tocqueville discovers that their habits of mind are not free but shaped by mass institutions: 'I do not know any country where, in general, less independence of mind and genuine freedom of discussion reign than in America … . There is no freedom of mind in America.'[52] In the second volume of the *Démocratie*, Tocqueville points out that the American, Cartesian habits of mind do not develop through extensive intellectual studies or Socratic dialogues, but the American mind receives a host of ready-made opinions 'from public opinion, which thereby relieves American citizens from the responsibility to form their own opinions'.[53] Tocqueville thinks that 'there is no country in the civilized world where they are less occupied with philosophy than in the United States'[54] and concludes that, though American democracy is free, thanks to its townships, due to its mass institutions 'the life of a mind in the United States' is 'small' and 'dull'.[55]

In France, as well, mass institutions shape revolutionary habits of the mind. In his *Souvenirs*, Tocqueville observes how, prior to and during the February Revolution (which, in his eyes, is ultimately a revolt of the masses), revolutionary opinions of populist parties, led by demagogues like Ledru-Rollin and Louis Blanc, had created restlessness in the mind and troubles in the heart of the French people. The mind of these socialist leaders, in Tocqueville's view, was deaf to truth, being governed by party ideologies. They assured the crowd that 'the goods of the wealthy were in some way the result of a theft committed against themselves' and that 'inequalities of fortune were as much opposed to morality and the interests of society as to nature'.[56] And the crowd wished to believe this. For, the last thing that the masses want from their demagogues is realism, principle or prudence. They desire 'audacity' and 'physical pleasures', not truth and liberty.[57]

The liberal disease: the revolt of the bourgeoisie

According to Tocqueville, 'truth lives, whatever one does, and liberty remains the greatest thing in this world'.[58] Truth and liberty go hand in hand. Only liberty ensures that truth can be sought and pursued, while it is truth that sanctifies liberty. Indeed, for Tocqueville, liberty is 'a *sacred* thing. There is only one thing else that better deserves the name: that is virtue. But then, what is virtue if not the *free* choice of what is good.'[59] The rule of the will to power and the no less dangerous love of well-being blind the human mind and heart, making them indifferent to truth and liberty, to the just and the good.[60] The one who is a 'slave of his passions'[61] cannot bear the labour and hardship, which are often required to acquire and practice the virtues.[62] Virtue, the habit of the mind and heart to prefer, to choose and to do what is good, is a prerequisite for liberty. At the same time, without the freedom, the right to perceive and choose the good, there can be no virtue. Such is Tocqueville's classical understanding of liberty.

For Tocqueville, it is only the citizen who is willing to listen to truth, to fight for true liberty and to live virtuously in the public domain.[63] He sees the bourgeois, however, as Rousseau did too, as the arch-enemy of the citizen.[64] The bourgeois, being ruled, not by reason, but by the will to power, does not have the passion to acquire the good habits of mind and heart for self-government, but is satisfied by 'the habit and taste of following their will alone in their particular actions'.[65] The bourgeois mind does not habitually seek what is good, but retreats in its own mediocre subjectivism, in which the classical virtues (and, therefore, the standards of democratic citizenship) disappear. This is what Tocqueville means by 'individualism'. Individualism, for him, is the political emancipation of the citizen into the private domain of the bourgeois.[66] Bourgeois individualism makes the classical virtues, necessary for an active public life, redundant. Hence, Tocqueville concludes that individualism (or emancipation) proceeds from 'an erroneous judgment' and has its source in 'the defects of the mind'.[67] Tocqueville, therefore, concludes that, though aristocratic societies are naturally unjust, the aristocratic citizens, having acquired the classical virtues, were more just.[68]

Molière's *Le bourgeois gentilhomme* probably had, given Tocqueville's taste and admiration for the artist, a decisive influence on the statesman's sociological imagination. Though Tocqueville seldom refers to his sources, and refers only once to Molière in *L'Ancien Régime et la Révolution*,[69] the classical satirist seems his teacher in understanding the social relationship between the bourgeois and the aristocrat. There is a striking resemblance between Molière's social satire and Tocqueville's depiction of the bourgeois passions, of the bourgeois who desires neither liberty nor democracy, but who wants to be the equal of the aristocrat. Tocqueville points at the old bourgeoisie desiring privileges like tax exemption. He points at their desire for the noble status, which they actually acquired by buying themselves offices from degenerate kings like Louis XI, who created and sold offices, to weaken the old nobility and enforce his own absolute rule.

As in Molière's play, Tocqueville describes how the system of ennoblements put the passions in disorder: the newly ennobled were repulsed by the old aristocrats because their conduct was not noble enough, while the common people found them too noble already.[70] Molière describes M. Jourdain, a caricature of the bourgeois, as an irredeemable *esprit bas*: while being preoccupied with his social mobility and newly acquired self-identity, he is totally insensitive to the needs of himself and of others.[71] Being ruled by his desire for nobility, even for kingship, M. Jourdain not only desires to be at the centre of the stage, but also demands to be the centre of all attention, imposing himself on others, compelling others to dance to his tune. His bourgeois habits of the heart (*esprit marchand*; M. Jourdain likes to keep accounts) unconsciously betray him in his futile attempt to be a real aristocrat. He is a rich parvenu, a poor imitation of genuine nobility – poor because he does not possess the sense of honour, moderation and tact, which define the original aristocrat.

Like Molière, Tocqueville makes it clear that the bourgeois is not an object of aristocratic scorn because of the social class he belongs to, but is undignified because he denies his true station. M. Jourdain's aspirations are so incongruous, so discordant with his political reality, that they amount to a kind of selfish perversity. Though M. Jourdain's autonomy, which he owes to his private wealth and his craving for independence, is in itself a great democratic good, he becomes a great democratic evil (a democratic despot) when he imposes his own bourgeois mediocrity, his *esprit bas*, on others. Since M. Jourdain is not willing to recognize any authority higher than his own and to let any 'superior wisdom', as Tocqueville calls it,[72] interfere in his own affairs, he denies himself the right and duty to improve, morally and politically. He falls prey to the power of his own will that is dominated by concupiscence.[73]

In his *L'Ancien Régime*, Tocqueville particularly seems to recognize M. Jourdain in Napoleon. Though Tocqueville greatly admires Napoleon as a military genius, 'his taste for the gaudy, false greatness, bombast, the gigantic' betrays him as a parvenu.[74] In American democracy, Tocqueville discovers the *esprit marchand* in the captains of industry. This 'manufacturing aristocracy' of millionaires, railway kings, oil kings, cattle kings only resembles the aristocracy in its privileges, not in its habits of mind and heart. The 'manufacturing aristocracy' does not constitute a real aristocracy because the captains of industry 'have neither common spirit nor objects, neither common traditions nor hopes'[75] Tocqueville points out that the democratic threat of the capitalist class is that this master fails to establish a genuine civic bond with its workers. The worker is dehumanized for *economic* purposes: the captain's 'goal is not to govern the latter [worker], but to make use of it'.[76] In aristocratic societies, Tocqueville points out, 'one would see inequality and misery in society, but souls were not degraded'.[77] By contrast, manufacturing aristocracies degrade the soul of the worker. They are not aristocratic, but oligarchic.

Tocqueville's classicism

Like the romantics of his age, Tocqueville has a taste for originality, novelty, grandeur and heroism. He believes in the power of the word, has a distaste for the 'abominable vulgarity' of popular mass culture, and he even shares the romantic admiration for Napoleon of Stendhal's Julien Sorel. And yet Tocqueville is not a romantic but a classical thinker. He does not share the philosophical idealism, historicism and commitment to art, aesthetics and literary criticism of the romantic movement. Unlike the idealists, he does not refer to man's creative and unique originality, but to his eternal capacity for reason and universal (Socratic) rationality. Unlike the historicists, he is not concerned with the historical individuality of events, but with abstracted universals of human nature, classes, principles, norms and functional requisites of society. Unlike the cultural critics, he does not seek the emancipation of the imagination to promote artistic work, but seeks the liberation of reason and will from oppression for the sake of the common good, through statesmanship and citizenship.[78] In his attempt to safeguard classicism, Tocqueville seeks to rescue liberty against a romantic type of democratic culture that is not inspired by that classical value.

According to Tocqueville, 'romanticism is not faithful; it is a bad guide if we want to know precise details of facts and particular motives which have caused action'.[79] Romanticism is not faithful because it does not believe that democracy is vouchsafed by the divine laws of providence, but is created by the passionate commitments of humans. Romantics do not believe in an overarching democratic order that awaits discovery by Socratic reason, but hold that all orders are created or imposed by human will and human imagination.[80] All orders, including aristocratic and democratic orders, are scattered worlds, scenes of conflict between divergent aesthetic values, in which the highest values compete with the lowest. Romantics substitute aesthetics for politics; they demand artistic freedom in place of political freedom. They are not so fond of citizens and statesmen, unless they have creative designs and artistic talent.[81] Thereby, romanticism destroys the civic self-government that Tocqueville defends.

The leader of the romantic movement in France, Victor Hugo, defined romanticism as 'liberalism in literature'. In this liberalism, so different from Tocqueville's 'new liberalism', aesthetics is substituted for politics, artful self-expression for political self-government. Hugo, like Voltaire,[82] saw the liberty of the creative imagination, in literature or art in general, as the foundation of liberty in society and liberty in the government.[83] Hugo's romantic liberalism in literature means that one takes the liberty to let the imagination, rather than classical reason, contemplate, to let one's thoughts wander and discover new worlds. Liberalism in literature opens up new horizons to experiment and to create one's own life through the novel. It also means that liberty demands that all limits to the free imagination, including the limits of classical natural law as imposed by the intellect, must be cast aside whenever these limit the creative desires of self-realization. For Tocqueville, this apolitical understanding of liberty, which detaches the beautiful from the good, poses a great threat to liberty. In Tocqueville's classical understanding, there can be no liberty without the classical virtues – the free decision for the good; and the good is what Socratic reason shows.

It is important to realize that Tocqueville had little admiration for the creations of the romantic mind in nineteenth-century literature.[84] Posterity has attached a huge cultural value to the great works of Victor Hugo, Stendhal, Honoré de Balzac, Georges Sand and Gustave Flaubert, but Tocqueville finds his contemporaries intellectually and morally mediocre. Even though he admires Alphonse de Lamartine's poetic style, he does not discover a Molière in him:

> [I]f Bossuet or Pascal were to come to life, they would think us receding into semi-barbarism; they would be unable to enter into the ideas of our fashionable writers; they would be disgusted with their style, and be puzzled by their language.[85]

In other words, the classical standards are guarded by writers like Bossuet and Pascal; and Tocqueville seeks to imitate them, in the classical criticism of his romantic contemporaries.[86] For, in his view, independently from the state of civilization, be it an aristocracy or a democracy, only the classical standards of thinking, feeling and acting support the classical values – liberty and human dignity.

The Tocquevillian judgement of democratic cultures

Tocqueville's judgement of democratic cultures from a theocentric point of view provides important guidance for the identification of the opportunities for, and threats to, liberty in democratic societies, including our own. The problems of democratic habits, the threats of mass democracy, M. Jourdain and romanticism to democratic culture, as envisioned by Tocqueville, are as relevant today as they were in Tocqueville's age. These problems ultimately go back to the very problem of democratic cultures, of how to reconcile liberty and equality. In America, Tocqueville observes how the Puritans have managed to safeguard the classical values liberty (self-government towards the good life) and human dignity in their New England township, in which, in his vision, an air of antiquity and a biblical perfume are combined. In America, liberty is threatened by mass society and the 'manufacturing aristocracy'. In Europe, he observes how the French Revolution continues destroying the old world, making it particularly difficult to reconcile democratic equality and classical liberty. In revolutionary Europe, many passions, except the passion for liberty, govern the conduct of nations. The social passions for self-realization, comfort and security weaken the political desire to suffer for self-government, while they inspire to lower standards for action – lower standards that cannot sustain liberty.

Classicism is a solution that Tocqueville offers for safeguarding the highest civic and religious standards of thought, feeling and action, without which a self-governing and democratic citizenry cannot be constituted. In terms of thought, classicism seeks to destroy the ideological mind that is not open to truth: only by complying to the high Socratic standards of thinking can reason be opened to truth, including the truth of democracy. Tocqueville seeks to raise awareness that humans are part of an overarching, providentially guided order that sets fixed limits on their actions. As providential history reveals to reason that democracy is part of the pre-given order, the European nations, to conform to God's will and become just, must raise themselves to constitute a democratic citizenry. In terms of feeling, classicism seeks to trigger the passion for liberty as the queen of the passions. Through his writings and statesmanship, Tocqueville seeks to inflame the 'sublime desire' for liberty in his public, making it clear that liberty must be understood as a divine gift that 'enters of itself into the great hearts that God has prepared to receive it'.[87] In terms of action, classicism seeks to inspire the exercise of the classical virtues, including the virtues of faith, charity and hope, in civic self-government. Tocqueville makes it clear that freedom demands high standards: a lot of effort, resistance, sacrifice, practical wisdom and statecraft, which are not obvious features of democratic cultures.[88]

Tocqueville offers a vision of the democratic 'narrow gate', which is not without hope. In the democratic era, it is very difficult to be free as a democratic citizenry in the Tocquevillian or classical high norm-governed sense. Aristocrats were used to govern themselves according to classical standards, but a democratic people must still acquire this political *habitus*. Aristocrats, accordingly, are teachers of liberty.[89] For the aristocrats, it was easier to govern themselves towards the good life because their freedom was strongly supported by their aristocratic culture of chivalry, and socially embodied in their local *corps intermédiares*, towns and communes. For a democratic people, it is more difficult to govern themselves because their democratic culture is constantly threatened by mass revolts and ideology, while the governmental response to these revolts has been the organization of security, equality and welfare on a large and abstract scale. In America, the small-scale Puritan township provides an example of how liberty and democracy can be reconciled, but this is so because the Puritans strongly believed that they were on a divine democratic mission and acted politically within the providential order. In Europe, on the other hand, the French Revolution continued.

In the *Souvenirs*, Tocqueville identifies the February Revolution as the continuation of the French Revolution. At that time, Tocqueville branded the newly born proletariat, driven by socialist class hatred vis-à-vis the ruling bourgeoisie rather than by the love of liberty, as 'the new barbarians'. Both bourgeoisie and proletariat subordinate freedom to other political ends, such as stability, security, comfort, prosperity, which are threats to liberty. As for Tocqueville 'only freedom can tear people from the worship of Mammon',[90] the subordination of liberty to other ends such as equality, peace and prosperity is indeed a barbarous act. It is barbarous because it destroys the classical norms that regulate the overarching order and sustain local self-government. As a member of the Chamber of Deputies under the bourgeois rule of Guizot and Thiers, Tocqueville, prior to the February Revolution, pressed for civic spirit in the bourgeois bodies, to become *worthy*, as a governor, of exercising power over the proletariat with prudence, moderation, justice and courage. 'For God's sake change the spirit of the government, for, I repeat, it is the spirit that is leading you to the abyss', he told the bourgeois in parliament.[91]

Clearly, for Tocqueville, it is always the quality of mind and heart, not politics, that confronts us with the deepest abyss. In Tocqueville's view, only a classical turn of mind and Christian change of heart can save us from the abyss of low standards. In his own age of the ruling bourgeoisie, of François Guizot and Adople Thiers, Tocqueville looked at the modern world from what he believed to be the point of view of God, through the eyes of his beloved French seventeenth- and eighteenth-century spokespersons and writers. Through their classical norms that he had made his own and accepted, quite dogmatically, as truth, he concluded that if these great philosophers, citizens, Christian moralists and comedians were to return to life, nothing would astonish them more than 'the dullness of modern society, and the mediocrity of modern books'.[92] Tocqueville and his teachers of the past – Bossuet, Molière, Pascal, Fénélon, Montesquieu – are relevant today as a classical tradition of thought because they supply us with permanent and high standards by which we are able to judge our own democratic culture, as Tocqueville judged his own contemporaries.

Notes

1　Alexis de Tocqueville, *Democracy in America*, trans. Harvey C. Mansfield and Delba Winthrop (Chicago: University of Chicago Press, 2000), p. 6.

2 'Providence has not created the human race entirely independent or perfectly slave. It traces, it is true, a fatal circle around each man, which he cannot leave; but within its vast limits man is powerful and free; so too with peoples.' *Ibid.*, p. 676.

3 *Ibid.*, p. 552.

4 Tocqueville, *The Old Regime and the Revolution, Vol. I: The Original Text,* ed. François Furet and Françoise Mélonio, trans. Alan S. Kahan (Chicago: University of Chicago Press, 1998), p. 190.

5 Françoise Mélonio states that 'Tocqueville's God was like Pascal's, a hidden one – but Nature carries within herself the knowledge of Good and Evil.' Mélonio, *Tocqueville and the French,* trans. Beth G. Raps (London: University Press of Virginia, 1998), p. 64.

6 Tocqueville, *Democracy*, p. 462.

7 Letter to Louis de Kergorlay, January 1835. All references from Tocqueville's letters, which I use here, can be found in Alexis de Tocqueville, *Selected Letters on Politics and Society,* ed. Roger Boesche, trans. James Toupin and R. Boesche (London: University of California Press, 1985). This quote can be found on page 93.

8 Françoise Mélonio reports that conservative Catholics were far from impressed by what they understood as 'providential politics' (p. 39). Custine, for instance, argued that, by relating Christ to democracy, Tocqueville confused the spiritual with the temporal. By pushing Christ into politics, Custine believed that Tocqueville exploited holy providence to promote carnal democracy. See Mélonio, *Tocqueville and the French,* p. 37.

9 Tocqueville, *Democracy*, p. 675.

10 Letter to Paul Clamorgan, 1 January 1839. *Selected Letters*, p. 132.

11 'After all, the will of God was to diffuse a mediocre happiness on the totality of men, and not to concentrate a large amount of felicity on some and allow only a small number to approach perfection.' Letter to Eugène Stoffels, 21 February 1835. *Selected Letters*, p. 99.

12 'Providence, which doubtless wished to present the spectacle of our passions and misfortunes as a lesson to the world.' Alexis de Tocqueville, *The Old Regime and the French Revolution. Volume II: Notes on the French Revolution and Napoleon,* trans. Alan S. Kahan (Chicago: University of Chicago Press, 2001), p. 65.

13 'Cicero, who utters such great groans at the idea of a citizen crucified, finds nothing to reproach in these atrocious abuses of victory. It is evident that, in his eyes, a foreigner is not of the same human species as a Roman.' Tocqueville, *Democracy*, p. 539.

14 *Ibid.*, p. 413.

15 Letter to John Stuart Mill, June 1835. *Selected Letters*, p. 102.

16 'Some may accuse me of displaying too strong a taste for freedom, which, I am assured, is hardly of concern to anyone in France today.' Tocqueville, *Old Regime*, I, p. 86.

17 'The lack of practical wisdom which ended up disorganizing everything.' *Ibid.*, II, p. 28.

18 Letter to Louis de Kergorlay, January 1835. *Selected Letters*, p. 94.

19 Letter to Francisque de Corcelle, 17 September 1853. *Selected Letters*, p. 294.

20 Tocqueville, *Democracy*, p. 275.

21 *Ibid.*

22   'If, in the course of this work, I have not succeeded in making the reader feel the importance that I attribute to the practical experience of the Americans, to their habits, to their opinions – in a word to their mores – in the maintenance of their laws, I have missed the principal goal that I proposed for myself in writing it.' *Ibid.*, p. 295.

23   Tocqueville, *The Old Regime*, II, p. 34.

24   Alexis de Tocqueville, *Recollections: The French Revolution of 1848*, ed. J.P. Mayer and A.P. Kerr (Oxford: Transaction Publishers, 1990), pp. 188–9.

25   'You may say that institutions are only half of my subject. I go farther than you, and I say that they are not even half. You know my ideas well enough to know that I accord institutions only a secondary influence on the destiny of men. Would to God I believed more in the omnipotence of institutions! ... I am quite convinced that political societies are not what their laws make them, but what sentiments, beliefs, ideas, habits of the heart, and the spirit of the men who form them, prepare them in advance to be ... .' Letter to Francisque de Corcelle, 17 September 1853. *Selected Letters*, p. 294.

26   Tocqueville, *Democracy*, pp. 28–9.

27   *Ibid.*, p. 32.

28   *Ibid.*, p. 275. See for a further elaboration on this specific theme, Ossewaarde, *Tocqueville's Moral and Political Thought: New Liberalism* (London: Routledge, 2004).

29   Tocqueville, *Democracy*, p. 32.

30   'The home of Puritanism continued to have its place in the middle classes; it was from the heart of the middle classes that most of the emigrants came.' *Ibid.*, p. 35.

31   *Ibid.*, p. 33.

32   'The township is the sole association that is so much in nature that everywhere men are gathered, a township forms by itself ... it is man who makes kingdoms and creates republics; the township appears to issue directly from the hands of God.' *Ibid.*, p. 57.

33   *Ibid.*, p. 55.

34   'The municipal institutions which in the thirteenth and fourteenth centuries had made the chief cities in Germany rich and enlightened little republics.' Tocqueville, *Old Regime*, I, p. 104.

35   Hence, Tocqueville is able to point out that the township also exists in aristocratic societies: 'the institution of township introduces democratic freedom into the heart of the feudal monarchy'. Tocqueville, *Democracy*, p. 5.

36   'I see the whole destiny of America contained in the first Puritan who landed on its shore, like the whole human race in the first man.' *Ibid.*, p. 267.

37   'The organisation and establishment of democracy among Christians is the great political problem of our time. The Americans have doubtless not resolved this problem, but they furnish useful lessons to whom wish to resolve it.' *Ibid.*, p. 298.

38   Agnès Antoine, *L'impensé de la démocratie: Tocqueville, la citoyenneté et la religion* (Paris: Fayard, 2003), pp. 172–4.

39   Tocqueville states that 'God prepares a firmer and calmer future for European societies.' Tocqueville, *Democracy*, p. 12. He says nothing about the African or Asian continents. Note that Tocqueville does not separate America from Europe: 'I cannot consent to separate America from Europe, despite the

ocean that divides them. I consider the people of the United States as the portion of the English people.' *Ibid.*, p. 429.

40 Arend Lijphart, *Patterns of Democracy: Government Forms and Performance in Thirty-six Countries* (New Haven: Yale University Press, 1999).

41 Tocqueville stresses that among a democratic people, 'dispositions of their mind soon lead them to scorn forms', including democratic forms. Tocqueville, *Democracy*, p. 404.

42 Tocqueville, *L'Inde*, in: *Oeuvres complètes*, ed. J.-P. Mayer (Paris: Gallimard, 1951-), 3, I, pp. 448–9. Hereafter abridged as OC.

43 As is well known, Tocqueville, like Aristotle, holds that isolation from the fellow citizens produces bestiality in men. Outside the city, humans cannot realize their political nature. In his *Recollections*, Tocqueville says: 'Nothing that I saw later that day [during the February Revolt] impressed me so much as that solitude in which one could, so to speak, see all the most evil passions of humanity at work, and none of the good ones.' Tocqueville, *Recollections*, p. 38.

44 Oliver Hidalgo, *Unbehagliche Moderne: Tocqueville und die Frage der Religion in der Politik* (Frankfurt: Campus Verlag, 2006), pp. 66–73.

45 Tocqueville, *Old Regime*, I, p. 163.

46 'I wish that citizens were introduced into public life to the extent that they are believed capable of being useful in it, instead of seeking to keep them away from it at all costs.' Letter to Eugène Stoffels, 5 October 1836. *Selected Letters*, p. 114.

47 'The crowd is so constituted that it gathers more willingly around an idea that is false but great, than around several ideas that are true but small.' Letter to Gustave de Beaumont, 6 November 1843. *Selected Letters*, p. 167.

48 'Parties are an evil inherent in free governments; but they do not have the same characteristics and the same instincts at all times'; 'America has had great parties; today they no longer exist.' Tocqueville, *Democracy*, pp. 166–7.

49 Tocqueville refers to the 'taste for statistics' as an indicator of mass society. Tocqueville, *Old Regime*, I, p. 139.

50 In a letter to Nassau Senior, Tocqueville says that nothing is more dangerous to liberty than universal suffrage of a slavish people in combination with centralized executive power. Letter to Nassau William Senior, 25 August, 1847. *Selected Letters*, p. 189.

51 The crowd believes that 'political life is no more than a game in which each person seeks only to win; that politics has nothing serious in it but the personal ambitions of which it is the means'. Letter to Gustave de Beaumont, 14 December 1845. *Selected Letters*, pp. 181–2.

52 Tocqueville, *Democracy*, pp. 244–5.

53 *Ibid.*, p. 409.

54 *Ibid.*, p. 403.

55 *Ibid.*, p. 461.

56 Tocqueville, *Recollections*, p. 137.

57 *Ibid.*, p. 203.

58 Letter to Gustave de Beaumont, 8 March 1855. *Selected Letters*, pp. 317–8.

59 Tocqueville, *Voyages en Angleterre et en Irlande de 1835*, in: OC, 5:ii, p. 91.

60 Tocqueville, *Democracy*, p. 153.

110   *Reading Tocqueville*

61   *Ibid.*, p. 242.
62   'There is nothing harder than the apprecenticeship of freedom.' *Ibid.*, p. 229.
63   Ossewaarde, 'Tocqueville's Christian Citizen', *Logos: A Journal of Catholic Thought and Culture* 8(3) (2005), pp. 5–17.
64   Interestingly enough, Tocqueville (contrary to Rousseau) recognizes Machiavelli as the teacher of the bourgeoisie, rather than as the teacher of the *citoyen* (whose teacher is Aristotle): 'one senses that Machiavelli, like so many people of our day, is endowed with a nature so flexible and so free of all principles that he would be capable of doing anything, even good, if the thing became profitable'. Letter to Pierre-Paul Royer-Collard, 25 August 1836. *Selected Letters*, p. 111.
65   Tocqueville, *Democracy*, p. 639.
66   'It brings relatives together at the same time that it separates citizens.' OC 3:i, p. 562.
67   'Selfishness is born of a blind instinct; individualism proceeds from an erroneous judgement rather than a depraved sentiment. It has its source in the defects of mind as much as in the vices of the heart.' *Ibid.*, p. 482.
68   'We have therefore moved far back from the point at which our fathers had arrived; for we allow to be done under colour of justice and consecrate in the name of law what violence alone imposed on them.' *Ibid.*, p. 99.
69   Tocqueville refers to Molière in his discussion of the relationship between the gentleman and the bourgeois. See Tocqueville, *Old Regime*, I, p. 153.
70   *Ibid.*, pp. 156–8.
71   My reading of Molière is based on David Whitton, *Molière: Le bourgeois gentilhomme* (London: Grant and Cutler, 1992).
72   Tocqueville, *Democracy*, p. 409.
73   Tocqueville typifies: 'the real French bourgeoisie, narrow, egoistic, and when it cannot govern solely by itself, preferring a master'. Tocqueville, *Old Regime*, II, p. 297. Also note his tiredness of 'our little democratic and bourgeois pot of soup'. Letter to Gustave de Beaumont, 9 August 1840. *Selected Letters*, p. 143.
74   Tocqueville, *Old Regime*, II, p. 188.
75   Tocqueville, *Democracy*, p. 532.
76   *Ibid.*, p. 532.
77   *Ibid.*, p. 8.
78   Francesco Spandri, 'Le rôle de l'imagination dans l'idéal égalitaire', in *Tocqueville et la Littérature*, ed. Françoise Mélonio and José-Luis Diaz (Paris: PUPS, 2005).
79   Tocqueville, *Correspondance avec son neveu Hebert*, 23 February 1857. *Selected Letters*.
80   Hence the relationship between revolution and imagination: 'what remains perhaps most alive in the original spirit of the Revolution is in the literature.' Letter to Gustave de Beaumont, 24 April 1856. *Selected Letters*, p. 329.
81   Tocqueville clearly recognizes the spirit of romanticism in the February Revolution when he says that 'what I call the literary spirit in politics consists in looking for what is ingenious and new rather than for what is true, being fonder of what makes an interesting picture than what serves a purpose, being very appreciative of good acting and fine speaking without reference to

the play's results, and, finally, judging by impressions rather than reasons.' Tocqueville, *Recollections*, p. 67.

82 Voltaire 'envied the English above all for their literary freedom, but hardly concerned himself for their political freedom, as if the first could ever exist for long without the second'. Tocqueville, *Old Regime*, I, p. 209.

83 Victor Hugo, *Hernani*, ed. C. Eterstein (Paris: Flammarion, 1996), preface.

84 Arthur Kaledin rightly points at Tocqueville's 'professed disdain for romanticism as a cultural movement (he believed it too would lead to a willful derangement of order and to decadence) and his refusal even to read its literature'. Kaledin, 'Tocqueville's Apocalypse: Culture, Politics, and Freedom in Democracy in America', in Laurence Guellec (ed.), *Tocqueville et l'esprit de la démocratie* (Paris: Sciences Po Les Presses, 2005), p. 55.

85 Tocqueville, 'Conversations avec Nassau Senior', 26 August 1850, in Tocqueville, *Correspondence and Conversations of Alexis de Tocqueville with Nassau William Senior from 1834 to 1859*, ed. M.C.M. Simpson (London: King, 1872).

86 Françoise Mélonio, 'Préface', in *Tocqueville et la literature*, pp. 9–11. In the same edition, Laurence Guellec argues that Tocqueville uses 'very classical models', but that he identifies the classical standard with 'La Bruyère, Montesquieu, Voltaire, Buffon, Pascal'. See Laurence Guellec, 'Tocqueville écrivain', p. 110. Elsewhere, Tocqueville suggests that the ancients have set the standard: 'all who aspire to literary excellence in democratic nations ought frequently to refresh themselves at the springs of ancient literature; there is no more wholesome medicine for the mind.' Tocqueville, *Democracy*, p. 63.

87 'Do not ask me to analyze this sublime desire, it must be felt. It enters of itself into the great hearts that God has prepared to receive it; it fills them, it fires them. One must give up on making this comprehensible to the mediocre souls who have never felt it.' Tocqueville, *Old Regime*, I, p. 217.

88 'One would therefore be wrong to believe that the old regime was a time of servility and subordination. There was much more freedom than in our day.' *Ibid.*, p. 179.

89 'One must still regret that, instead of bending the nobility under the yoke of the law, we have slaughtered it and alienated it. In acting thus, we have deprived the nation of a necessary part of its substance, and given liberty a wound which can never be healed.' *Ibid.*, p. 173.

90 *Ibid.*, p. 88.

91 Tocqueville, *Recollections*, p. 13.

92 'If the brilliant talkers and writers of that time [eighteenth century] were to return to life, I do not believe that gas, or steam, or chloroform, or the electric telegraph, would so much astonish them as the dullness of modern society, and the mediocrity of modern books.' Tocqueville, 'Conversations avec Nassau Senior', 10 April 1854, in *Correspondence and Conversations of Alexis de Tocqueville with Nassau William Senior*.

7
A Secular Reading of Alexis de Tocqueville

Paul Cliteur

Introduction

Alexis de Tocqueville is sometimes presented as an almost prophetic political thinker, Annelien De Dijn and Raf Geenens write in their introduction to this book. This is an appropriate observation, indeed. On law, politics, philosophy and other subjects he has presented new ideas that only much later got the recognition that they deserve. According to many commentators this also applies to his ideas on religion. After the relentless onslaught of some radical Enlightenment thinkers on religion (especially Holbach),[1] Tocqueville was one of the most impressive nineteenth-century commentators who tried to reconcile modern democracy with religion.[2]

My aim in this chapter is to assess the validity of Tocqueville's ideas on religion within the context of the recent upsurge of religious ideas. What can we learn from Tocqueville? Can his approach to religion serve as a source of inspiration to the way modern European states can deal with religion, more particularly religious diversity? Is religion indeed, as Tocqueville contends, important for the maintenance of the democratic political order? If so, why? If not, what are the alternatives? And are Tocqueville's ideas, as is often contended, the counterpoint to the Enlightenment or is his work indebted to the secular tradition as well?

These are the questions I will try to answer in this chapter. I will not concentrate on whether Tocqueville was sincere in his belief. This is the subject of a long discussion among Tocqueville scholars. What exactly did he believe himself? Some commentators speak of his 'indestructible faith'.[3] According to Joachim Wach, Tocqueville repeatedly indicated his views on life and politics were 'firmly rooted in religious conviction and religious faith'.[4] His stance is that liberty cannot be established without morality and morality not without faith.[5] This faith is not every faith in general, but religious faith in particular, Wach tells us.

This may be true, but it does not mean that Tocqueville himself was a firm believer. According to other scholars Tocqueville was an 'agnostic' and a 'spiritualist'.[6] Jean-Louis Benoît points out that, although Tocqueville remained within the Catholic Church, he was very critical of Catholic political parties, severely criticized the papal hierarchy of Pius IX, found dogmatic thinking abhorrent in general and rejected important religious ideas such as the Immaculate Conception and original sin.[7] He admired the evangelical stories and values incorporated in those stories, but the central idea of the incarnation and divine character of Jesus Christ remained alien to him.[8] So even as a 'Christian' thinker his claims are not very strong.[9] In contemporary vocabulary, popularized by secularist thinkers such as Daniel Dennett and Richard Dawkins, the position of Tocqueville could perhaps best be qualified as 'belief in belief'.[10] Someone who has 'belief in belief' sees belief as a fiction worth maintaining.

The reasons for this can be diverse: rational calculation as in Pascals Wager,[11] emotional need as with William James,[12] or political expediency.[13] Tocqueville's acknowledgement of religion fitted into the last category: religion was necessary to uphold the democratic order. In that sense his ideas were similar to, although not identical with, those of the greatest Enlightenment thinker, Voltaire.

Voltaire was very close to the position that religion, in the sense of belief in the existence of God, is necessary for political reasons (much closer than his reputation as an anti-religious writer warrants).[14] Voltaire calls himself a 'theist'. But this is not belief in the personal God that manifested His will in Holy Scripture and sent his son to the earth to redeem the sins of mankind, but a more abstract almighty God that takes revenge on evil-doers that escape earthly justice.[15] In his 'Epître à l'auteur du livre des Trois Imposteurs', Voltaire presents us his notion of a God that would be socially beneficial.[16] Voltaire thinks that all peoples have sustained the notion of an almighty and perfect God that was the foundation of social order and justice and the terror of the potential criminal (and tyrant). So useful is the belief in such a God that if he would not exist he should be invented ('Si Dieu n'existait pas, il faudrait l'inventer'). Philosophers in particular should widely circulate this useful belief ('croyance utile').[17] Not only Voltaire, but also many other Enlightenment thinkers took this position. In that sense they were not far from their nineteenth-century conservative detractors, Burke one of the first, who proclaimed: 'We know, and what is better we feel inwardly, that religion is the basis of civil society, and the source of all good and comfort.'[18]

What is Tocqueville's position in this discussion? The public role of religion is not the subject of a separate volume in the work of Tocqueville but his remarks on religion are dispersed throughout his many writings.[19] The most important passages on the public role of religion are to be found in his main book, *De la démocratie en Amérique*,[20] and in his correspondence, in particular the correspondence with another great nineteenth-century thinker: Arthur de Gobineau (1816–1882).[21]

In what follows I will first give an overview of Tocqueville's ideas on the public role of religion, analyze his recommendations and present a critique of his stance. The conclusion of my analysis will be that although Tocqueville makes many interesting comments on the historical foundation of the American Republic, some of his ideas on religion as foundational for the political and moral order are difficult to apply to modern societies, living, as we do, in a multicultural and multireligious context. A commonwealth inspired by (and founded in) one specific religion was perhaps a possibility in Tocqueville's time, but it is no longer a possibility in our pluralist times. In modern societies the unifying bond can only be found (as I will try to demonstrate in the following pages) in a set of secular republican ideas.

Does that make Tocqueville's ideas on religion and social cohesion obsolete? Certainly not, because, as we will see, Tocqueville's work includes many clues to the possibility of a more 'secular reading'. In some passages Tocqueville does not exclusively refer to one specific religion as the source of social cohesion (Christianity), but seems to leave open the option of a purely secular 'religion' or a public philosophy as a 'civil religion'. In this last interpretation, his ideas are not only relevant for contemporary discourse, but may well be indispensable.

The correspondence with Gobineau

The correspondence with Gobineau starts with Tocqueville's assignment of Gobineau as what we would now call his 'research assistant'.[22] When the correspondence starts (in 1843) Tocqueville is 38 years old and their exchange of letters continues to his death in 1859. At the start of their relationship Gobineau is 27 years old, an ambitious young philosopher, eager to be accepted by the French intellectual public and hoping for the help of the 'arrivé' Tocqueville. Gobineau is expected to inform Tocqueville on new developments in the field of ethics and morals in the broad sense of these words (so also covering political philosophy).[23] The result is an impressive exchange of letters on religious thought, contemporary philosophers and related matters. In particular the public role of Christianity is discussed by these two giants of the nineteenth century.

Regarding the public role and essence of Christianity the two thinkers vehemently disagree. Gobineau is critical of Christianity; Tocqueville is a defender of the Christian faith, especially the thesis that Christianity is in some form essential for the maintenance of American democracy. Tocqueville contends that Christianity has caused a revolution in the field of rights and duties of the people. Christianity, Tocqueville says, did not bring new duties into existence, but it changed the relationship of the duties among each other. The 'soft virtues' ('vertus douces'), such as compassion, humanity and forgiveness were not held in high esteem in antiquity. Christianity changed all this.[24] Moreover, Christianity not only meant a revolution for the *substance* of morals, but also for its *foundation*. After Christianity, the sanctioning of morality had completely changed. The meaning of life was seen not in this life any longer, but in the life hereafter ('Il plaça le but de la vie après la vie'). And because of this change of emphasis, morality got a firm foundation, much better than would be the case when morality had to stand on its own feet, as was the case in classical antiquity.[25] All the ingredients of Christianity were preexistent before the appearance of Christ, but because of Christianity they got a different colouring and they were seen as a unity.[26] It made of these moral elements a 'religion', Tocqueville writes. This new appreciation of religion as the basis of morals was widespread in the nineteenth century. After the onslaught on religion made by some of the eighteenth-century *philosophes* many nineteenth-century political philosophers revaluated the role of religion as the necessary social bond of society.[27] In France this can be found with Chateaubriand,[28] Joseph de Maistre[29] and even Benjamin Constant.[30]

Tocqueville is most impressed by the supernatural foundation of morals in religion. A more worldly foundation of morals seems to him – in the correspondence with Gobineau – a mere 'second best'. When the supernatural foundation of morality had become shaky, he writes, only self-interest rightly understood was seen as a basis for morals. This 'revolution'[31] was accomplished by the British utilitarians (Bentham,[32] later Mill[33]), who made it a focal point of their moral theory. Tocqueville's intention is to counter this development, which had started in the eighteenth century.[34] Gobineau cannot agree with his older mentor on this specific topic. 'I have to confess you that I have a completely different opinion on Christianity than you,' Gobineau wrote.[35] Sometimes the temperature rises in the correspondence and the reader wonders whether their relationship will survive the deep theoretical differences. But the letters always end with the good wishes to the mutual wives.

The two correspondents also tackle the difficult question how to cope with the misdeeds that have been perpetrated in the name of religion.[36] Tocqueville indicates that the Christian religion has gone through barbaric times and has been affected by those times. But we should not reproach Christianity with that. All the criticism that has been made of Christianity has no relevance for the central message of the Christian creed, which is that we should love our neighbour like ourselves.[37]

There is much discussion regarding whether Tocqueville was a sincere believer. As we have seen, Wach speaks of the 'Frenchman's indestructible faith'.[38] This faith is certainly not just faith in general, but *religious* faith in particular. In a letter to one of his friends he writes:

> What has always struck me about my country ... has been to see lined up on one side the men who prize morality, religion, order, and on the other those who love freedom and the equality of men before the law. This sight has struck me as the most extraordinary and most deplorable ever offered a man's view; for all these things which we separate are, I am certain, indissolubly united in the eyes of God. They are all *holy* things, if I can express myself so, because the greatness and happiness of man in this world can come only from the simultaneous combination of them all.[39]

Wach notes: 'This combination was the great Frenchman's ideal all through his life.'[40] Wach is only one commentator of many who emphasized the religious, almost apologetic nature of Tocqueville's writings. There is, of course, a firm basis for such an interpretation, as we will see, but there is some counter-information as well.

Why is religion so important for a democracy like the United States of America? And would religion also be indispensable for all modern democracies? To answer these questions we have to put the ideas of Tocqueville in the context of his view on the development of American democracy as described in his major work on the subject.

Democracy, equality and Christianity

The first sentence of *De la démocratie en Amérique* is well known: 'Among the new things that attracted my attention during my stay in the United

States, none struck me more forcefully than the equality of conditions.'[41] Equality is a broad principle for Tocqueville. It seems to encompass also individual freedom and autonomy. In words that prefigure John Stuart Mill's essay *On Liberty* (1859)[42] Tocqueville proclaims that each individual is the best judge of what concerns himself alone.[43]

Another observation that Tocqueville made and that is closely connected to his comment on equality is that the social state of the Americans is eminently democratic. It has had this character since the birth of the colonies and it had it even more at the time Tocqueville was writing *De la démocratie en Amérique*.[44] The principle of popular sovereignty 'looms over each and every aspect of the Anglo-American political system', Tocqueville asserts.[45] Every page of his book will reveal new applications of this doctrine, the writer tells us.

His views on political equality and democracy are clearly based on a view of man. 'Each individual is supposed to be as enlightened, as virtuous and as strong as every other individual.'[46] Why does the individual obey society? He obeys society because union with his fellow men seems useful to him, and because he knows that such union cannot exist without a regulatory power.

> In everything to do with the duties of citizens to one another, he has therefore become subject. In everything that regards himself alone, he remains master. He is free and owes an account of his actions only to God. Whence this maxim: the individual is the best as well as the only judge of his own interest, and society has the right to direct his actions only when it feels injured by his activities or when it requires his cooperation.[47]

What has this to do with religion, Christianity in particular? The relation between democracy and its core principle equality on the one hand and Christianity on the other, is made clear when Tocqueville writes: 'Christianity, which made all men equal in the sight of God, will not shrink from seeing all citizens as equal in the eyes of the law.'[48] This observation had been made before by Tocqueville and would be reiterated after him countless times:[49] Christianity is the most egalitarian religion.[50] So 'champions of freedom' should hasten to invoke the aid of religion, 'for they must know that without morality freedom cannot reign and without faith there is no basis for morality'.[51]

In some ways Christianity is identical to the American founding idea: equality. All the great writers of antiquity belonged to the slave-owning aristocracy. It took the coming of Jesus Christ to make people understand that all members of the human race are by nature similar and equal, Tocqueville writes.[52] Not only Christ is the linchpin between equality and religion, the same could be said of God. 'Men who are similar and equal readily conceive of the notion of a single God who imposes the same rules on each of them and grants them future happiness at the same price.'[53] The idea of the unity of the human race continually brings men back to the idea of the unity of the Creator, Tocqueville contends. Sober, skeptical and sometimes even cynical political commentator as Tocqueville is, he sounds lyrical when he sketches a common future under one God:

> It seems to me that the more the barriers that divide the nations of mankind and the citizens of each nation disappear, the more the human mind tends, as if by its very nature, to embrace the idea of a single, all-powerful being imposing the same laws in the same way on everyone equally.[54]

As can be expected, Tocqueville also dwells on the historical origin of the American Republic and the significance religion had for the founding fathers. There is, as is well known, the relation between the Christian colonies and democracy.[55] 'All the new European colonies invariably contained at least the germ, if not the mature form, of a complete democracy', Tocqueville tells us.[56] Those immigrants or 'pilgrims' belonged to an English sect with austere Christian principles. Tocqueville is perfectly right that Puritanism was not just a religious doctrine, but that it virtually coincided with the most absolute democratic and republican theories.[57] When the immigrants landed on the shores of the new country in 1620 they adopted a covenant, which read:

> We, whose names follow, who, for the glory of God, the development of the Christian faith, and the honor of our fatherland have undertaken to establish the first colony on these remote shores, we agree in the present document, by mutual and solemn consent, and before God, to form ourselves into a body of political society, for the purpose of governing ourselves and working towards the accomplishment of these designs; and in virtue of this contract, we agree to promulgate laws, acts and ordinances, and to institute as needed officials to whom we promise submission and obedience.[58]

Here we see the new spectacle of a society 'homogeneous in all its parts', Tocqueville writes.[59] Not even classical democracy could dream of such a social cohesion, based on the acceptance of common principles.

These facts are of course well known. There is a historical connection between Christianity and the birth of America and there are conceptual correlations between Christianity and the ideal of equality (all believers equal in the eyes of God). But that does not imply, to be sure, that religion was the sole or even the most important factor contributing to the success of the American Republic. Neither does it imply, of course, that religion would still be the most viable candidate for fostering social cohesion in contemporary democracies. In the remainder of this chapter I want to elaborate on the significance of Tocqueville's ideas for contemporary society. Many followers of Tocqueville, or those inspired by his thought, seem to think that on the basis of what Tocqueville wrote in the nineteenth century they can still contend that religion or Christianity could be useful as an instrument for social cohesion. Is that true? Why, in contemporary pluralistic society where Jews, Muslims, Christians, Hindus, Buddhists and unbelievers live under the protection of the American Constitution, should one specific religion be acknowledged and privileged as the supposed foundation of the democratic order? That requires some explanation indeed. And would Tocqueville, if he had lived in the twenty-first century, still have attributed to Christianity the prominent place it took in mid-nineteenth-century America? These are some questions I hope to answer in the pages that follow.

An analysis of Tocqueville's ideas and assessment of his significance for contemporary social problems

In order to answer these questions, let us now turn to a more close analysis of Tocqueville's ideas on the importance of religion for the political order. The first thing to be noted is that Tocqueville presupposes more than he explicitly argues for. In the correspondence with Gobineau, for instance, he presupposes that moral ideas would float in the air, so to say, if they did not have the support of religion. This is the grist of his critique of English utilitarians like Bentham and Mill.[60] After the supernatural foundation of morals had been demolished, the only thing that was left was a secular or utilitarian foundation for morals. Tocqueville considers this to be a shaky foundation. But is such a negative judgement justified? And what would be the alternative?

The obvious alternative for a purely philosophical or secular foundation of morals as provided by the utilitarians is, of course, an ethical theory known as divine command morality.[61] Why is something good? Because it has been commanded by God. Why is something morally rejectionable? Because it has been forbidden by God. According to adherents of divine command morality only the divine will can provide us with a secure basis for morality. But is that true? Further analysis of the theory presents us with a host of problems.[62] First, there is the problem of the arbitrary character of the divine will. God has forbidden theft and violence, but what if God had commanded the torture of innocent children? Would that make torture morally right? Most people, including believing Christians, will have problems with that position. But if they do, they presuppose an autonomous idea of good and evil. And this means that they subscribe to the position that religion is not the basis of morals, but rather morals the foundation of religion. This simple objection[63] is in fact a substantial critique of the religious foundation of morals.[64]

That Tocqueville did not recognize this point as something that discredits his ideas on the social and political significance of religion is strange, because he was well aware of the vicissitudes of lawmaking based on religion. In *De la démocratie en Amérique* Tocqueville comments on the plans of Connecticut's lawmakers to base their law on sacred texts. Tocqueville calls that a 'strange idea' ('In drafting those laws, they hit on the strange idea of drawing upon sacred texts').[65] But is this really so strange after Tocqueville's eulogizing of the Christian influence on law and politics? 'Whoever shall worship any deity other than the Lord God shall be put to death', the Connecticut lawmakers proclaimed. They continued with provisions taken literally from Deuteronomy, Exodus and Leviticus. In harmony with what they had learned from those sacred texts they also declared blasphemy, witchcraft, adultery and rape punishable by death.[66] A son who failed to honour his father and mother? This was subject to the same penalty, and social intercourse between unmarried individuals was subject to severe censure.[67]

Tocqueville comments: 'Thus the laws of a rude and half-civilized people were carried over into a society of enlightened spirit and gentle mores.'[68] These penal laws were 'profoundly marked by narrow sectarian thinking'.[69] He seems shocked because these Puritan legislators proclaimed 'even death for Christians who wished to worship God in some way other than their own'.[70] Apparently Tocqueville does not reckon these precepts from Holy Scripture to be 'Christian' in the sense he is advocating when he declares Christianity indispensable for democracy.

He takes the lawmakers to task because they 'intruded upon the realm of conscience'[71] and 'were totally oblivious of the great principles of religious freedom'.[72]

These comments could be expected from a consistent secularist as Holbach, but how do they fit in with Tocqueville's approach? How can Tocqueville list all these problematic texts and still say: 'in America, it was religion that showed the way to enlightenment; it was respect for divine law that showed man the way to freedom'? Those lawmakers took the divine will seriously, so it seems, according to Tocqueville perhaps a little too seriously. What his treatment of the Connecticut lawmakers shows us is that a considerable part of divine inspired texts from Scripture has to be ignored and left behind before real freedom and civilization can emerge. So Tocqueville can only maintain his thesis on the intricate connection of religion and politics when being at the same time very selective with regard to the religious sources of inspiration for the American constitutional and political order. When Tocqueville writes that in America somehow the 'spirit of liberty' and the 'spirit of religion' have been combined we have to gauge what exactly is that 'spirit of religion'. Apparently, it is not making penal laws on the basis of God's word. The spirit of religion must be something different from that. But what? Tocqueville does not give us a clear answer to that question.

The position that we need religion for the maintenance of moral and political order, can also be criticized on from a more pragmatic angle. Adherents of this position usually are vague as to the question *what religion* is supposed to fulfil that role. Tocqueville uses the words 'Christianity' and 'religion' interchangeably, but if we canvass his entire oeuvre it is clear that he does not consider every religion suitable for that function. He vehemently rejects Islam for instance.[73]

The protagonist of the claim that religion should be the basis of the moral order could, of course, take the position that the religion of the majority would be best qualified to fulfil the function of the social bond. But the problem is that most contemporary societies are multicultural or multireligious. And the prospects for one religion gaining the upper hand are not very good, to say the least. Besides, non-establishment clauses like the first amendment of the American Constitution prohibit state-churches and official state religions. In combination with freedom of belief, these are a firm foundation of modern constitutions and this makes the chances of a majority religion very slim. This would imply that Tocqueville's ideas on Christianity as the foundation of American democracy – whatever their value was in the nineteenth century – would hardly be an option in contemporary societies. Because the pluralistic or multicultural composition of the people is a hard fact in contemporary life, the question is: 'what unites all civilians with different religions?' As religion can only unite people from the same group yet disunites society as a whole, we have to look for a new source of inspiration that can bind the people together.

For post-Enlightenment thinkers like Edmund Burke, Chateaubriand, Joseph de Maistre and also Tocqueville (although I will qualify this statement hereafter) the republican principles of the French Revolution or Enlightenment could not function as the new civil religion. Some of these nineteenth-century thinkers advocated a return to religion as the foundation of the political and moral order as had been the case in the pre-Enlightenment period. But globalization and demography has now made this nineteenth-century option obsolete. A longing for one religion as the unifying factor of contemporary societies is a romantic illusion, a nostalgic desire for a time and culture that no longer exist.[74] As we have seen, Tocqueville dreams of 'the idea of a single, all-powerful being imposing the same laws in the same way on everyone equally'.[75] But this is no longer the world we are living in and probably never will be. The adherents of the different denominations will probably never overcome their differences as to the nature of their God.[76] More likely is that, if religion is mixed up with politics, a protracted discussion over the nature of God will lead us into wars of religion, as we have witnessed in sixteenth- and seventeenth-century Europe.

If these critical remarks on the social and political function of religion are justified, then we have to reconsider a kind of secular or denominationally neutral civil religion. And the next question is: do we find hints at such a secular civil religion in Tocqueville's work? Or had he bet all his cards on the religion of Christianity as some other counter-revolutionary thinkers like Joseph de Maistre had done?

The secular reading of Tocqueville

Tocqueville is a complex and, it seems to me, not always consistent thinker. In a majority of passages in *De la démocratie en Amérique* and other books he stresses the need for a religious backup of the moral order and he appears to be skeptical about the autonomy of ethics and politics. Yet there seem to be some footholds for independent politics and ethics in his work as well, more specifically when he uses the word 'religion' in a very broad and non-sectarian way. In Volume One, Part II, Chapter 10, he comments on his favourite subject, popular sovereignty, as an idea that impregnates the whole American mind. The idea, or, as Tocqueville writes, the 'dogma' of popular sovereignty is 'the last link in a chain of opinions that rings the whole Anglo-American world'.[77] But then his discourse makes an interesting twist in the direction of reason (and not faith). Tocqueville writes: 'Providence equipped each individual ... with the degree of reason necessary to guide his conduct in matters of exclusive interest to himself alone. This is the great maxim on which civil and political society in the United States is based.'[78]

Let us read these words carefully: Providence endowed man with reason. Tocqueville continues by telling us that reason and the republic seem intimately connected, because the republic penetrates into the ideas, opinions and general habits of the Americans, and 'in order for them to change their laws, they would in a sense have to change themselves through and through'.[79] Apparently, it is not only uncritical acceptance of dogma that is extolled in the work of Tocqueville. Man can reason about the political order. It is reason that makes it possible to review the laws in the light of the idea of popular sovereignty. And then Tocqueville introduces a new conception of 'religion' that is much broader than Christianity or even theism. He writes:

> In the United States, the religion of the majority is itself republican. That religion subjects the truths of the other world to individual reason, just as politics leaves the interests of this world to the good sense of all, and it allows each man free choice of the path that is to lead him to heaven, just as the law grants each citizen the right to choose his government.[80]

Here religion in the traditional sense is completely evaporated. This is the civil religion of the Enlightenment thinkers. Tocqueville does not advocate Christianity or Catholicism as the bond uniting all the citizens of the Republic, but their faith in reason and in popular sovereignty. The republican conviction is here portrayed as the 'religion' that animates the American political order.

In this passage the great aristocratic Frenchman subscribes more to the Enlightenment ideas of the eighteenth-century radicals than to the enlightened conservatism of thinkers like Burke and Chateaubriand that resonates in other parts of his oeuvre. The only thing, even in this passage, that reminds us of his predilection for the 'dogmatism' that animates the rest of his work, is that the republican principle itself is proclaimed as a dogma that cannot be scrutinized by reason: 'The republican principle reigns in America today as the monarchical principle dominated France under Louis XIV.'[81] The republican principle, Tocqueville adds, is accepted in America without combat, without opposition, without proof: 'by a tacit accord, a sort of *consensus universalis*'.[82]

On the basis of these passages it is possible to interpret Tocqueville not only as the founding father of the 'Christian view' that links the American Republic to Christianity, but also to see him as the expounder of the notion of a 'civil religion' that is much broader than religion in its confessional meaning.

Let us go back to an older commentator on Tocqueville's work, John Nef. Nef writes: 'Beliefs have played and are playing compelling parts in history. All of us believe in something.'[83] Indeed, *in something*. But judging from the Tocqueville passage quoted above, this can just as well be a secularist philosophy. It may also be possible to refer to common values as the binding element in contemporary societies, such as faith in democracy, in human rights, or in the rule of law. Apologists for belief tend to ignore or disavow the unifying potential of secular creeds. Yet Nef as well comes very close to the view that secular creeds can fulfil this function, as is clear from the following words:

> If belief is an inevitable part of individual experience, nothing is perhaps of greater moment than the question whether men and women generally have accessible any belief capable of uniting rather than dividing them, any belief that will nourish the gentle virtues and help justice, charity, compassion and love, rather than hatred, jealousy, fear, and the lust for power, to gain, and now (if given reign) almost inevitably to destroy the world.[84]

This is indeed the central question: is there 'any belief capable of uniting rather than dividing' the people that have to share the territory of the state? This question cannot be answered by simply proposing your own religious conviction.

So Tocqueville is important, not because of what he has written about the specific importance of Christianity for democracy, but because of his emphasis on what we now call a 'civil religion'. Sanford Kessler writes: 'Perhaps the most important conclusion to emerge from the contemporary civil religion debate so far is that religion in some form is essential for a well-ordered democratic polity.'[85] I stress 'in some form'. Kessler cites Will Herberg, who contends that every society requires a shared religious faith, which gives its citizens the basic ideas, values, rituals and symbols that make common political life possible.[86] Using one of the existing world religions for that purpose would demean that religion and cause civil strife in a multireligious society.[87] Thus, if we want to make Tocqueville relevant for our contemporary democracies we have to interpret him as the propounder of a civil religion, not as advocating Christianity as social mooring. Fortunately, there are several passages that make this 'civil-religion reading' of Tocqueville viable.

Another passage where Tocqueville indicated that the success of the American Republic results from much more than religion, in the narrow sense of the word, is to be found in Chapter 8 of the first book of *De la démocratie en Amérique*. Tocqueville writes:

> The thirteen colonies that simultaneously threw off the English yoke at the end of the last century shared the same religion, the same language, the same mores, and almost the same laws; they fought a common enemy; they should therefore have powerful reasons to unite closely with one another and consolidate as a single nation.[88]

It is clear from this passage that the first Americans shared much more than just 'religion', in the confessional sense that Tocqueville, in other passages of *De la démocratie*, singles out as the foremost if not sole factor of social cohesion. What about the motivating factor of sharing a common history, for instance? Tocqueville is aware of a 'harmony between fortune and human efforts' in America.[89] What was the source of that harmony? Was it a shared religion? Tocqueville answers: 'America was a new nation, yet the people who lived there had long been accustomed to the exercise of liberty elsewhere. These were two great causes of domestic order.'[90] In other words, it had novelty and the sense of freedom in its genes. That is what distinguished America from other nations – not religion in the narrow sense.

In yet another passage Tocqueville points out that the founding fathers of the American Republic were outstanding and independent thinkers: 'the men who framed the laws of the Union were almost all remarkable for their enlightenment and still more remarkable for their patriotism'.[91]

I do not want to contend that my 'secular reading' of Tocqueville is the only one possible. There are many passages where Tocqueville seems to understand confessional religion or even Christianity as the firm foundation of the American republic. In many places Tocqueville presents us with sweeping generalizations such as:

> It was religion that gave birth to Anglo-American societies. This must always be borne in mind. Hence religion in the United States

is inextricably intertwined with all the national habits and all the feelings to which the fatherland gives rise. This gives it a peculiar force.[92]

In such passages Tocqueville apparently overlooks that historical influence and viability for the future are completely different things. It may be true that Christianity exerted a great historical influence on the founding of the American republic but that nonetheless only a secular state has prospects for the future. Tocqueville's admirer and contemporary, John Stuart Mill, understood this very well. He wrote some insightful essays on the relationship between morals and religion that are in some respects more subtle than the ideas of the great Frenchman. Mill wrote:

> They say, that religion alone can teach us what morality is; that all the high morality ever recognized by mankind, was learnt from religion; that the greatest uninspired philosophers in their sublimest flights, stopt far short of the Christian morality, and whatever inferior morality they may have attained to (by the assistance, as many think, of dim traditions derived from the Hebrew books, or from a primeval revelation), they never could induce the common mass of their fellow citizens to accept it from them. That, only when a morality is understood to come from the Gods, do men in general adopt it, rally round it, and lend their human sanctions for its enforcement. That granting the sufficiency of human motives to make the rule obeyed, were it not for the religious idea we should not have had the rule itself.[93]

Mill is not reluctant to acknowledge this: 'There is truth in much of this'. But he adds one important proviso: 'There is truth in much of this, *considered as a matter of history*.'[94] Ancient peoples have generally understood their morals, their laws, their intellectual beliefs and even their practical arts of life as revelations from superior powers.[95] That does not mean, however, that this is necessarily the case. When people were savages, moral precepts needed god-given sanctions. But as civilization advances, it must be possible to uphold moral values without divine sanctions. The secularist position is clearly stated by Mill when he writes: 'Are not moral truths strong enough in their own evidence, at all events to retain the belief of mankind when once they have acquired it?'[96] Mill points out that much of what is considered specifically Christian morality is equalled in the *Meditations* of Marcus Aurelius, which we have no ground for believing to have been in any way indebted to Christianity.[97] Yet whatever may be the source of some moral precepts, the relevant question is whether they can stand on their own feet. Even if some of the precepts of Jesus were an original contribution to our moral heritage, it has become the property of humanity and cannot now be lost by anything short of a return to primeval barbarism.[98]

In his correspondence with Gobineau, Tocqueville indicated that he considered the ideas of the 'utilitaires anglais' as rather shallow.[99] I do not think this judgement is very judicious. Mill understood better than Tocqueville what the future had in store for us, although also in the work of Tocqueville there are moorings for a civil religion of a non-denominational character. A secular reading of Tocqueville seems possible and probably this aspect of his work has greater significance for the future than many scholars seem to realize.

Notes

1 Paul-Henri Thiry d'Holbach, *Histoire Critique de Jésus Christ ou analyse raisonnée des Evangiles* [1770], ed. Andrew Hunswick (Geneva: Librairie Droz SA, 1997). Paul-Henri Thiry d'Holbach, 'La contagion sacrée, ou histoire naturelle de la superstition ou tableau des effets que les opinions religieuses ont produits sur la erre [1768]', in Paul-Henri Thiry d'Holbach, *Premieres oeuvres*, ed. Paulette Charbonnel (Paris: Éditions Sociales, 1971), pp. 139–75. For other radical currents and thinkers within the Enlightenment tradition, see Catherine Secrétan, Tristan Dragon and Laurent Bove (eds), *Qu'est-ce que les Lumières 'Radicales'? Libertinage, athéisme et spinozisme dans le tournant philosophique de l'âge classique* (Paris: Éditions Amsterdam, 2007).
2 See Joshua Mitchell, 'Tocqueville on Democratic Religious Experience', in Cheryl B. Welch (ed.), *The Cambridge Companion to Tocqueville* (Cambridge and New York: Cambridge University Press, 2006), pp. 276–302.
3 Joachim Wach, 'The Role of Religion in the Social Philosophy of Alexis de Tocqueville', *Journal of the History of Ideas*, 7(1) (1946), pp. 74–90. See p. 75 in particular.
4 *Ibid.*, p. 76.
5 *Ibid.*
6 Jean-Louis Benoît in Alexis de Tocqueville, *Notes sur le Coran et autres textes sur les religions*, ed. Jean-Louis Benoît (Paris: Bayard, 2007), p. 10.
7 *Ibid.*, p. 10.
8 *Ibid.*, p. 10: 'In that sense, he had no faith'.
9 It all depends, of course, on what makes a 'Christian'. Bertrand Russell writes: 'I think that you must have a certain amount of definite beliefs before you have a right to call yourself a Christian.' These beliefs are: (1) belief in the existence of God, (2) belief in life after death, (3) belief that Christ has a specific significance. Cf. Bertrand Russell, *Why I Am Not a Christian. And Other Essays on Religion and Related Subjects* (London and New York: Routledge, 2004), p. 2.

10   Daniel C. Dennett, *Breaking the Spell. Religion as a Natural Phenomenon* (New York: Allen Lane, Penguin Books, 2006), pp. 200–46. Richard Dawkins, *The God Delusion* (London and Johannesburg: Bantam Press, 2006), p. 301.

11   See fragment 233 (in the Brunschvicg edition) of Blaise Pascal, *Pensées* [1670] (Fragment 418 in the Lafuma edition). This fragment is also included in countless introductions to the philosophy of religion, see for instance: Blaise Pascal, 'The Wager', in Michael Peterson, William Hasker, Bruce Reichenbach, David Basinger (eds), *Philosophy of Religion. Selected Readings* (New York and Oxford: Oxford University Press, 1996), pp. 63–5.

12   See William James, 'The Will to Believe', in William James, *Writings 1878–1899* (New York: Library of America, 1984), pp. 457–79.

13   Going back on Plato's 'Noble Lie', a religious myth told to the people to motivate them to do what is good and right. In contemporary political thought this idea was forcefully defended by Leo Strauss. See Shadiah B. Drury, *The Political Ideas of Leo Strauss* (New York: Palgrave MacMillan, 2005 [1998]), pp. 65ff.

14   According to Burke, Voltaire was a blasphemous thinker. See Edmund Burke, *Selected Letters of Edmund Burke*, edited and with an introduction by Harvey C. Mansfield Jr (Chicago and London: University of Chicago Press, 1984), p. 268. For Maistre he was the most despicious writer. See Joseph de Maistre, *Du Pape*, 2nd edn (Tournai: J. Casterman, 1820), p. 264.

15   Voltaire, *Dictionnaire philosophique*, ed. René Pomeau (Paris: Garnier-Flammarion, 1964 [1764]). See the article 'Theist'.

16   Voltaire, 'Epître à l'auteur du livre des Trois Imposteurs', in Voltaire, *Oeuvres complètes de Voltaire* (Paris: Garnier, 1877–85), Tome 10, pp. 402–5.

17   See also Voltaire, 'Athée, athéisme' in Voltaire, *Dictionnaire philosophique*, eds. Julien Benda and Raymond Naves (Paris: Éditions Garnier Frères, 1764), avec introduction, variantes et notes par Julien Benda, texte établi par Raymond Naves (Paris: Éditions Garnier Frères, 1764), pp. 36–44. See p. 40 in particular.

18   Edmund Burke, *Reflections on the Revolution in France*, ed. Conor Cruise O'Brien (Harmondsworth: Penguin Books, 1982 [1790]), p. 186.

19   Jean-Louis Benoît brings these texts together and provides excellent commentary. See Tocqueville, *Notes sur le Coran*.

20   Alexis de Tocqueville, *Democracy in America*, translated by Arthur Goldhammer (New York: Library of America, 2004).

21   Alexis de Tocqueville and Arthur Gobineau, *Correspondence entre Alexis de Tocqueville et Arthur de Gobineau, 1843–1859*, ed. L. Schemann (Paris: Librairie Plon, 1909).

22   See André Jardin, *Tocqueville. A Biography* (New York: Farrar Straus Giroux, 1988), pp. 431–2.

23   Cf. 'Qu'y a-t-il en définitive de *nouveau* dans les travaux ou les découvertes des moralistes modernes?' in Tocqueville and Gobineau, *Correspondence*, p. 4.

24   *Ibid.*, p. 5.

25   *Ibid.*: Christianity gave 'un caractère plus pur, plus immatériel, plus désintéressé, plus haut à la moral'.

26   *Ibid.*, p. 6: 'Lui seul en fit un ensemble, en lia toutes les parties et faisant tourner cette nouvelle morale en religion … .'

27   As I already made clear, not all of the Enlightenment thinkers were hostile to religion. Only the defenders of what Jonathan Israel has called 'radical

Enlightenment' were. See Jonathan I. Israel, *Enlightenment Contested. Philosophy, Modernity, and the Emancipation of Man 1670–1752* (Oxford: Oxford University Press, 2006), and Jonathan I. Israel, *Radical Enlightenment. Philosophy and the Making of Modernity 1650–1750* (Oxford and New York: Oxford University Press, 2001).

28 See his critique on the French *Encyclopédie* and its secularist leanings in: Chateaubriand, *Essai historique, politique et moral sur les révolutions anciennes et modernes, considérées dans leur rapports avec la Révolution française*, ed. Maurice Regard (Paris: Gallimard, 1978 [1797]), p. 358.

29 Joseph de Maistre, *Essai sur le principe générateur des constitutions politiques* (Lyon: M.P. Rusand, 1833).

30 See Benjamin Constant, 'De la religion considérée dans la source, ses formes et ses développements', in Benjamin Constant, *Oeuvres*, ed. Alfred Roulin (Paris: Gallimard, 1957 [1824]), pp. 1365–95. See p. 1370 on Holbach.

31 On the revolution of the utilitarians, see Elie Halévy, *The Growth of Philosophic Radicalism* (London: Faber and Faber, 1972 [1928]).

32 Jeremy Bentham, *An Introduction to the Principles of Morals and Legislation*, ed. J.H. Burns and H.L.A. Hart (London and New York: Methuen, 1982 [1789]).

33 John Stuart Mill, 'Utilitarianism', in John Stuart Mill, *On Liberty and Utilitarianism* (New York: Alfred A. Knopf, Everyman's Library, 1992), pp. 113–72.

34 Cf. Alexis de Tocqueville, *L'ancien régime et la Révolution*, ed. J.-P. Mayer (Paris: Gallimard, 1967), p. 242: 'On peut dire d'une manière générale qu'au XVIII siècle le christianisme avait perdu sur tout le continent de l'Europe une grande partie de sa puissance.'

35 Tocqueville and Gobineau, *Correspondence*, p. 12: 'Je vous avoue que je professe une opinion absolument contraire à la vôtre sur le christianisme.' Tocqueville and Gobineau also clashed on Islam. Gobineau had a rather favourable opinion of Islam, Tocqueville was a vehement critic. See Tocqueville, *Notes sur le Coran*, pp. 37ff.

36 A matter that was, of course, widely discussed among Enlightenment authors. See: Paul-Henri Thiry d'Holbach, 'La Contagion Sacrée, ou Histoire Naturelle de la Superstition ou Tableau des Effets que les Opinions Religieuses ont produits sur la Terre' [1768], in Paul-Henri Thiry d'Holbach, *Premieres oeuvres*, pp. 139–75. On p. 170 he writes: 'on nous dira peut-être que ce n'est point à la religion elle-même, mais à l'abus de la religion, que sont dus les excès dont nous avons parlé'.

37 Tocqueville and Gobineau, *Correspondence*, p. 13: 'Aimez Dieu de tout votre coeur et votre prochain comme vous-même, ceci renferme la loi et les prophètes.'

38 Wach, 'The Role of Religion'. See p. 75 in particular.

39 Alexis de Tocqueville, 'Letter to Eugène Stoffels, on His Love of Freedom and New Kind of Liberalism' (24 July 1836), in *The Tocqueville Reader. A Life in Letters and Politics*, ed. Olivier Zunz and Alan S. Kahan (Malden, MA: Blackwell, 2002), p. 152.

40 Wach, 'The Role of Religion', p. 76.

41 Tocqueville, *Democracy in America*, p. 3.

42 Mill, *On Liberty*.

43 Tocqueville, *Democracy in America*, p. 72.
44 *Ibid.*, p. 52.
45 *Ibid.*, p. 72.
46 *Ibid.*
47 *Ibid.*
48 *Ibid.*, p. 12.
49 And criticized for that, for instance by Nietzsche. See Friedrich Nietzsche, *Der Antichrist*, [1888–9], in Friedrich Nietzsche, *Sämtliche Werke. Band 6*, ed.Giorgio Colli und Mazzino Montinari (Munich: De Gruyter, Deutscher Taschenbuch Verlag, 1999), pp. 165–255.
50 Page Smith, *Rediscovering Christianity. A History of Modern Democracy and the Christian Ethics* (New York: St Martin's Press, 1994), p. 132.
51 Tocqueville, *Democracy in America*, p. 12.
52 *Ibid.*, p. 496.
53 *Ibid.*, p. 505.
54 *Ibid.*, p. 506.
55 See George Jellinek, *Die Erklärung der Menschen- und Bürgerrechte*, ed.Walter Jellinek (Munich and Leipzig: Duncker & Humblot, 1927).
56 *Ibid.*, p. 34.
57 *Ibid.*, p. 37.
58 *Ibid.*, p. 40.
59 *Ibid.*
60 Mill had also reviewed *De la démocratie en Amérique* with enthusiasm. He asked Tocqueville to contribute to a magazine he had started. See Jardin, *Tocqueville*, p. 235.
61 For a historical overview of the different forms, see: Janine Marie Idziak, 'Divine Command Morality: A Guide to the Literature', in Janine Marie Idziak, *Divine Command Morality: Historical and Contemporary Readings* (New York and Toronto: Edwin Mellen Press, 1979), pp. 1–38.
62 See Kai Nielsen, 'Ethics without Religion', in Michael Peterson, William Hasker, Bruce Reichenbach, David Basinger (eds), *Philosophy of Religion. Selected Readings* (New York and Oxford: Oxford University Press, 1996), pp. 536–44.
63 Only roughly formulated here. For a more elaborate treatment, see the texts comprised in Idziak, *Divine Command Morality*, or Philip Quinn, 'The Recent Revival of Divine Command Ethics', *Philosophy and Phenomenological Research*, 50 (Supplement) (1990), pp. 345–65.
64 Already developed in Plato, *Euthyphro*, 4e. See also A.E. Taylor, *Plato. The Man and His Work* (London: Methuen, 1977 [1926]), p. 151.
65 Tocqueville, *Democracy in America*, p. 42.
66 *Ibid.*
67 *Ibid.*, p. 43.
68 *Ibid.*, pp. 42–3.
69 *Ibid.*, p. 44.
70 *Ibid.*
71 *Ibid.*, p. 43.
72 *Ibid.*
73 Tocqueville, *Notes sur le Coran*, p. 37.
74 Some of the romantics were well aware of this. See Novalis, *Die Christenheid oder Europa* (Ditzingen: Reclam, 1984 [1799]).

75 Tocqueville, *Democracy in America*, p. 506.
76 As the German theologian Hans Küng advocates in: Hans Küng and Karl-Josef Kuschel, *Erklärung zum Weltethos*. *Die Deklaration des Parlamentes der Weltreligionen* (Munich and Zurich: Piper, 1993).
77 Tocqueville, *Democracy in America*, p. 458.
78 *Ibid.* On the use of the term 'providence', see Benoît: 'Quand on étudie en détail l'ensemble du *corpus* tocquevillien, il apparaît clairement que cette croyance à la 'Providence' est diffuse; Tocqueville est bien éloigné du providentialisme de Bossuet ou des penseurs contre-révolutionnaires: Bonald et Joseph de Maistre, contrairement à ce que peut penser le lecteur.' Tocqueville, *Notes sur le Coran*, p. 21.
79 Tocqueville, *Democracy in America*, p. 458.
80 *Ibid.*, p. 459.
81 *Ibid.*
82 *Ibid.*, p. 460.
83 John Nef, 'Truth, Belief and Civilization: Tocqueville and Gobineau', *Review of Politics*, 25(4) (1963), pp. 460–82. See p. 463 in particular.
84 *Ibid.*, p. 464.
85 Sanford Kessler, 'Tocqueville on Civil Religion and Liberal Democracy', *The Journal of Politics*, 39(1) (1977), pp. 119–46. See p. 120 in particular.
86 Kessler, 'Tocqueville on Civil Religion', p. 120.
87 By concentrating on the political utility of religious belief to the point of indifference as to its content, Lively and Zetterbaum argue, Tocqueville undermines the very belief he finds necessary to the preservation of liberty. As a result, Tocqueville's position is untenable according to these authors. See Jack Lively, *The Social and Political Thought of Alexis de Tocqueville* (Oxford: Clarendon Press, 1962), pp. 196–7. Marvin Zetterbaum, *Tocqueville and the Problem of Democracy* (Stanford, CA: Stanford University Press, 1967), pp. 120–4. According to Catharine Zuckert, by contrast, Tocqueville's position is internally consistent. See Catherine Zuckert, 'Not by Preaching: Tocqueville on the Role of Religion in American Democracy', *Review of Politics*, 43(2) (1981), pp. 259–80.
88 Tocqueville, *Democracy in America*, p. 126.
89 *Ibid.*, p. 148.
90 *Ibid.*
91 *Ibid.*, p. 172.
92 *Ibid.*, p. 486.
93 John Stuart Mill, *Three Essays on Religion* (Amherst NY: Prometheus Books, 1998 [1874]), p. 96.
94 *Ibid.*
95 *Ibid.*
96 *Ibid.*, p. 97.
97 The same idea is elaborated with a wealth of material in Joseph McCabe, *Sources of the Morality of the Gospels* (London: Watts & Co., 1914).
98 Mill, *Three Essays on Religion*, p. 98.
99 Tocqueville and Gobineau, *Correspondance*, p. 7.

8
Democracy and Religion: Some Tocquevillian Perspectives

Agnès Antoine

Tocqueville and the question of religion

In the French culture, where secularism has long been associated with anti-religiousness, Tocqueville's analyses of religion have often been neglected, overlooked and even criticized as a shadow upon his otherwise enlightened modern approach to egalitarianism and its defining characteristics. In opposition to this view, I would like in what follows to emphasize the interest of Tocqueville's analyses on the nature of religion, its possible role in democracy and the relationship between Christianity and democratic principles. Even more importantly, I would like to show how the question of religion is central to his thought. Though this question seems to take up relatively little room in his works, it is in fact intrinsically related to Tocqueville's reflections on democracy, as the other side (or underside) of the democratic coin. The reconciliation of democracy and religion – or, more specifically, of democracy, morality and religion – is the underlying theme that runs through all Tocqueville's works as well as his political views. One has only to think of his programmatic introduction to *De la démocratie en Amérique*, which is very explicit in this respect, presenting his project through a detailed account of the questions that inspired it and which he wants to address to the French people. Why are democrats – particularly, French ones – so often anti-religious, that is, anti-Christian in this case? And why are believers – Christians again, and more particularly, Catholics – so often anti-democratic?[1]

I should also mention two other particularly significant texts that frame Tocqueville's intellectual and political career. The first is his famous letter to Eugene Stoffels from 24 July 1836, where Tocqueville defines himself as a 'liberal of a new kind'. What does this mean? By 'liberal'

Tocqueville means a 'friend of liberty', a friend of the liberties that can come to flourish in a democracy, and thus a true democrat; but of a 'new kind' in that, for him, being a democrat does not mean renouncing all moral regulation or defying any authority, as seems to be called for by the most radical democrats. In unveiling what he calls his 'programme' and also his 'plan as a whole' to his friend, Tocqueville writes:

> What has always struck me about my country ... has been to see lined up on one side the men who prize morality, religion, order, and on the other those who love freedom and the equality of men before the law. This sight has struck me as the most extraordinary and most deplorable ever offered a man's view; for all these things which we separate are, I am certain, indissolubly united in the eyes of God. They are all *holy* things, if I can express myself so, because the greatness and happiness of man in this world can come only from the simultaneous combination of them all. Since then I have realized that one of the most beautiful enterprises of our times would be to show that all these things are not at all incompatible; that on the contrary they are necessarily linked to one another, so that each of them is weakened by being separated from the others.[2]

The second text I want to mention shows from a retrospective standpoint the steadfastness of Tocqueville in this 'beautiful enterprise': a letter from 1853 to his friend Corcelle, where he once again declares he is convinced 'man's true grandeur lies only in the harmony of the liberal sentiment and religious sentiment' – he 'whose passion for thirty years has been to bring about this harmony'.[3]

Most importantly, however, I would go so far as to say that the types of questions Tocqueville poses to democracy arise out of a religious sensibility and a theological framework that implicitly underlie his sociological method. Unsurprisingly in an avid reader of Pascal, Rousseau and even Montesquieu, Tocqueville's approach to the human condition is Augustinian in that his questions are mainly addressed to the 'heart' of the democrat, towards the object of his love. In Augustine, the fundamental choice at work in human freedom is expressed in the two cities symbolizing the two conflicting orientations in the heart of every human being and of humanity as a whole: the 'City of Man', ruled by a self-love that turns away from God; and the 'City of God', ruled by a love of God that turns away from the self. Tocqueville himself proposes an analysis of the democratic city starting from the equality of conditions as a 'generating fact'. This objective approach, however, is doubled by a moral and metaphysical questioning into the possible fate of a humanity that has given up on organizing communal life according to any kind of religious foundation. Thus, *De la démocratie en Amérique* (and particularly the second volume from 1840) can be read as a broad reflection on the fate of an equality without God. In this sense, the question of religion pervades Tocqueville's works, even though he argues from a non-theological, sociological and utilitarian (as he is often reproached) standpoint – the very standpoint that is accessible to a man of equality without God. Yet, Tocqueville does not disassociate himself from this kind of democrat. His questioning of democracy is also a questioning of the self as an individual conditioned by egalitarian culture and sharing, more specifically, in modernity's doubt or perplexity with respect to the 'supernatural'. Also shaped by the aristocratic culture, however, Tocqueville hears another voice within him: the voice of greatness. This is why, he tells us, he has gone to the trouble of elevating himself to meditative heights from which he can contemplate the path of humanity and subsequently bear his enlightened viewpoint back down to the democratic city.[4]

The fate of an equality without God

Tocqueville sees the progressive generalization of equality among human beings as the work of providence, first, because it seems to be unavoidable and irreversible, but also because it has allowed a more shared and thus more equitable notion of liberty to arise. Democracy is the institutionalization of *equal liberty* for all human beings, and its expression in 'human rights' gives rise to 'natural' virtue or law, which replaces the former rule of customs, with all their peculiarity and variability. Thus, it is the advent of a more just and universal morality, as well as its concrete achievement in new political institutions where each citizen – as sovereign – is called to participate in elaborating a common destiny. The democrat has integrated this foundational equality of human beings into his way of thinking. He has a feeling of similarity that was lacking in his predecessors, and this allows him to see himself as belonging to a unified and single humanity. He is able to feel sympathy and even compassion for his fellows because he easily identifies with them. And in comparison to the sometimes cruel practices of aristocratic societies, customs have a general tendency to become more gentle.

Yet, Tocqueville underlines that the democratic heart only *seems* to grow bigger through this feeling of similarity. In fact, the notion of humanity the democrat harbours henceforth in his mind can remain an abstract idea: it does not necessarily lead to an awareness of one's neighbours, nor to a feeling of collective belonging in a shared enterprise. Where, then, is the democratic heart headed? What is the aim of its love?

Tocqueville answers that, in his heart, the democratic man is first devoted to himself, and then to his nearest and dearest, to family and friends – this is to define *individualism* as the main characteristic of egalitarianism. His desires, on the other hand, are mostly directed towards the seeking of material goods and the improvement of his well-being – in other words, *materialism* is the second trait characterizing democratic man. His sphere of preoccupations is mostly private, and he invests his energy into material and 'short-term' goals that provide immediate satisfaction. This is not to say that his heart is lacking in ambition, but rather that his ambition is literally 'earthly': infinite desires have been replaced by an unlimited pursuit of smaller desires. Tocqueville thus worries that the heart of democratic man will end up 'narrowing', 'contracting', 'hardening' and 'closing up' on itself, and that his soul will shrink, weaken and atrophy. From an Augustinian perspective, it seems the democratic condition – left to its natural 'tendencies' – pushes democratic man towards self-love, rather than love of God, neighbour, or community. 'The soul gradually adapts itself to the objects that occupy it', writes Rousseau in his *Discours sur les sciences et les arts*.[5] And it was already written in the Gospel: 'For where your treasure is, there will your heart be also.'[6]

To capture the tendency Tocqueville found so worrisome in desire, it is useful to look at the psychoanalytic concept of narcissism (taken in a very general sense) in connection with the problematic relationship between individual and world. Freud and Augustine – important transmitters of the Judeo-Christian tradition (though a reluctant one in the former case) – are to my mind the best guides for reading Tocqueville, along with other 'Augustinians' like Pascal and Rousseau. All these thinkers see the human being as a desiring being, divided between self-love and the love of Love, narcissism and object-love, personal drives and cultural sublimation, life drives and death drives, the angel and the beast.

The strength of Tocqueville's analysis is that he manages to present the potential for narcissism as more properly a result of social conditioning than a moral choice of modernity – as is suggested, for instance, by Lamennais in his *Essai sur l'indifférence en matière de religion*. Tocqueville is careful to distinguish between individualism and egoism: a moral vice of the human heart consisting in a 'passionate and exaggerated love of self'. Individualism, on the other hand, is a 'reflective and tranquil sentiment' brought about by the egalitarian way of life and 'that disposes each citizen to cut himself off from the mass of his fellow men'.[7] In fact, by establishing equality between human beings, democracy undoes prior existing relationships. 'Aristocracy,' writes Tocqueville, 'linked all citizens together in a long chain from peasant to king; democracy breaks the chain and severs the links'.[8] 'Severs the links': henceforth, social relationships are no longer straightforward, but involve a more voluntary participation in their construction than when they were simply imposed and transmitted by the very organization of society. 'Severs the links' also means a break with traditions and inherited cultures; and this is the source of democratic rationalism, with its intellectual and individualistic tendencies. Finally, 'severs the links' means the disappearance of any fixed framework for material existence, accompanied by a legitimate quest of the democratic individual for a place in the world as source of his preoccupation with material goods and his unlimited passion for comfort and well-being – in a word, his materialism.

Individualism, rationalism and materialism characterize a scientific, commercial and industrial society that at first places its trust in state institutions for the managing of public affairs. In a kind of vicious circle, this society re-enforces the narcissistic tendencies of the individual arising out of the egalitarian condition. Withdrawn into their private activities, human beings risk losing the ability to represent reality to themselves in similar ways and create common projects. This could give way to a kind of indifference to public affairs, an alienation from the political. Paradoxically, however, this happens at the very moment where politics, in the strong sense, first becomes possible; that is, at the very moment when every individual acquires the liberty to participate in determining communal goals. The danger of an equality without God is the danger of a humanity that, 'though constantly on the move', no longer makes progress and, far from choosing its own path, is rather possessed and imprisoned by its own reflection and 'acquiesce[s] in [its] fate without offering any resistance'.[9]

Tocqueville points out that there is nothing in democratic culture that could naturally counterbalance these tendencies, awakening democratic man to responsibility and heightening his awareness of communal life. Not only does religion lose its structuring role, but – more importantly – the very foundations of morality, and subsequently of communal obligations and reciprocal rights and duties, become problematic. 'Do you not see that religions are on the wane and that the *divine* notion of rights is disappearing? Does it not strike you that mores are crumbling and that, along with them, the *moral* notion of rights is fading away?'[10] How then to get the democrat to willingly turn his attention away from himself? How to integrate a sense of transcendence and magnitude – constitutive of human nature and indispensable to civilization, according to Tocqueville – without returning to the idealization at work in aristocratic cultures?

A political science for democracy

The aim of the 'new political science' Tocqueville is seeking to create is to answer these questions; and it cannot help but be 'new', for it applies specifically to the world of equality. In fact, the spontaneously narcissistic tendencies of democratic society can only be counterbalanced by artificial means. These means are provided by the art of politics, which is by its very nature an art of balancing, of preserving the middle ground, and above all an art versed in the human passions, according to Tocqueville. One must suggest something that is neither too elevated, nor too base to the democratic heart. Neither the unattainable values of old – which Tocqueville understood (before Nietzsche) were first and foremost created to give legitimacy to the elite that was in power – for they forced human beings to become disembodied angels. Nor, as only source of morality, the seeking of material goods and immediate satisfaction to one's individual needs, for this would be to reduce the human being to a beast blindly driven by its need for self-preservation.

To open up the heart of democratic man, Tocqueville develops his thought in two main directions, and these are related to the question of a 'moral' or 'divine' notion of the rights mentioned above. To begin with, Tocqueville wants to show that democracy is capable of an authentic civic 'virtue' different from the morality of devotion and sacrifice in bygone societies ruled by honour. Though democratic man has somewhat lost the ability to sublimate, though he has little sense of duty in return for the rights he has acquired, it is still possible to offer him a 'natural' morality. This would be a morality without religious foundation and made to the measure of man, that is, made to the measure of what primordially moves human beings when the masks of aristocracy have fallen away: self-interest. The key is to make sure this self-interest is 'rightly understood': democratic man has to come to understand that, in taking up a standpoint of common interest, he is also serving his personal interest, that it is more useful to him to work towards the common interest than to neglect it. However, Tocqueville maintains that this morality of self-interest rightly understood can only be effective if it moves beyond theory: to be internalized, it would have to be taught through practice. He believes more strongly in educating human sensibilities than in inculcating a rationalistic catechism into the democratic mind. Reason is insufficient and even dangerous when it pretends to be able to humanize man all by itself, for it does not take into account the desiring nature of human beings, human beings as beings of the flesh. Tocqueville hopes to provide the democrat with what he calls 'the spirit of the city' through the concrete practice of citizenship activities that can be *embodied* and, through force of habit, come to be loved for themselves. In a word, it is by practising citizenship that one becomes a citizen. The more opportunities there are for participating in communal affairs, the broader will become the public space. And the more democrats integrate care for the common good, the more likely it will become one of their love objects. Tocqueville's reflections on the decentralization of political institutions fall within this framework. But they are only one part of a much broader reflection on the necessity of encouraging association in a society that has a structural tendency towards dissociation. The science of association – that is, association as an art, as well as reflections on the means necessary to its achievement – is put forward as the 'mother science' required by democracy, its primary political art. In particular, Tocqueville emphasizes the role of voluntary associations, which always have a strong political dimension, independently of whether their goals are explicitly political or not. Further, not only is the relation between equality and association a necessary one for Tocqueville, but associative practices need to be developed in proportion to any increases in equality. In this way, it is possible for the democrat to reappropriate the sovereignty he has been too quick to hand over to representatives of the political majority or of the power of the state – the two symbols of collective rationality. It is only through the involvement of his whole body as sensible that the democrat learns to take into account the existence of other human beings, to discover different points of view, and to get a true feel for his fellows, that is, to 'feel with' them and thus progressively broaden his intellectual and moral awareness. Tocqueville writes: 'Feelings and ideas are renewed, the heart expands, and the human spirit develops only through the reciprocal action of human beings on one another'.[11] Like Rousseau, he places particular emphasis on the constitution of morality as progressive in nature, on the importance of proximity to our love objects. As such, we only begin to become members of humanity at large after having been citizens in smaller communities. But through association, Tocqueville puts into place a kind of mediation between the particular and the universal, the individual and the communal, that was lacking in Rousseau's theory of sovereignty. In an equal and individualizing society, association underpins the concrete process of mutual recognition through which humanity can truly come into its own.

The role of religion

Along with his reflections on the conditions for a modern moral and civic education, Tocqueville considers the role that might be played by religion in bringing equilibrium to democratic civilization. Though political power rests upon the principle of sovereignty rather than on the divine, and though a progressive emancipation of morality and law from religious authority takes place in democratic cultures, this does not mean that religion disappears from society – even if the democrat, through his intellectual and sensible structure, has little predisposition towards belief and religious experience. For religious sensibility is universal, according to Tocqueville, insofar as it arises out of a feeling of finitude common to all human beings. Awareness of mortality leads to a desire for immortality or eternity, a desire to move beyond the earthly. This is why Tocqueville also speaks of a 'religious instinct' in relation to the human heart in its restlessness and longing for the infinite, its desire to surpass or transcend itself. Moreover, the spirit of religion is not necessarily contrary to the spirit of democracy. This is demonstrated by the example of America, where democracy arose in harmony with religion, unlike in France, where freedom was only achieved by overthrowing both the power of the king and of the Catholic Church. Indeed, did equality not arise out of Christian culture, even though other spiritual trends may have prepared the way, and even though Christianity has not been solely responsible for the spread of equality in all its forms in the history of Europe?

Tocqueville believes that religion can still have a political effect in modern societies, as long as we understand that this effect is indirect and should remain so. Paradoxically, the political and the spiritual can only develop in a complementary way once they have been clearly separated on an institutional and legal level, that is, once all danger of one power dominating the other has been removed. True to his sociological and utilitarian approach, Tocqueville points out the interest of religion's powers of sublimation for democratic politics and culture. Even though the community of believers that remains in democracy is rather small, religion maintains a few points of reference in a society that is otherwise morally unstable and without limits in its desire for rational mastery of the world. Moreover, religion can have a 'dematerializing' effect on democratic society by making visible love objects that differ from the ones suggested by the surrounding culture – love objects that mostly arise out of the seeking of material pleasures, the longing for possessions and a market mentality. Finally, in relation to this dimension of immateriality, Tocqueville brings to the fore the role religion can play in broadening the democratic conception of temporality, one that focuses on the present – a present of short, juxtaposed instants, of endlessly renewed little desires – to the detriment of the past and the future. By its very nature, religion projects human being towards the future, for it symbolizes the 'beyond'. Religion teaches human beings to consider the long term, the slowly winding road, and thus encourages great projects and vast enterprises. It is also a strong carrier of hope – though it is not the only one – and can thus contribute to maintaining a dimension so important for human and societal vitality. Most importantly for Tocqueville, religion is a break in the closure of democratic society: it guarantees that the alterity it symbolizes is maintained in a culture that has a tendency to confuse equality and uniformity, similarity and homogeneity.

How, then, are we to give religion its rightful place? First, by reestablishing its cultural dignity, suggests Tocqueville in addressing democrats hostile to religion and who try, in the name of tolerance, to impose their atheistic vision of the world and suppress the religious: believers should neither have to hide their beliefs in shame, nor to exhibit them. Second, by reforming religions and making them more democratic, suggests Tocqueville, this time speaking to believers and representatives of religious institutions who tend towards conservatism. Certain symbols, rites, moral principles and even dogmas that may only be the result of historical sedimentation upon the 'core' religious truths, uselessly offend democratic sensibilities. Religion has to be lived differently in democratic societies than in hierarchical ones.

Yet, do we not run the risk of reducing religion to a morality that serves democratic principles, and of thus losing the prophetic dimension that allows the religious to cut through worldly thinking? Do we not risk creating a kind of religion that is to be 'rightly understood' – what Tocqueville himself observed in some Americans? Perhaps. But Tocqueville prefers to imagine an influence in the opposite direction. In a democratic society where politicians and moralists are able to reawaken a sense for the future and for great ambitions in their fellows, it may be that this 'civic' detour leads men back to religious faith. For Tocqueville, the political is the possibility of an authentic meeting place for human beings, no matter what their beliefs, as well as a locus that converges towards the general concept of humanity in all its mysteriousness. In attempting to reconcile civic humanism with religious humanism, Tocqueville occupies an original place in the history of ideas that continues, for this reason, to be disturbing and largely misunderstood. In the 'Platonic' branch of the Christian tradition, which has long dominated the West and which gives a biased interpretation of Augustine's two cities, believers are called to devote themselves entirely to their salvation and to heavenly things. Earthly concerns are to be rejected as worldly vanities – especially politics, with the power- and glory-seeking it implies. Conversely, the civic tradition, with Machiavelli as its paradigmatic figure, gives exclusive pride of place to the political, although it has also been known to make instrumental use of religion in consolidating power: earthly citizenship has precedence over the heavens. Tocqueville's own view, however, is that '[t]he heart of man is vaster that people imagine':[12] having two loves – of city and of God – does not necessarily amount to serving two masters, for in certain conditions these loves can move in the same spiritual direction. The choice democrats are faced with is not one of choosing for democracy against religion, or for religion against democracy, for the earth against the heavens or the heavens against the earth. Instead, out of the plurality of their equal liberties, the choice is one of inhabiting democratic creation rather than falling back into the state of nature.

Notes

1 'Religious men do battle against liberty, and friends of liberty attack religion,' Tocqueville writes in his introduction to *De la démocratie en Amérique*. Alexis de Tocqueville, *Democracy in America*, trans. Arthur Goldhammer (New York: Library of America, 2004), p. 13. For a more in-depth discussion of the themes explored in this chapter, see Agnès Antoine, *L'impensé de la démocratie. Tocqueville, la citoyenneté et la religion* (Paris: Fayard, 2003).
2 Alexis de Tocqueville, 'Letter to Eugène Stoffels, on His Love of Freedom and New Kind of Liberalism' (24 July 1836), in *The Tocqueville Reader. A Life in Letters and Politics*, ed. Olivier Zunz and Alan S. Kahan (Malden, MA: Blackwell, 2002), p. 152.
3 Alexis de Tocqueville, 'Letter to Claude-François de Corcelle' (17 September 1853), in *Selected Letters on Politics and Society*, trans. James Toupin and R. Boesche, ed. Roger Boesche (Berkeley: University of California Press, 1985), p. 295.
4 Cf. Tocqueville, *Democracy in America*, p. 470.
5 Jean-Jacques Rousseau, *Discourse on the Sciences and the Arts (First Discourse) and Polemics*, trans. Judith R. Bush, Roger D. Masters, and Christopher Kelly ed. Roger D. Masters and Christopher Kelly (Hanover, NH: University Press of New England, 1992), p. 21.

6   St Luke 12.34 (King James Version).
7   Tocqueville, *Democracy in America*, p. 585.
8   *Ibid.*, p. 586.
9   *Ibid.*, pp. 759–60.
10 *Ibid.*, p. 274 (my italics).
11 *Ibid.*, p. 598.
12 *Ibid.*, p. 637.

9
Tocqueville, European Integration and Free Moeurs

Larry Siedentop

Introduction

There are three questions that I want to address. Where are we today in Europe? How did we get here? What should be done now? I shall discuss these questions relying, as much as possible, on the 'help' of Tocqueville – that is, on his insights, categories and values. Obviously, what follows is not a detailed analysis of his thought, but rather an attempt to apply some of his ideas to the process of European integration. If I were to claim more than that, it would be presumption.

So let us start. The first thing that strikes me is that Tocqueville, when confronted with the European Union, would probably have gone through the whole gamut of emotions. He might have started with surprise or even astonishment. For he would have been familiar with only two sorts of project for integration: forcible projects, projects for empire in the fashion of Charles V, Louis XIV and Napoleon; or utopian projects in the fashion, say, of the Abbé de Saint Pierre. A process of peaceful integration of nation-states, backed by powerful and often ancient national identities, would have seemed, to say the least, novel to Tocqueville.

The second emotion Tocqueville might well have felt is warm approval. But in saying that, I think we must fall back on the distinction that runs through and helps to organize Tocquevillian thinking – that is, the distinction between 'la condition sociale' and 'les institutions politiques', between civil society and government. Only then can we begin to address, with Tocqueville's help, my first question: where are we now in Europe – what is the condition of the European Union?

Consumerism

As a convinced liberal, Tocqueville would have been impressed by the extraordinary changes in civil society that have accompanied and been made possible by European integration in recent decades: the freer movement of persons, goods, services and capital, as well as the wider horizons that have been their subjective counterpart.

Yet his initial approval might soon give way to a kind of puzzlement. For Tocqueville would be struck by how little credit the European Union gets for helping to have brought about these changes. Among the younger generation of Europeans especially, these changes often seem to be simply taken for granted. There is little or no gratitude felt towards the European Union. Why is that? And what that does it tell us about the process of European integration hitherto?

Tocqueville would not fail to notice the extent to which for several decades Europe was constructed largely on an economic agenda. That became especially clear with the acceleration of integration from the late 1980s – after the Single European Act, with the Maastricht and Amsterdam treaties and the creation of a common currency. After all, the latter was often seen as a convenient, relatively uncontroversial 'back door' entry into federalism, as virtually entailing a federalist outcome without stirring up too much political controversy in the meantime.

Tocqueville would, I suggest, have been dismayed by the prolonged absence of adequate public debate about the nature of the political project for an integrated Europe – about its constitutional implications for member states. What are the prospects of self-government in Europe? That is the question that mattered most to him. Educated in a political tradition, which, as in Montesquieu, tended to see a continental scale of political organization as a threat to self-government, Tocqueville would put that question first.

I suspect that Tocqueville would have connected the noticeable lack of gratitude towards the European Union to widespread public uncertainty about the nature of the political project for Europe – to fears that integration may develop at the expense of self-government. He would certainly have deplored those changes in liberalism, which tend to present it more in economic or market terms than in political terms. For rights-based liberalism rather than utilitarianism was his credo. Indeed, perhaps Tocqueville's deepest conviction was that liberalism and its corollary, representative government, can be a means of restoring idealism to the modern world – of offsetting the materialism or, as we might describe it, the 'consumerism' that seems intrinsic to a democratic society. For Tocqueville, satisfying consumer wants should not exclude trying to improve the quality of those wants – particularly through the claims and exercise of citizenship.

Using this insight of Tocqueville, and applying it to the condition of Europe today, we can guess at his first conclusion. Markets do not create gratitude, whereas political institutions, at their best, may do so. Europe has paid a high price for being constructed largely on an economic agenda. Political idealism has not been nurtured. 'Getting richer together' has instead been the leitmotiv.

By contrast, idealism about the potential of civil liberty, representative government and citizenship was at the very core of Tocqueville's political thinking. In his view, the democratic social revolution – an egalitarian revolution in social structure – would only reach its 'natural' conclusion when it was crowned with free institutions, with representative government in the fullest sense, with citizens' participation at the local, regional and national level. Unfortunately, the democratic social revolution could yield two very different political outcomes, self-government on the one hand, or bureaucratic tyranny on the other. The postwar communist dictatorships in Eastern Europe would have confirmed his fears about the ever-present threat of the latter.

Centralization, in Tocqueville's eyes, was the pathology of the democratic social revolution – the Achilles' heel, so to speak, of a democratic social structure. The destruction of intermediate institutions, the withering of the habit of association, was conjured up whenever he spoke of the 'atomization' of society and of 'individualism'. And class conflict provided the mechanism. Achieving democracy by destroying an aristocratic society, with its involuntary associations and localism, involved a serious risk: that the struggle against privilege might lead to an excessive concentration of authority and power at the centre, in a bureaucratic state machine. After all, Tocqueville flagged bureaucratic tyranny as the great threat associated with modern democracy long before Max Weber.

It was the over-centralized or bureaucratic form of the French state that first led Tocqueville to become interested in American federalism – and to draw from it his celebration of the benefits of local liberty. And, of course, crucial to his didactic use of American examples – particularly the New England township – was his insight that the absence of an *ancien régime* in America, of any prolonged struggle against aristocracy or social privilege, meant that America had happily escaped the pathology of the democratic social revolution.

The crisis of democratic legitimacy

Let me suggest a second conclusion. Today Tocqueville might well fall back on an argument that he had encountered in Guizot's lectures and the *Doctrinaires*, in order to identify and assess political dangers attending the process of European integration. The argument he encountered in the 1820s and made his own was that centralization, the destruction of local autonomy in France, had been an *unintended consequence* of the long struggle against social privilege, against aristocracy and its local power.

How might Tocqueville have adapted this argument to today's Europe? I think he might argue that the greatest danger attending the process of European integration is that democratic political cultures may be weakened where they already exist, in the member states, without being replaced at the European level. In other words, the weakening of national democratic political cultures may prove to be an unintended consequence of the process of integration.

Recent popular and nationalist reactions to European integration – which are by no means confined to the French and Dutch referenda results on the constitutional treaty – may be a sign that the public is more sensitive to this danger than the political classes of Europe. The failure of the European Parliament to establish any significant hold over public opinion may be another symptom.

The democratic legitimacy of the European Union is at risk. Opinion polls suggest that it is in danger of being perceived as an elite-driven enterprise and a bureaucratic menace to national autonomy. This is in part the price now being paid for the long postponement of constitutional issues – followed by the rather sudden attempt to make up for lost time, to 'wrap up' the constitutional question once and for all. Did years of constitutional neglect contribute to a premature constitutional exercise under Giscard d'Estaing? Perhaps.

We are living through the crisis of European integration, which is a crisis of democratic legitimacy. This crisis of democratic legitimacy is an unintended consequence of the process of European integration. It could also be described as the crisis of the European nation-state. But here we must be careful. A crisis of democratic legitimacy is not the same thing as a 'democratic deficit'. Yet the two are often confused. Distinguishing between the two is a prerequisite for clear thinking.

Given the mobility of public opinion and the difficulty of accurately charting its movements, there is a sense in which representative democracies are always in deficit. Nor is that all. Liberal democratic systems are often designed, constitutionally, to ensure the occasional deficit, by constraining the majority principle in important respects – to protect individuals and minorities through a bill of rights, for example. A crisis of legitimacy is different. It can be said to exist when there is no widely understood and accepted framework for public decision-making. That, I think, could be Tocqueville's assessment of the political condition of Europe today. Power has shifted. But has authority?

A crisis of legitimacy may be said to have been the fact that dominated Tocqueville's political life and thinking – though, of course, the crisis that preoccupied him was at the national level rather than European level. It was the inability of successive nineteenth-century French regimes to establish their legitimacy – which is to say that the French Revolution had not been 'closed', that the revolutionary tradition remained a constant obstacle to the achievement of self-government in France.

Couldn't one say that the process of European integration since 1945 has created a kind of peaceful revolutionary tradition – and contributed to problems that give Tocqueville's thought a new relevance and profundity today? I believe it to be so. For the process of integration raises questions that are closely related to two of Tocqueville's key conceptions: *centralization* and *free moeurs*.

Tocqueville deploys these terms to argue that self-reliance and the habit of association are fostered and sustained by local and regional autonomy – by the experience of self-government. Moreover, the attitudes and habits fostered by local and regional autonomy spill over into civil society, giving it a vigour and autonomy that limits the growth of central power.

By contrast, when local government is reduced to an instrument of central government – when it becomes merely local administration – self-reliance and the habit of association are compromised. Looking to the state machine to deal with most problems then becomes a vicious habit. In that sense, centralization develops at the expense of free moeurs. This is the moral perspective that would, it seems to me, inform Tocqueville's judgements about the political condition of the European Union today.

A federal outcome?

How would Tocqueville describe the European Union in its present form? Is it a confederation? Tocqueville considered that traditionally confederations, lacking any means of direct action on individuals, were marked either by chronic weakness or were in fact dominated by one member state. He might perhaps have considered that the latter was true of the European Union during the years when it was dominated and shaped by France. But I suspect he would conclude that today the transfer of power in certain spheres to Brussels has lifted the European Union beyond the category of traditional confederations.

Does the European Union belong rather to a newer political category, what we have come to call 'federalism' on the American model? Here Tocqueville would probably hesitate, for the European Union has not – at least as yet – consecrated a formal division of sovereignty between the centre and member states. In that sense the constitutional position remains ambiguous – an ambiguity sustained by talk of its member states 'sharing their sovereignty'. For Tocqueville, that formal division of sovereignty between the federal government and the states in America marked a profound innovation. For it provided the basis for federal government acting directly on individuals in certain respects, and so acquiring an administrative machine separate from those of the states. Clearly, this has not yet happened within the European Union, and so it falls short of 'federalism' on the American model.

And yet the formal supremacy of EU law in certain spheres does bring the Union closer to federalism, insofar as it obligates the executives and courts of the member states to apply its rules. In fact, this can introduce what Tocqueville considered one of the great innovations of the American political system, the power of judicial review. The supremacy of EU law as decided by the Luxembourg Court opens the door, at least in theory, to further centralization – to extending the writ of the Union when faced with conflicts of jurisdiction. In that way the European Union already displays a tacit constitutionalism. For identifying different spheres of authority enables the European Union to constrain member states by relying on their own administrative and judicial systems.

While recognizing that such judicial review can become an agent of centralization, Tocqueville also saw it as the means of reconciling the unity of a political system with administrative decentralization. By means of judicial review, local and regional agencies of government can be held to account without subordinating them in a single bureaucratic hierarchy. For Tocqueville, that was the genius of American institutions – something he hoped might provide inspiration for reform of the French state. If commenting on the development of the EU, he would doubtless have relied on this distinction between governmental centralization and administrative centralization in order to combat the 'enemy', a bureaucratic form of the state developing at the expense of local and regional autonomy and free moeurs.

So it is important to notice that Tocqueville was not a critic of political centralization as such, provided it did not become merely the agent of bureaucratic government. In the case of nation-states, this emerges in Tocqueville's admiration for England and its administrative decentralization. But he also foresaw that the struggle against aristocracy in England might later undo this combination of governmental centralization ('the supremacy of the King in Parliament') with administrative decentralization. Then England, like France, would face the difficult problem of recreating free moeurs when they have been lost, due to over-centralization or bureaucracy.

Economism

Having looked at the first question (where are we today in Europe) and identified a danger (that national democratic cultures may be weakened by the process of integration), let me now explore briefly the second question I mentioned at the outset, again with Tocqueville's 'help'. How did we get here? Why were basic constitutional questions postponed for such a long time?

Here the answers are more obvious. At first the circumstances of post-1945 Europe ruled out an overly federalist agenda – not least because of the pariah status of Germany. So economic innovations and cooperation provided a less contentious way forward – 'getting richer together' became the name of the game. Before long, the unprecedented prosperity that resulted reinforced this bias. The result was what, in *Democracy in Europe*, I have called 'economism', which is the habit of subordinating political (and especially constitutional) argument to economic argument.[1] This mindset helped to turn successive EU treaties into technical exercises – not sufficiently designed to appeal to or shape public opinion.

Tocqueville would have been struck by this marked change in the character of liberal thinking in the later twentieth century – by what I am tempted to call the 'infiltration' of liberalism by economic reductionism, by a liberal version of historical materialism through the impact of Marxism on liberalism. That infiltration reinforced an attitude that if the economics were 'got right', then other aspects of integration would almost take care of themselves. That reductionist assumption made it easier to postpone discussion about the proper political destination for Europe.

Yet under the cover of this liberal reductionism, a fierce political competition was in fact going on – a competition I describe in

Democracy in Europe as a competition between three forms of the state to provide the model for Europe as a whole.[2] British opposition to anything like the federalist model espoused by Germany and the Netherlands ruled out such an outcome. Yet the custom-based, 'common law' nature of the British state made its model impossible to export. Didn't that leave the door open for a bureaucratic model, which was 'second nature' to the French political and administrative class – which also had in the first decades of integration the advantage of Germany still being a pariah state and Britain having been excluded by De Gaulle's veto?

Constitutionalism

Let us move on to the third question I asked at the beginning – what is to be done? The challenge is to overcome the crisis of legitimacy affecting European integration today – to overcome what, put most simply, is a widespread perception that 'Europe' is something happening to Europeans, rather than something they are doing. People in the street are not fools. They sense, even if they cannot give details, that there has been a significant shift of power away from the nation-states to the centre, to Brussels. Estimates are that more than two-thirds of social and economic regulation in member states now originates in Brussels.

The acceleration of integration since the later 1980s has involved not merely institutional changes – such as the single market and the abolition of national currencies – but has also threatened important changes in personal identity – in the ideas and loyalties that govern individual conduct. The political cultures attached to the nation-states of Europe were formed only slowly and with great difficulty. But they succeeded to some extent in creating a sense of mutual obligation among citizens, a willingness to make sacrifices for others. Can the European Union create in a few years what it took the nation-states centuries to develop? Can it foster European citizenship?

I am convinced that Tocqueville would think that only through constitutionalism can Europe rise to the challenge. But I also think that, quite apart from the referenda results in France and the Netherlands, he would conclude that the constitutional treaty was overly ambitious, too bureaucratic in character and premature. For decades EU treaties were not really for public consumption. They were put together by civil servants, for other civil servants. Little wonder that the Union has acquired a technocratic reputation! 'A civil servant's dream; a citizen's nightmare' would not be an unfair caricature of the past conduct of EU affairs.

Careful reading of Tocqueville suggests, I think, that there is only one way forward. A constitutional sense must be fostered across Europe – for such a constitutional sense would mark the first appearance of a truly European public opinion as well as the advent of a new legitimacy. However, this conclusion involves rejecting two other viewpoints; the first being that fostering such a constitutional sense is unnecessary, the second that it is impossible. The first is the view of those academics (neo-realists) who believe that an essentially technocratic approach to the construction of Europe will gradually yield popular consent through results. The second is the view of euro-sceptics who believe that Europe is too large and diverse for there ever to be anything resembling a European public opinion.

Now I believe that fostering such a constitutional sense is both necessary and possible. But I also believe that it can only be done slowly and with great difficulty. Overcoming the crisis of legitimacy will take great patience, skill and even cunning. There are both formal and informal conditions that will have to be satisfied, if such a constitutional sense is ever to develop. Here Tocqueville's *De la démocratie en Amérique* offers invaluable help – though I think even he underestimated the importance of one factor at the Philadelphia Convention in 1787 which brought the formal and informal conditions together. That is, the delegates inherited a kind of constitutional sense. There was a 'ghost' at the Convention, the ghost of the London government. For in many respects the delegates to the Philadelphia Convention saw the new federal government as inheriting some of the functions once performed by the government in London. That made their task easier. They did not have to create a constitutional sense ex nihilo.

As we have seen, Tocqueville's final criterion for judging any suggested constitutional arrangements for the European Union would be its likely impact on free moeurs. Will the European Union sustain and encourage their development, or does it develop at their expense? What arrangements – what distribution of authority and power – will best serve that goal?

Let us notice, by the way, how distinctive this Tocquevillian conception of free moeurs is – joining, as it does, personal autonomy and self-reliance with the habit of voluntary association. For that joining makes it notably different from some conceptions of liberty which preceded him, notably Rousseau's General Will, Benjamin Constant's conception of modern liberty in 'De la liberté des anciens comparée à celle des modernes', as well as more recent conceptions such as that of Isaiah Berlin in 'Two Concepts of Liberty'.

How would Tocqueville have applied his distinctive test of free moeurs? Did he have a method to apply? Certainly, Tocqueville did not have a 'methodology' – having the good fortune to live in a pre-professional age. If Tocqueville can be said to have had a method, we can perhaps locate it in some of the propositions that shaped his argument in *De la démocratie en Amérique*:[3]

- Laws are more important than physical circumstances.
- Moeurs are more important than laws.
- Moeurs depend finally on shared beliefs.

Tocqueville was therefore closer to the school of historical idealism than to historical materialism in approaching social explanation. Agreeing with these propositions, I tried – in my own book – to identify in *De la démocratie en Amérique* a number of informal conditions which underlay and contributed to the success of American federalism – and which Europe must satisfy if it is to approach even a quasi-federal political outcome.[4] They were (1) a robust tradition of local and regional autonomy, (2) a shared language, (3) an open political class, in which lawyers play a leading part, and (4) shared moral beliefs, providing a basis for distinguishing between public and private spheres – what should be done by government and what should be left to individuals. To what extent can Europe today match these informal conditions? My conclusion was that considerable progress had been made on the first two fronts, but worrying little on the last two.

What about the formal conditions? What legal arrangements should the European Union now promote, if it is even to begin to create a constitutional sense across the continent? Let me suggest a few.

First, a right of exit from the EU – in order to establish the voluntary character of the Union; making a contrast with American federalism as understood since the Civil War.

Second, a far clearer and more constraining definition of the subsidiarity principle – a definition far removed from the 'shared competences' of the proposed constitutional treaty, in which members states were allowed to exercise authority in a range of spheres only the European Union had chosen not to act. The presumption should be against central action rather than in its favour.

Third, the inflation of the language of 'rights' must be resisted. The most effective way of building a rights-based political culture across Europe – indispensable if European democracy is to be 'liberal' and the majority principle constrained – is to introduce a relatively short charter of rights. The proposed European charter of rights inflates the language of rights, turning what may or may not be desirable social and economic goals into the language of rights. If the appeal to 'rights' is to have the moral and legal force it should have, then it must not be confused with 'utility'.

Fourth, Europe must introduce, sooner rather than later, bicameralism. For it is no accident that federal systems rely on it. Having two chambers, one of which represents the population (or majority) principle, while the other represents a territorial principle (which may constrain the majority principle), is the most effective way of educating a population into the formalities of a political system on a continental scale, made up of member states.

Fifth, bicameralism would offer another advantage, if membership of the upper house were drawn from leading members of national parliaments who retained their national roles. Perhaps the greatest problem facing the European Union is that national political classes have used the existence of the European Parliament as an excuse to distance themselves from the European project – something that has helped to create the crisis of legitimacy in Europe, by weakening that precarious sense of empowerment which the nation-states of Europe had managed, with great difficulty, to create among their citizens through representative institutions.

Sixth, such an upper house for the European parliament ought to share responsibility with the European Court for defending the principle of subsidiarity. That is, there should be two locks on the door that leads to centralization. The judicial lock is not, by itself, an adequate protection against centralization. The history of the American Supreme Court, under John Marshall, provides a salutary warning in that respect, with its consistent interpretation of the constitution in favour of the federal government. The bias of the highest court can so easily come to favour extending the jurisdiction of the centre against that of the periphery.

All of these measures, designed to protect and foster free moeurs might, slowly, begin to foster a constitutional sense across Europe. And such a sense is the real prerequisite for anything like a constitution for Europe.

Notes

1 Larry Siedentop, *Democracy in Europe* (London: Allen Lane, Penguin, 2000), p. 33.
2 *Ibid.*, pp. 102–21.
3 See Chapter 9 of the first volume of *De la démocratie en Amérique*. Alexis de Tocqueville, *Democracy in America*, trans. Arthur Goldhammer (New York: Library of America, 2004), pp. 319–64.
4 Siedentop, *Democracy in Europe*, pp. 122–50.

10
Tocqueville and European Federalism: A Reply to Larry Siedentop

Wilfried Swenden

Introduction

In this chapter, I critically assess the preceding contribution by Larry Siedentop on 'Tocqueville, European Integration and Free Moeurs'. Prior to engaging with some of Siedentop's considerations, I should emphasize that I try to formulate my remarks with an important methodological point in mind. It is important to mention it here, for it goes to the heart of Tocqueville's logic of enquiry. In my view, the brilliance of Tocqueville's analysis of American democracy stems from his ability to move back and forth between detailed empirical observations and general theoretical propositions. Furthermore, the uniqueness of American democracy is illustrated by contrasting nineteenth-century America with Europe, and France, in particular. Therefore, Tocqueville is in many ways a 'comparative political scientist' *avant la lettre*. Corollary, if we wish to remain honest to Tocqueville's legacy, we cannot but compare the European Union with other contemporary international regimes (such as UN, WTO, NAFTA) or with other national democracies, in particular 'federations'. Notions of 'centralization', 'free moeurs' (mores), 'local autonomy' can only be fruitfully applied to the European Union if they are sufficiently detached from their nineteenth century context.

Keeping this observation in mind, it is not difficult to see why I will argue that *by today's standards*, the European Union is far from heading towards the bureaucratic tyranny which Tocqueville (and Siedentop) fear(ed) so much. Furthermore, nearly two centuries after his first trip to America, many more states have democratized (and in more inclusive ways than Tocqueville ever experienced) and other international regimes (which were largely absent during his lifetime) have emerged. The 'new political science' which Tocqueville proclaimed has improved

155

our understanding of the conditions under which states or federations form, democracy collapses and authoritarian regimes emerge.

In the following section, I first review how the contemporary reality of the European Union measures up against Tocqueville's predictions and Siedentop's analysis. I will argue that the European Union is neither a state, nor a bureaucratic tyranny. Second, I will argue that 'federalism' is possibly the best institutional paradigm with which to compare the present European Union, and also that the practice of federalism does not necessarily mean that the European Union should be read as a 'centralizing' endeavour. In this sense, I believe that Siedentop's analysis stays too close to the empirical evidence which Tocqueville relied upon when he formulated his ideas. Third, I will nuance Siedentop's statement that the European Union should primarily be seen as a 'utilitarian' endeavour. Fourth, although critical of Siedentop's characterization of the contemporary European Union, I share his view that the European Union lacks the 'constitutional' sense that is required for turning it into a constitutionalized polity. Furthermore, I partially endorse his concern that European integration somehow reduced the health of EU member-state democracy. However, I do not share most of his institutional suggestions to revive EU democracy. Instead, I endorse some recent proposals by Follesdal and Hix, bearing in mind that their implementation may require a new Treaty, and therefore, the likely consent of the population in some member-states. The basic tenet of their suggestions, however, is correct: EU policies need to be more politicized before a full-blown constitutionalization of the European Union can be contemplated.

Why the European Union is not a federation, let alone a bureaucratic tyranny

A federal state is the most *decentralized* form of state-hood. In a confederation, the member-states retain their external sovereignty, in a regionalized, or decentralized state the centre formally retains all sovereignty. So, by Tocqueville's standards, what would the European Union be, and how does he define federalism?

In *De la démocratie en Amérique*, Tocqueville described post 1789 United States as a form of 'incomplete' government. He also uses the term 'federal' differently from how it is used today.

> Several nations form a permanent league and establish a supreme authority. This authority does not act directly on ordinary citizens, as

a national government might do, but it does act on each of the confederated peoples taken as a body. Such a government, so different from all others, is called federal.[1]

The type of state which Tocqueville describes is not yet a full-fledged federation because in a federation the centre can take decisions which *directly* bind all citizens across the state, albeit only within its constitutionally allocated competencies.

In this sense, what by contemporary standards is commonly understood as a *federal* government is what Tocqueville refers to as an 'incomplete national government'. In the case of an incomplete national government, 'the central government acts directly on the people it governs, administering them and judging them as national governments do, but it does so only within a limited sphere'.[2] Tocqueville does not specify the powers of the centre in such an 'incomplete national government' in much detail, but on the basis of what he observes in America, such powers are the right to *make peace or war*, to *raise money* or to *raise troops*, to provide for the *general needs* and to regulate the common interests of the nation.

Tocqueville's definition of an 'incomplete national government' clarifies that he links federalism to a particular type of state-format. He does not, unlike what is common practice in contemporary federal theory, consider federalism as *any* mode of governance in which elements of shared and self-rule are combined.[3] Therefore, his understanding of federalism approximates that of what theorists today define as a 'federation'. This is an important nuance because authors who conceive federalism as a form of governance which can be detached from a *state* routinely consider the European Union as 'federal' already.[4]

One only needs to take a cursory look at Tocqueville's definition of an 'incomplete government' to realize that the European Union is *not* yet federal. Member-states have retained external sovereignty. True, EU treaties and laws are supreme and have direct effect, but most European legislation still has to be transposed into national law. Furthermore, the European Union is not genuinely involved in making war beyond its borders, it has no tax-raising autonomy, but is entirely dependent from member-state contributions instead, and it cannot raise troops. In addition, the American states which united in 1789, so Tocqueville observed, agreed not only that the federal government dictated laws, but also that it executed those laws itself. By contrast, the European Union is not normally engaged in implementing its own competencies and it has very few administrators (as the comparatively small size of the Commission attests). Rather, the European Union relies on the cooperation of the member-states and the national Courts. Indeed, the European Court of Justice has played a major role in enforcing the supremacy of EU law by skillfully building alliances with national courts. The latter have used the 'preliminary ruling procedure' to strengthen their position vis-à-vis the highest national courts.[5] In fact, other than the European Court of Justice, the Court of First Instance and the Court of Auditors the European Union does not control any courts itself.

Next to the rather weak administrative underpinning of the European Union compared with that of the centre in a federal state, the EU member-states retained a much larger grip on the governance of the EU centre than the regions of a federation on the centre of their state. This is made apparent by considering the 'structural' and 'procedural' guarantees which EU member-states possess.[6] For instance, the so-called 'intergovernmental institutions' (European Council, Council of Ministers) retain the biggest legislative stake in EU policy-making and overpower the European Parliament. 'Supranational' institutions such as the Commission or European Court of Justice are composed on the basis of national quota (a restriction that is absent from the composition of most federal executives or courts). In procedural terms, member-state autonomy is guaranteed by prescribing unanimity for treaty reform and for many legal changes that touch upon issues of high political salience (security and foreign policy, fiscal co-ordination, social policy matters etc.). Even when the European Union decides on issues that do not require unanimity, the procedural threshold (qualified majority) is generally much higher than is the case for most federal states. The strength of member-state autonomy is further made apparent by observing the right of member-states 'to opt out' of certain policy areas. The quarrels in 2005 on determining the size of the EU budget for the period 2007–2012 not only reveal the comparatively small size of the EU budget but also the ability of individual member-states to block proposed amendments. The limited spending capacity of the European Union leads to its virtual absence in redistributive policies, the core feature of most centres in federal states. I think Tocqueville would find this an interesting observation, for if he were to compare contemporary democracies with one another, he would notice that even central governments in federal states without a large social-democratic party such as the United States spend a great deal of money on social assistance programmes or health care.

The European Union, as the above analysis demonstrates, is still far removed from a federal state structure. On balance, the European Union is closer to being confederal than federal (in a Tocquevillian sense). By itself, this makes the fear of a bureaucratic tyranny far-fetched; a fear that is more alive in the perception of the public (and in the spinning minds of British tabloid press editors) than something which social scientists (the intellectual heirs to Tocqueville) would be able to observe. Although the European Union is not a 'bureaucratic tyranny', could it be in danger of becoming one? Not on the basis of what Tocqueville perceived as the main causes of a bureaucratic tyranny. The class cleavage shaped the party systems of most European states (where party systems are primarily aligned along left-right divides), but the threat of a social revolution has disappeared. The National and Industrial Revolutions which swept through Europe in Tocqueville's lifetime produced lasting patterns of state and party nationalization, but they did not generate centralized authoritarian regimes.[7] True, the Nazi and authoritarian or communist regimes could not have materialized without the levels of social unrest which Tocqueville predicted. Yet, Social-Democratic parties now participate in many member-state governments (and thus the 'labour class' is no longer excluded from political participation) and on the whole the class cleavage has lost much of its salience.

Furthermore, rising discontent with the process of European integration is likely to strengthen pressures for 'renationalizing' some policy sectors or to increase the use of softer forms of Europeanization. For instance, despite fears of a race to the bottom and tax dumping, there has been little willingness, let alone consensus among the member-states of the European Union to coordinate social policies. The open method of coordination applies benchmarking as a cautious mechanism to achieve wider social policy goals across EU member-states, for instance in fighting poverty or combating unemployment.[8] However, the open method of coordination (OMC) does not produce a harmonization, let alone a centralization of EU social policy.

Similarly, notwithstanding European integration, representative government is still alive at the local, regional and national levels (and albeit in a less complete form at the EU level). Therefore, there is no justified fear of a destruction of local autonomy, which as Tocqueville observed, would be the unintended consequence of the struggle against social privilege.

Federalism as an unlikely, yet more likely outcome than a bureaucratic tyranny

Perhaps more than just providing a static picture of how the European Union compares with contemporary federations, we should consider the direction in which the European Union is heading. After all, the involvement of the European Union in social policy (through the OMC method), justice and home affairs or peace-keeping operations is relatively new, and perhaps a federation could emerge as a matter of time? In line with Tocqueville, Siedentop argues that federal structures require a civil society and government (*la condition sociale* and *les institutions politiques*) which are conducive to federalism. This statement begs in fact two questions. First, what are the conditions of federalism; second does the absence of one or several of these conditions necessarily imply that federalism or a federation cannot take hold?

In my view, Siedentop's reading on the conditions of federalism are coloured too much by the conditions that made the American federation possible. Here federalism emerged as a 'centripetal' movement, a gradual coming together of states which shared a common history as former colonies of Great Britain: 'Not only do the various [American] states share almost the same interests, origin and language, but they are also civilized to the same degree, so that it is usually easy for them to come to agreement.'[9]

Like the formation of the United States, the European Union follows a largely centripetal direction (the coming together of member-states into 'an ever closer' union). Yet, the motives for coming together are different. For instance, unlike what Riker pointed out as a crucial drive for explaining the formation of America, it is more difficult to assert that the European Union was formed to fight off an external threat (unless the Soviet Union was perceived as such), or to aggrandize territory (member-states applied to join the Union, in general, the Union has not been actively seeking to expand its membership).[10] More importantly, not long after 1840, the year in which Tocqueville published his second volume of *De la démocratie en Amérique*, two important events took place which put his conditions under which federalism is possible somewhat into perspective.

First, the slavery issue, which Tocqueville rightly identified as one of the vulnerable American spots, sparked a civil war. The outcome led to a recalibration of central-state relationships. The powers of the federal government were enhanced and the authority of the federal government to make 'final' decisions in its constitutionally assigned areas of competence was recognized. In this sense, the conditions underpinning the formation of the American federation were not sufficient to *sustain* it.[11]

Second, in 1848 Switzerland became Western Europe's first state with a federal constitution. Multilingual and multireligious Swiss society defied most of Tocqueville's favourable conditions for federalism. Although a brief (but less bloody) civil war was needed to uphold the Swiss federal bargain, the Swiss case demonstrates that a sovereign state can flourish despite the presence of significant social and cultural fault lines. More recent experiences with (centrifugal) federalism in Belgium and Spain show that federalism can go hand in hand with a multilingual or multiethnic context.

What lessons can be learned from the above observations for the European Union?

First, the European Union certainly lacks some of the favourable conditions of federal state-building which Tocqueville identified: after the Cold War, an imminent military threat (Soviet Union) has disappeared; closer economic integration continues, but it is not matched by a shared history and language which creates strong enough ties to produce a common state structure (Swiss cantons were united in a confederal union prior to federalization and faced powerful neighbours to the north, east and west with aggrandizing ambitions). Arguably, although a 'European public sphere' is not entirely absent, it is not sufficiently strong to create a federal polity in the Tocquevillian (i.e. American) sense.[12] However, this is not problematic, given that the European Union does not aspire to the type of statehood which characterizes a federation, let alone a unitary state. The member-states of the European Union have retained a very strong institutional capacity as they, and not the newly created European institutions have the largest tax-raising powers, control public spending in welfare and education and raise troops.[13] Therefore, if the European Union ever were to acquire state attributes, it could hardly be anything different from a *federal* state.

Second, federal structures are not inherently centralizing. The rationale behind federalism in Belgium and Spain is a centrifugal one. Furthermore, the division of powers between the centre and the regions in a federal state is not necessarily fixed. For instance, the founding fathers of the Canadian federation had a more centralized polity in mind than the United States, but in reality the opposite occurred: the Canadian federation transformed into one of the most decentralized federations, while the United States has moved into a more centralizing direction. This comparison illustrates that authority in a federal state can 'migrate' back and forth between the centre and the regions. To discuss the causes of (de)centralization *after* a federal state has formed falls beyond the scope of this chapter, but the crucial point is that if the European Union were to acquire the traits of a federation, it could well be on the brink of further centralization *or* revert to more sub-European autonomy. The pendulum can swing back and forth between centralization and decentralization.

Third, in the complex polity which the European Union inevitably is, centralizing competencies can go hand in hand with decentralizing tendencies. The contemporary Belgian, Italian, Spanish and even British polities demonstrate that political authority does not necessarily spread out in one direction, but can simultaneously move upwards and downwards. In this sense, a more accurate description of the European Union is to see it as a 'poly-centric' polity[14] or a system of Multi-Level Governance[15] in which functions are dispersed and shared across various levels of authority, without producing the 'centralizing' implications which Tocqueville (and Siedentop) seemed to fear so much.

Finally, the process of European integration primarily follows the trajectory of negative integration. In the economic realm, European integration seems to promote the removal of trade-barriers, the imposition of harder budget constraints in order to coordinate fiscal policies, and the opening of public services to competition (such as the railway and postal services). Although such a process of European economic integration may be contested because it rests on 'neo-liberal' principles, it does lend further support to the thesis that the 'bureaucratic' state may be unravelling further, not only up- and downwards, but also laterally (from the state to the market).[16]

The European Union and sheer utilitarianism

Europe, so Siedentop argues, was constructed on a liberal, economic agenda, with the principle aim of 'getting richer together'. This would surprise Tocqueville who advocated rights-based ideas rather than sheer utilitarianism.

There is some truth in this statement. As I have just argued the European Union has pursued an ambitious agenda of 'negative integration', in which trade barriers were progressively reduced and a free market of goods, people, capital and ultimately also services has been taking shape. Much has been said of the difficulty of the European Union to become active in positive integration. For instance, different 'worlds' of welfare (the Anglo-Saxon, the Rhineland model and the Scandinavian) and differences in the extent of social coverage (often linked to national variations in levels of socio-economic development) prevent a powerful social Europe from taking shape.[17] Yet, in my view, to argue that Europe is constructed on sheer utilitarianism is too one-sided.

First, for the founders of the then European Economic Community, closer economic integration was a means to an end: the incremental achievement of political integration. Although the so-called 'functionalist' or Monnet method may not have reached its objective, the outcome is not sheer utilitarianism. It is no coincidence that the process of economic integration kicked off in state-sensitive areas such as coal, atomic energy and steal; production factors that played a crucial role in the build up to the Second World War.

Second, the EU Treaties (and the draft constitutional Treaty) demonstrate that the European Union shares a tradition which respects human rights, the rule of law and democracy.[18] Candidate member-states which do not comply with any of these principles cannot enter the Union; member-states which fail to observe them can be suspended from the Union. If the EU was only about economic cooperation or sheer utilitarianism, such conditions would not matter. Indeed, similar conditions are largely absent from trade organizations such as NAFTA, ASEAN or Mercosur.

Third, following Maastricht, the European Union sought to develop the notion of a 'European citizenship'.[19] Although European citizenship does not add much to the 'lowest common denominator' of national citizenships, it emphasizes a number of rights and duties that all citizens of the European Union must observe or can rely on. Examples of these are the right to vote and stand in local and EP elections; the right to diplomatic and consular protection; the right of petition to the EP and appeal to the ombudsman; the right of accessing most documents which emanate from the European institutions; the right of addressing EU institutions in any of the official languages, the ability to access public services in EU countries; non-discrimination by reason of nationality, sex, race or ethnic origin, religion or belief, disability, age or sexual orientation. Candidate member-states are thoroughly screened on these matters. For instance, Turkey could not claim membership as long as it failed to comply with some of these criteria.

Fourth, in the past decade, the European Union has become active in the military domain, albeit very cautiously. In 2007, the European Union is involved in peace-keeping missions in Macedonia and Kosovo. Not much notice is given to these missions, but this is probably more a function of their relative success than of their insignificance.[20]

Fifth, the most important recent legal and institutional developments have occurred in the field of justice and home-affairs (the so-called third pillar of the European Union). Partially driven to control immigration into the European Union and to protect it against terrorism, justice and home affairs is more than just a 'utilitarian' policy.[21] Similarly, recent efforts to create a European space of higher education (albeit, strictly speaking beyond the framework of the European Union) are not solely inspired on economic grounds, but also on the conviction that a process of knowledge transfer will serve the interests of EU citizens, economic and non-economic alike.

Finally, in some sense one can see the European Union as a collective European answer to the challenges of globalization. As Stefano Bartolini puts it, 'national competitiveness becomes the dominant political imperative and program as national regimes are exposed to competition that can no longer be contained either at the national level'. This may have visible consequences: (1) shift of taxation from mobile to immobile factors; (2) shift of financing of the welfare state from employers' contributions to general tax revenues; (3) ruling out of state aids and subsidies to domestic industries for employment protection; (4) pushes towards privatization of previously nationalized industries that protected sectors of the labour force; (5) constraints on public borrowing and the overall public deficit and (6) rising autonomy of central banks no longer allowed to extend credit to governments.'[22] Although the European Union can be seen as 'utalitarian, and neo-liberal' insofar as it fosters a logic of economic competition among its member-states, Europeanization can also be seen to 'cushion' globalization effects by shifting macro-economic decisions to a level where they could generate a more profound collective impact.

The European Union: reasons to worry?

That the European Union is neither a federal state nor a bureaucratic tyranny does not mean that there are no reasons to be concerned with the contemporary state of the Union in general and its democratic health in particular. Siedentop argues that the process of European integration has unintentionally reduced democracy in its member-states (without generating a European democracy instead). One can see two reasons for this, both of which were noticed by Tocqueville: the first is inherent to all polities which enlarge; the second is of specific importance to the European Union.

Tocqueville already noticed that, other things being equal, the larger the polity (in terms of the number of citizens which it addresses) the smaller the input of each individual citizen in collective decisions of the centre. The sheer size of the European Union means that EU decisions *directly affect* a much larger group of citizens than decisions which member-state government take separately. Therefore, *even if European citizens were to have a strongly developed constitutional sense,* the European Union could never succeed in involving its citizens more closely than their member-states. Therefore, what may be gained in terms of effectiveness by adding a European tier of decision-making may be lost in terms of participatory democracy. Or, more 'supranational' democracy cannot entirely make up for 'lost' domestic democracy since the relative weight of individual voters in collective decision-making decreases. Tocqueville observed it as one of the main difficulties that ensue from building up a 'federal' government.[23]

But next to darker prospects for participatory democracy in large polities, Tocqueville also predicted that larger polities face more difficulty in building workable majorities: 'the more the population grows, and the more diversified minds and interests become, the more difficult it is to form a cohesive majority.'[24] This makes confederal polities more prone to instability, possibly anarchy and authoritarianism (as Tocqueville observed in Mexico despite the adoption of a constitutional blueprint that mirrored that of its northern neighbour).

In all the confederations that preceded the American Union as we know it today, the federal government was obliged to rely on the separate governments included in the confederation in order to meet its own needs. If a prescribed measure displeased one of those governments, it could always circumvent the requirement to obey. If strong, it could resort to arms; if weak, it could tolerate resistance to the laws of the union that it had accepted as its own, invoke its very weakness as a pretext, and rely on the force of inertia to have its way.

Thus, inevitably, one of two things came to pass: either the most powerful of the united peoples seized the powers of the federal authority and dominated the others in its name; or the federal government was abandoned to its own forces, anarchy established itself among the confederates, and the union lost the power to act.[25]

In the view of Tocqueville, what prevented the United States (unlike Mexico) from going down this path (at least after the civil war!) was its capacity to build workable or 'unified' majorities and to make outvoted minorities tolerate or comply with the majority verdict. To some extent, the multiple checks and balances in the US political system as well as political package-deals such as the *Connecticut* and *Missouri* compromises (which respectively balanced small and large state or slave and non-slave state representation in the Senate) contributed to this aim.

More importantly however, has been the presence of *shared habits or mores* among US citizens *across* the union.

Siedentop borrows from Tocqueville insofar as in his opinion, the 'mores' which EU citizens hold are not sufficiently alike (and free) to generate a constitutional sense that is thick enough to wield a genuinely democratic 'Government of the Union'. Put differently, the European Union is still too much a *demoi*cracy instead of a *demos* in its own right.[26] As Siedentop correctly argues, the current level of European integration is primarily the product of an elitist consensus. The same applies to most other multilateral organizations, such as NAFTA, ASEAN or Mercosur, but as earlier paragraphs illustrated, the European Union has outgrown the classic features of a 'utilitarian' trade organization. The permissive public consensus no longer prevails, as was made obvious in early referendums on the Maastricht Treaty and EMU in Denmark and France, respectively, and the more recent rejection of the constitutional Treaty in France and the Netherlands.

The absence of a constitutional sense should not worry us if the European Uniion does not have ambitions to deeper integration, or if its citizens and governments were not concerned with potentially 'unravelling' some aspects of the present *acquis communautaire*. However, it would be hard not to expect such a constitutional sense as a prerequisite for more positive integration (for instance by transforming mere coordination efforts in social policy into binding legislation), the development of a proper EU tax-raising capacity, a European defence force or foreign policy authority. Furthermore, some economists have argued that the European Union requires more political integration ('a European government') if the monetary union is to hold.[27]

Creating a 'constitutional' sense requires politicizing the European Union

Without the appropriate 'mores' or 'constitutional sense' Tocqueville would probably predict that the European Union, should it venture into the areas outlined above, would be in danger of succumbing to one of his two 'confederal' doom scenarios. Either some of its most powerful members could constitute a 'directoire' and impose common interests upon the other member-states *or* the process of European integration would slowly unravel and the judicial enforcement of the *acquis communautaire* could no longer be guaranteed. It seems that in the present state, the prospect of 'unraveling' is more realistic than that of a 'bureaucratic despotism'.

What then are some of the appropriate mechanisms to strengthen the 'mores' of European citizens? Citizens *are* already involved in EU decision-making of course. Some commentators have even argued that the input of the directly elected European Parliament or the presence of a Council composed from member-state executives suffices to 'legitimize' EU policy-making. The European Parliament is the only EU institution which is directly elected. Yet, the continuous rise of its powers since 1979 coincided with a steady drop in voter turnout. Hence, strengthening the European Parliament would not necessarily accommodate the legitimacy problems from which the current European Union suffers. Arguably, individual voters can relate more easily to EU decisions when these are taken by ministers (whom they can familiarize with due to their role in domestic politics and the media attention which they receive there) than by directly elected MEPs.

Next to their involvement in EP decisions, citizens (of some member-states) also occasionally vote on EU Treaties. Votes on treaties frequently pertain to large political or constitutional issues, and they leave voters with a clear but very limited choice (yes or no). In fact, one could argue that the *key* to more citizen participation (and the development of a constitutional sense) lies in a partial politicization of European issues *beyond* the grand constitutional questions. Just as a child must learn to walk before it starts running, the public needs to be involved more in daily EU decision-making before it is expected to engage with the grand constitutional debates. Low public involvement is not so much (or not only) the result of the low salience of EU legislation or the nature of its policies as regulatory rather than redistributive.[28] Low public involvement can also stem from misconceived institutional design, or by the non-politicization of decision-making on issues that should be (partially) politicized.[29] Thus, the sequencing of events for which public deliberation and indeed politicization is required ought to be correct. The European Union may not be ripe to jump on the constitutionalization boat, but the 'mores' of its citizens can be enhanced by improving the way in which decisions are taken in *non-constitutional* matters. Without politicizing the micro-politics of the European Union (the making of daily policies and the accountability thereof) first attempts to politicize its macro-politics (European constitution-building) are practically doomed to fail. What are potential ways of 'politicizing' the Union, and in the process, developing the 'mores' that are required to consolidate or strengthen European integration?

First, the accountability of EU policies needs to be improved. In part, accountability is blurred by entrusting the regulation and implementation of EU policies to two different layers of government and by the lack of EU powers to fund its policies on the basis of proper taxes.[30] Although the absence of EU fiscal autonomy and the role of the member-states in implementation cannot be changed easily, the transparency of Council decisions could be enhanced (in this regard I also concur with Siedentop's remarks). Council decisions and votes should be made public, so that ministers cannot blame unpopular positions on colleagues from other member-states. Furthermore, to the extent that the role of the European Council increases in relation to the Council, similar mechanisms are needed to down- and upstream information to and from the member-states. National parliaments have an important role to play in structuring and preparing the European debate and in holding their ministers to account. Strengthening the input of national MPs or at least increasing their control on members of the executive could mediate that distance.

However, increasing transparency of Council decisions will not generate a more politicized Union but merely increase the accountability of its policies. The additional institutional suggestions which Siedentop puts forward will in my view not contribute to developing the right set of mores. At one extreme, he proposes to entrust the member-states with a right of voluntary (and unilateral) exit. To create a right of voluntary exit is to open the door to instability: member-states could credibly threaten to leave the union as a means to constantly renegotiate existing equilibriums to their own benefit. At the very least, such threats should require the consent of a majority of MEPs and a majority of the member-states. Siedentop also puts much faith in the creation of a bicameral legislature. Arguably, the European Union is already bicameral: the two main players in the legislative game are the Council (which acts as a powerful broker of national interests) alongside a democratically elected European Parliament. The European Union institutional machinery would be seriously overloaded if most or all legislative decisions also required the consent of a third chamber that is composed from members of national parliaments. Since pre-selecting MEPs is the responsibility of national parties and national pre-selectorates, MEPs already frequently operate as agents of national (party) interests. Is a permanent chamber of national MPs really needed when members of national executives and to a more limited extent MEPs already protect national interests? Instead, subsidiarity can be used as a more valuable protection against policy centralization, without requiring a third 'parliamentary chamber'. The suggestion of the failed draft constitutional Treaty made sense in this regard: the national parliaments could serve as an *ad hoc* collective subsidarity watchdog by 'voting' against the consideration of EU legislative proposals before they are introduced in the Council or European Parliament.

Follesdal and Hix suggest some additional changes that would generate a more politicized European Union (and thus in my view could contribute to a strengthening of European mores). As they see it the European Union suffers from a legitimacy deficit because we cannot be sure that the answers which it produces to complicated questions would have been similar if they had been more open to political contestation. It is worth quoting Follesdal and Hix here in full:

> A key difference between standard democratic and non-democratic regimes is that citizens form their views about which policy options they prefer through the process of deliberation and party contestation that are essential elements of all democracies. Because voters' preferences are shaped by the democratic process, a democracy would almost definitely produce outcomes that are different to those produced by 'enlightened' technocrats. Hence, one problem for the EU is that the policy outcomes of the EU may not be those policies that would be preferred by a political majority after a debate about those policies. Without the articulation of positions on several sides of a policy debate, no wonder that a debate over a particular policy area does not exist, and that issues lack voter salience ... . Because there is not a visible quasi opposition to EU policies, citizens cannot distinguish between opposition to the current EU policy regime and opposition to the EU system as a whole. Anti EU parties and movements do not simply oppose the current policy balance at the European level, but they advocate root and branch reform or even abolition of the EU system.[31]

Opening up Council decisions to national parliamentary and public scrutiny is a first and necessary, but insufficient step to politicize the Union. Follesdal and Hix rightly point out that occasional referendums on proposed treaty changes or on increasing the powers of the European Parliament will not constitute valid alternatives. The former do not open up the possibility of a real debate on policy issues and substance, but emphasize the scope and machinery of EU decision-making instead. By itself, increasing the relevance of the European Parliament will not generate higher turnouts, without also changing the political relationship between the EP and Commission. Instead, both authors argue that there is sufficient scope for a partial politicization of the European

Commission and for establishing a stronger link between the Commission and Parliament. This can be achieved by separating the more 'technocratic' from the 'political' functions which the Commission currently performs. Where the Commission operates as a merger control authority or monitors the enforcement of EU law, its functions could be taken over by independent agencies. However, where it drafts legislation it acts a body of potentially great political significance. Here, Follesdal and Hix suggest to elect the European Commission president by national parliaments or citizens, or to present potential candidates for Commission leadership prior to EP elections: 'the potential impact of more democratic competition could be more or less policy from the European Union, depending on the type of contest that develops and the candidate who wins'.[32]

From politicization to constitutionalization?

A meaningful discussion on the constitutionalization of the European Union is only within reach after citizens have familiarized themselves with the daily issues of EU policy making and realized that their opinions matter. This is not to deny that changing the way in which the current Commission is elected, or adjusting the balance of powers between the various branches of EU governance is going to be difficult. Resistance to such proposals would emerge from actors who would lose out in absolute or relative terms (national ministers for instance). Furthermore, changing the way in which the Commission is composed or more clearly separating the executive and legislative roles of the Commission cannot be done without changing some Treaty provisions first. Finally, the successful politicization of daily issues does not of course guarantee the public endorsement of more profound constitutional amendments. However, as Cindy Skach illustrated with regard to constitution building in Brazil, where constitution-making occurs in a context in which a large scale population has been unaware of the various ways of organizing a democracy it is more likely to defer to the opinion of elite groups and political entrepreneurs.[33] Partial politicization could make citizens more aware of the issues at stake and indeed in time make them less deferential to the opinion of domestic elites and political entrepreneurs.

Are there, nonetheless, reasons to be optimistic? Tocqueville would have observed that the failure to adopt the constitutional treaty may have been the European Union's deepest crisis so far, but certainly not its only one. For instance, the 'lameduck' appearance of the then

European Community in the late 1960s and 1970s concurred with initiatives that paved the way to later economic and monetary integration in decades ahead. Furthermore, as Philippe Schmitter put it, the current *Zeitgeist* is not (yet) favourable to profound constitutional change, *domestic and European*:

> the timing for constitutionalization is simply wrong. In the absence of revolution, coup d'etat, liberalization from foreign occupation, defeat or victory in international war, armed conflict between domestic opponents, sustained mobilization of urban populations against the ancien regime and/or impending political collapse, no EU member state has been able to find the 'political opportunity space' for a major overhaul of their ruling institutions. The EU is built more as a process than as an event and the EU polity is not sufficiently linked to clear stateness and nation-hood which would enable the processes of democratization and federalization (constitutionalization) to occur with it in time.[34]

If anything, European integration has been a very incremental process. At the start of 2007, the German presidency considered revamping some of the less radical institutional changes that were proposed in the draft constitutional Treaty. Where suggestions provide opportunities to strengthen the involvement of the public in a structured political debate on European issues Tocqueville would be pleased rather than consider them as evidence of a European bureaucratic despotism at work.

Conclusion: learning from Tocqueville

It is hard to predict how Tocqueville would have assessed the present European Union. However, we can only gauge his thoughts if we apply his logic of enquiry to the present day situation. That logic was neatly summarized (albeit it in a different context) and applied by Follesdal and Hix, in their assertion that studies of European integration should 'in fact ditch abstract normative assertions in favour of careful normative reasoning and the assessment of empirical evidence'.[35]

If we follow this logic, we have reason to believe that Tocqueville would have realized that the European Union certainly is not a multi-tiered state (rather, to borrow from Schmitter, a poly-centric polity). He would observe that the conditions which led to a 'centralization' of the European Union along the American model are simply not there, and that the European Union is far removed from the levels of centralization which are characteristic for most contemporary federations. He would admire the procedural checks and balances in the EU centre and he would be dazzled by the smallness of the EU bureaucracy. In this sense, I think Tocqueville would put Siedentop at ease.

However, he would possibly find some reasons to be worried: the decoupling of regulatory, fiscal and administrative responsibilities could diminish overall levels of accountability. He might disapprove of the importance of the European Central Bank or European Court of Justice, given that both institutions lack explicit political control. Furthermore, he would probably recognize the challenges of enlargement and with it, the challenge of further increasing the distance between decision-makers and citizens. Finally, he would understand that the European Union is more than a simple trade organization and that if the European Union were to raise (or possibly even uphold) its goals, it would need to develop a 'constitutional' sense. I think that, at least in this regard, Tocqueville and Siedentop would share the same concerns. Perhaps Tocqueville would have been puzzled by the resilience of European national executives and parliaments as the main repositories of democratic legitimacy, despite their now much smaller grip on world events.

We can only speculate about the suggestions Tocqueville would put forward to develop a European constitutional sense. Maybe he would argue that such a sense *cannot* be institutionally engineered, cannot be acquired but should develop endogenously. Therefore, he may well have argued against more integration, not so much concerned that a bureaucratic tyranny could follow, but rather a backlash leading to disintegration. Quite possibly, he would be happy with the current 'reflection' period and welcome piecemeal institutional reforms instead.

Whatever suggestions Tocqueville may have put forward, in this contribution I argued that if his/our main concern is to develop a 'European sense' that is strong enough to carry the present or higher levels of European integration', not a constitutional debate, but rather a partial politicization of the European Union is required first. In this sense, I have endorsed the suggestions by Follesdal and Hix and took stance against Siedentop's proposed unilateral exit and 'third chamber' options.

After Tocqueville, social science witnessed an exponential growth. We now possess analytical tools and sources which Tocqueville could only dream of. Yet, knowledge has become more compartmentalized. Social science is broken up into various disciplines and within political science political philosophy has become increasingly detached from comparative politics, political sociology and international relations. Yet, understanding the complexity of the European Union requires that researchers transcend the comfort zones of their own disciplinary approaches. There is probably no 'Tocqueville' of European studies out there, but by collectively pooling our resources, we can keep the spirit of his work alive.[36]

Notes

1 Alexis de Tocqueville, *Democracy in America*, trans. Arthur Goldhammer (New York: The Library of America, 2004), p. 178.
2 *Ibid.*, p. 178.
3 Cf. Daniel Elazar, *Exploring Federalism* (Alabama: University of Alabama Press, 1987).
4 See for instance Kalypso Nicolaïdis and Robert Howse, *The Federal Vision. Legitimacy and Levels of Governance in the United States and the European Union* (Oxford: Oxford University Press, 2001), Daniel Keleman, *The Rules of Federalism. Institutions and Regulatory Politics in the EU and Beyond* (Cambridge, MA: Harvard University Press, 2004), and Anand Menon and Martin Schain, eds, *Comparative Federalism. The European Union and the United States in Comparative Perspective* (Oxford: Oxford University Press, 2006).
5 Cf. Alex Stone-Sweet, *Governing with Judges. Constitutional Politics in Europe* (Oxford: Oxford University Press, 2000).
6 Cf. Wilfried Swenden, 'Is the European Union in need of a competence catalogue? insights from comparative federalism', *Journal of Common Market Studies*, 42.2 (2004) pp. 371–92.
7 Cf. Seymour M. Lipset and Stein Rokkan, *Party Systems and Voter Alignments* (New York: the Free Press, 1967) and Daniele Caramani, *The Nationalization of Politics: The Formation of National Electorates and Party Systems in Western Europe* (Cambridge: Cambridge University Press, 2004).
8 Simon Hix, *The Political System of the European Union* (Basingstoke: Palgrave-Macmillan, 2005), pp. 245–9.
9 Tocqueville, *Democracy*, p. 190.
10 Cf. William H. Riker, 'Federalism' in Fred Greenstein and Nelson Polsby, eds, *Handbook of Political Science Vol. 5: Governmental Institutions and Processes* (Reading, MA: Addison-Wesley, 1975) and William H. Riker, *The Development of American Federalism* (Boston: Kluwer, 1987).
11 More recently, Daniel Ziblatt has argued that analysts frequently conflate arguments explaining state-formation (for instance why did Italy unify) with motives accounting for federal institutions building (why did Italy, unlike Germany, not adopt a federal constitution after unification). In his view, federal institution-building after unification requires units with a sufficiently strong institutional (economic, administrative and tax-raising) capacity. If a majority of the sub-units lack institutional capacity, the unit(s) initiating state-building (for instance Piedmont in the Italian case) will be forced to impose a unitary state structure upon the remaining units in the state. See Daniel Ziblatt, *Structuring the State. The Formation of Italy and Germany and the Puzzle of Federalism* (Princeton: Princeton University Press, 2006).

12   For a historical analysis of the European public sphere, see Hartmut Kaelble, 'The historical rise of a European public sphere?', *Journal of European Integration History*, 8.2 (2002) pp. 9–22.

13   For the notion of 'institutional capacity', see Ziblatt, *Structuring the State*.

14   Cf. Philippe Schmitter (2004), 'Is Euro-federalism a solution or a problem? Tocqueville inverted, perverted or subverted' in Lynn Dobson and Andreas Follesdal, eds, *Political Theory and the European Constitution* (London: Routledge, 2004).

15   Cf. Liesbet Hooghe and Gary Marks, *Multi-Level Governance and European Integration* (Lanham: Rowman & Littlefield, 2001).

16   For a succinct analysis, see Stefano Bartolini (2004), 'Old and New Peripheries in the Processes of European Territorial Integration', in C. K. Ansell and G. Di Palma, eds, *Restructuring Territoriality. Europe and the United States Compared* (Cambridge: Cambridge University Press, 2004).

17   Cf. Gøsta Esping-Anderson, *The Three Worlds Of Welfare State Capitalism* (Princeton: Princeton University Press, 1990) and Fritz W. Scharpf, *Governing in Europe. Effective and Democratic?* (Oxford: Oxford University Press, 1999).

18   Cf. Philip Alston, Mara R. Bustelo, and James Heenan, eds, *The EU and Human Rights* (Oxford: Oxford University Press, 1999).

19   Cf. Lynn Dobson, *Supranational Citizenship* (Manchester: Manchester University Press, 2006).

20   Cf. Ronald Dannreuther, ed., *European Union Foreign and Security Policy. Towards a Neighbourhood Strategy* (London: Routledge, 2003).

21   Cf. Hix, *The Political System of the European Union*, pp. 344–61.

22   Bartolini, 'Old and New Peripheries', p. 30.

23   For comparable observations, see Robert A. Dahl, *On Democracy* (New Haven: Yale University Press, 2000), pp. 100–99 and Robert A. Dahl and Edward Tufte Edward, *Size and Democracy* (Palo Alto, CA: Stanford University Press, 1973).

24   Tocqueville, *Democracy*, p. 181.

25   *Ibid.*, pp. 176–7.

26   Cf. Kalypso Nicolaïdis, 'We ... the Peoples of Europe', *Foreign Affairs*, 83.6 (2004) pp. 97–110.

27   Cf. Paul De Grauwe (2006), 'What have we learnt about monetary integration since the Maastricht treaty?', *Journal of Common Market Studies*, 44.4 (2006) pp. 711–30.

28   Cf. Andrew Moravcsik, 'In Defence of the "Democratic Deficit": Reassessing the Legitimacy of the European Union', *Journal of Common Market Studies*, 40.4 (2002) pp. 603–24.

29   Cf. Andreas Follesdal and Simon Hix, 'Why there is a Democratic Deficit in the EU: a Response to Majone and Moravcsik', *Journal of Common Market Studies*, 44.3 (2006) pp. 533–62.

30   For comparisons with German federalism, see Fritz W. Scharpf, 'The Joint-Decision Trap: lesson from German federalism and European Integration', *Public Administration*, 66.3 (1988) pp. 239–78.

31   Andreas Follesdal and Simon Hix, 'Why there is a Democratic Deficit in the European Union: a response to Majone and Moravcsik', *European Governance Papers* (EUROGOV), No. C-05–02 (2005) http://www.connex-network.org/eurogov/pdf/egp-connex-C-05–02.pdf, p. 13.

32 Follesdal and Hix, 'Why there is a Democratic Deficit in the European Union (2006), pp. 551–6.
33 Cindy Skach, 'We, the Peoples? Constitutionalizing the European Union', *Journal of Common Market Studies*, 43.1 (2005) pp. 161–2.
34 Schmitter, 'Is Euro-federalism a solution or a problem?', pp. 20–1.
35 Follesdal and Hix, 'Why there is a Democratic Deficit in the EU' (2006), p. 557.
36 The author would like to thank Raf Geenens for his insightful and detailed comments. The usual disclaimers apply.

Bibliography

Antoine, Agnès, *L'impensé de la démocratie: Tocqueville, la citoyenneté et la religion* (Paris: Fayard, 2003).

Aron, Raymond, *Paix et guerre entre les nations* (Paris: Calmann-Lévy, 1962).

——, 'Tocqueville retrouvé', *The Tocqueville Review/La Revue Tocqueville*, 1.1 (1979) pp. 8–23.

——, 'De l'existence historique,' *Cahiers de philosophie politique et juridique de l'Université de Caen*, 15 (1989) pp. 147–62.

Audier, Serge, *Tocqueville retrouvé. Genèse et enjeux du renouveau tocquevillien français* (Paris: Vrin/EHESS, 2004).

——, 'Les républicains français ont-ils ignoré Tocqueville?', *Respublica*, 40 (2004) pp. 61–75.

——, *Machiavel, conflit et liberté* (Paris: Vrin/EHESS – Contextes, 2005).

——, ed., *Henry Michel: l'individu et l'état*, special edition of *Corpus*, 48 (2005).

——, 'Tocqueville et la tradition républicaine,' *Cahiers de philosophie de l'Université de Caen* (2007), forthcoming.

Barber, Benjamin, *Strong democracy: participatory politics for a new age* (Berkeley: University of California Press, 1984).

——, *Jihad vs. Mac World* (New York: New York Times Book, 1995).

——, ' "Moderno repubblicanesimo?" La promessa della società civile', in *Libertà politica e virtù civile. Significati e percorsi del repubblicanesimo classico*, ed. Maurizio Viroli (Turin: Edizioni Fondazione Giovanni Agnelli, 2004) pp. 261–82.

Bartolini, Stefano, 'Old and new peripheries in the processes of European territorial integration', in *Restructuring territoriality. Europe and the United States compared*, eds, Christopher K. Ansell and Giuseppe Di Palma (Cambridge: Cambridge University Press, 2004) pp. 19–44.

Bellah, Robert N., Richard Madsen, William M. Sullivan, Ann Swidler and Steven M. Tipton, *Habits of the heart: individualism and commitment in American life* (Berkeley: University of California Press, 1985).

Bentham, Jeremy, *An introduction to the principles of morals and legislation*, eds, J.H. Burns and H.L.A. Hart (London and New York: Methuen, 1982 [1789]).

Benoît, Jean-Louis, *Comprendre Tocqueville* (Paris: Armand Colin, 2004).

——, *Tocqueville: un destin paradoxal* (Paris: Bayard, 2005).

Benoît, Jean-Louis and Eric Keslassy, *Alexis de Tocqueville, textes économiques, anthologie critique* (Paris: Pocket/Agora, 2005).

Boesche, Roger, *The strange liberalism of Alexis de Tocqueville* (London: Cornell University Press, 1987).

——, 'The dark side of Tocqueville: on war and empire', *Review of Politics*, 67 (2005) pp. 737–52.

Bosetti, Giancarlo and Sebastiano Maffettone, eds, *Democrazia deliberativa: cosa è* (Rome: Luiss University Press, 2004).

Boudon, Raymond, *Tocqueville aujourd'hui* (Paris: Odile Jacob, 2005).

Boulbina, Seloua Luste, 'Présentation', in *Tocqueville: sur L'Algérie*, ed. Seloua Luste Boulbina (Paris: Flammarion, 2003) pp. 7–41.

Bove, Laurent, Catherine Secrétan, and Tristan Dragon, eds, *Qu'est-ce que les Lumières 'radicales'?* *Libertinage, athéisme et spinozisme dans le tournant philosophique de l'âge classique* (Paris: Éditions Amsterdam, 2007).

Broglie, Victor de, 'Discours d'ouverture', *Assemblée générale annuelle de la Société de la morale chrétienne* (Paris, 1825).

Bugeaud, Thomas-Robert, *Par l'épée et par la charrue*, ed. Paul Azan (Paris: PUF, 1948).

Burke, Edmund, *Reflections on the revolution in France*, ed. Conor Cruise O'Brien (Harmondsworth: Penguin Books, 1982).

——, *Selected letters of Edmund Burke*, ed. Harvey C. Mansfield Jr. (Chicago and London: The University of Chicago Press, 1984).

Caramani, Daniele, *The nationalization of politics: the formation of national electorates and party systems in Western Europe* (Cambridge: Cambridge University Press, 2004).

Chateaubriand, René de, *Essai historique, politique et moral sur les révolutions anciennes et modernes, considérées dans leur rapports avec la Révolution française*, ed. Maurice Regard (Paris: Gallimard, 1978 [1797]).

Constant, Benjamin, 'De la religion considérée dans la source, ses formes et ses développements', in Benjamin Constant, *Œuvres*, ed. Alfred Roulin (Paris: Gallimard, 1957 [1824]) pp. 1365–95.

Dahl, Robert A., *On democracy* (New Haven: Yale University Press, 2000).

——, 'Political equality, then and now,' *The Tocqueville Review/La Revue Tocqueville*, 37.2 (2006) pp. 461–78.

Dahl, Robert A. and Edward Tufte, *Size and democracy* (Palo Alto, CA: Stanford University Press, 1973).

Dannreuther, Ronald, ed., *European Union foreign and security policy. Towards a neighbourhood strategy* (London: Routledge, 2003).

Dennett, Daniel C., *Breaking the spell. Religion as a natural phenomenon* (New York: Allen Lane – Penguin Books, 2006).

Dobson, Lynn, *Supranational citizenship* (Manchester: Manchester University Press, 2006).

Drescher, Seymour, 'Tocqueville and Beaumont: a rationale for collective study', in *Tocqueville and Beaumont on social reform*, ed. Seymour Drescher (New York: Harper and Row, 1968) appendix, pp. 201–17.

——, 'L'Amérique vue par les tocquevilliens', *Raisons politiques*, 1 (2001) pp. 62–76.

Drury, Shadiah B., *The political ideas of Leo Strauss* (New York: Palgrave MacMillan, 2005).

Dumont, Louis, *Homo hierarchicus: the caste system and its implications*, trans. George Weidenfeld and Nicolson Ltd. (Chicago: University of Chicago Press, 1980).

Edward, Bob and Michael W. Foley, 'Civil society and social capital: a primer', in *Beyond Tocqueville: civil society and the social capital debate in comparative perspective*, eds, Bob Edward, Michael W. Foley and Mario Dani (Hanover, NH: University Press of New England, 2001) pp. 1–14.

Eichthal, Eugène d', *Alexis de Tocqueville et la démocratie libérale* (Paris: Calmann-Lévy, 1897).

Elazar, Daniel, *Exploring federalism* (Alabama: University of Alabama Press, 1987).

Esping-Anderson, Gøsta, *The three worlds of welfare state capitalism* (Princeton: Princeton University Press, 1990).

Ferrara, Alessandro, *Modernity and authenticity: a study of the social and ethical thought of Jean-Jacques Rousseau* (Albany, NY: State University of New York Press, 1993).

Ferry, Jean-Marc, *L'Europe, l'Amérique et le monde* (Nantes: Editions Pleins Feux, 2005).

Fishkin, James, *Democracy and deliberation: new directions for democratic reform* (London: Yale University Press, 1991).

———, *The voice of the people* (London: Yale University Press, 1995).

Fishkin, James and Bruce Ackerman, *Deliberation day* (London: Yale University Press, 2004).

Follesdal, Andreas and Simon Hix, 'Why there is a democratic deficit in the European Union: a response to Majone and Moravcsik', *European Governance Papers* (EUROGOV), No. C-05–02 (2005) http://www.connex-network.org/eurogov/pdf/egp-connex-C-05–02.pdf.

———, 'Why there is a democratic deficit in the EU: a response to Majone and Moravcsik', *Journal of Common Market Studies*, 44.3 (2006) pp. 533–62. [slightly revised version of above paper]

Frederickson, George, *The comparative imagination: on the history of racism, nationalism, and social movements* (Berkeley: University of California Press, 1997).

Furet, François, 'The intellectual origins of Tocqueville's thought', *The Tocqueville Review/La Revue Tocqueville*, 7 (1985–86) pp. 117–29.

Furet, François and Mona Ozouf, eds, *A critical dictionary of the French Revolution* (Cambridge, MA: The Belknapp Press of Harvard University Press, 1989).

Gauchet, Marcel, 'Tocqueville l'Amérique et nous', *Libre*, 7 (1980) pp. 43–120.

———, *La religion dans la démocratie* (Paris: Gallimard/Le débat, 1998).

———, *La démocratie contre elle-même* (Paris: Gallimard, 2002).

———, *La condition politique* (Paris: Gallimard, 2005).

Guellec, Laurence, 'Tocqueville écrivain', in *Tocqueville et la littérature*, eds, Françoise Mélonio and José-Luis Diaz (Paris: PUPS, 2005) pp. 105–24.

De Grauwe, Paul, 'What have we learnt about monetary integration since the Maastricht treaty?', *Journal of Common Market Studies*, 44 (2006) pp. 711–30.

Habermas, Jürgen, *Between facts and norms*, trans. William Rehg (Cambridge: Polity Press, 1996).

Habermas, Jürgen, *The inclusion of the other*, eds, Ciaran Cronin and Pablo De Greiff (Cambridge, Mass.: The MIT Press, 1998).

Halévy, Elie, *The growth of philosophic radicalism* (London: Faber and Faber, 1972).

Hereth, Michael, *Alexis de Tocqueville: threats to freedom in democracy* (Durham: Duke University Press, 1986).

Holbach, Paul-Henri Thiry d', *Histoire critique de Jésus Christ ou analyse raisonnée des Evangiles*, ed. Andrew Hunswick (Geneva: Librairie Droz S.A., 1997).

———, 'La contagion sacrée, ou histoire naturelle de la superstition ou tableau des effets que les opinions religieuses ont produits sur la terre', in Paul-Henri Thiry d' Holbach, *Premières oeuvres*, ed. Paulette Charbonnel (Paris: Éditions Sociales, 1971) pp. 139–75.

Holmes, Stephen, *Benjamin Constant and the making of modern liberalism* (New Haven, Connecticut: Yale University Press, 1984).

Hooghe, Liesbet and Gary Marks, *Multi-level governance and European integration* (Lanham: Rowman & Littlefield, 2001).

Hix, Simon, *The political system of the European Union* (Basingstoke: Palgrave-Macmillan, 2005).

Hugo, Victor, *Hernani*, ed. C. Eterstein (Paris: Flammarion, 1996).

Israel, Jonathan I., *Radical enlightenment. Philosophy and the making of modernity 1650–1750* (Oxford and New York: Oxford University Press, 2001).

——, *Enlightenment contested. Philosophy, modernity, and the emancipation of man 1670–1752* (Oxford: Oxford University Press, 2006).

Jardin, André, *Tocqueville: a biography*, trans. Lydia Davis (New York: Farrar Straus Giroux, 1988).

Jennings, Lawrence C., *French anti-slavery: the movement for the abolition of slavery in France 1802–1848* (Cambridge: Cambridge University Press, 2000).

Kaelble, Hartmut, 'The historical rise of a European public sphere?', *Journal of European Integration History*, 8 (2002) pp. 9–22.

Kelemen, Daniel, *The rules of federalism. Institutions and regulatory politics in the EU and beyond* (Cambridge, MA: Harvard University Press, 2004).

Küng, Hans and Karl-Josef Kuschel, *Erklärung zum Weltethos. Die Deklaration des Parlamentes der Weltreligionen* (München and Zürich: Piper, 1993).

Le Strat, Claire and Willy Pelletier, *La canonisation libérale de Tocqueville* (Paris: Editions Syllepse, 2006).

Lipset, Seymour M. and Stein Rokkan, *Party systems and voter alignments* (New York: the Free Press, 1967).

Idziak, Janine Marie, 'Divine command morality: a guide to the literature', in Janine Marie Idziak, *Divine command morality: historical and contemporary readings* (New York and Toronto: The Edwin Mellen Press, 1979) pp. 1–38.

James, William, 'The will to believe', in William James, *Writings 1878–1899* (New York: The Library of America, 1984) pp. 457–79.

Jardin, André. *Tocqueville. A biography* (New York: Farrar Straus Giroux, 1988).

Jaume, Lucien, 'Tocqueville et le problème du pouvoir exécutif en 1848', *Revue française de science politique*, 41.6 (1991) pp. 739–55.

——, 'Tocqueville: un utilitarismo temperato', *Contemporanea*, 2.1 (1999) pp. 119–25.

——, 'Problèmes du libéralisme. De Mme de Staël à Tocqueville', *Droits*, 30 (January 2000) pp. 151–62.

——, 'Tocqueville et la perspective libérale sur le jury', *La cour d'assises. Bilan d'un héritage démocratique* (Paris: La Documentation Française, 2001) pp. 111–24.

——, 'Tocqueville dans le débat entre le droit de l'Etat et le droit de la société', *La pensée juridique d'Alexis de Tocqueville*, eds, Manuel Carius, Charles Coutel and Tanguy Le Marc'hadour (Arras: Artois Presse Université, 2005) pp. 27–39.

——, 'Tocqueville face au thème de la "nouvelle aristocratie". La difficile naissance des partis en France', *Revue française de science politique*, 56.6 (2006) pp. 969–83.

Jellinek, George, *Die Erklärung der Menschen- und Bürgerrechte*, ed. Walter Jellinek (München and Leipzig: Duncker & Humblot, 1927).

Julien, Charles-André, *Histoire de l'Algérie contemporaine* (Paris: PUF, 1964).

Kaledin, Arthur, 'Tocqueville's apocalypse: culture, politics, and freedom in *Democracy in America*', in *Tocqueville et l'esprit de la démocratie*, ed. Laurence Guellec (Paris: Sciences Po Les Presses, 2005) pp. 47–102.

Kessler, Sanford, 'Tocqueville on civil religion and liberal democracy', *The Journal of Politics*, 39.1 (1977) pp. 119–46.

Kielstra, Paul Michael, *The politics of slave suppression in Britain and France, 1814–48: diplomacy, morality, and economics* (New York: St. Martin's Press, 2000).

Lamberti, Jean-Claude, *Tocqueville and the two democracies*, trans. Arthur Goldhammer (Harvard: Harvard University Press, 1989).

Lacroix, Justine, *Michael Walzer, le pluralisme et l'universel* (Paris: Michalon/Le bien commun, 2001).

Lacroix, Justine and Jean-Marc Ferry, *La pensée politique contemporaine* (Brussels: Bruylant, 2000).

Lawlor, Mary, *Alexis de Tocqueville in the Chamber of Deputies* (Washington: Catholic University of America Press, 1959).

Lefort, Claude, 'From equality to freedom: fragments of an interpretation of *Democracy in America*,' in Claude Lefort, *Democracy and political theory*, trans. David Macey (Minneapolis: University of Minnesota Press, 1988) pp. 183–209.

———, 'Préface', in Alexis de Tocqueville, *Souvenirs* (Paris: Gallimard, 1999) pp. I–L.

———, *Writing. The political test* (Durham and London: Duke University Press, 2000).

Lively, Jack, *The social and political thought of Alexis de Tocqueville* (Oxford: Clarendon Press, 1962).

Lijphart, Arend, *Patterns of democracy: government forms and performance in thirty-six countries* (New Haven: Yale University Press, 1999).

Lipovetsky, Gilles, *L'ère du vide. Essai sur l'individualisme contemporain* (Paris: Gallimard, 1983).

Maistre, Joseph de, *Du Pape*, (Tournai: J. Casterman, 1820).

———, *Essai sur le principe générateur des constitutions politiques* (Lyon: M.P. Rusand, 1833).

Mancini, Matthew, *Alexis de Tocqueville and American intellectuals: from his times to ours* (Lanham: Rowman and Littlefield Publishers, 2006).

Marx, Karl, *Eighteenth Brumaire of Louis Bonaparte* (New York: International Publishers, 1969).

Mayer, Jacob Peter, *Prophet of the mass age. A study of Alexis de Tocqueville* (London: J.M. Dent & Sons, 1939).

McCabe, Joseph, *Sources of the morality of the gospels* (London: Watts & Co., 1914).

Mélonio, Françoise, *Tocqueville et les Français* (Paris: Aubier, 1993).

———, 'Nations et nationalismes', *The Tocqueville Review/La Revue Tocqueville*, 18.1 (1997) pp. 61–75.

———, *Tocqueville and the French*, trans. Beth G. Raps (London: University Press of Virginia, 1998).

Mélonio, Françoise and José-Luis Diaz, eds, *Tocqueville et la littérature* (Paris: PUPS, 2005).

Menon, Anand and Martin A. Schain, eds, *Comparative federalism. The European Union and the United States in comparative perspective* (Oxford: Oxford University Press, 2006).

Mill, John Stuart, *On Liberty* (Harmondsworth: Penguin Books, 1977 [1859]).

———, 'Utilitarianism', in John Stuart Mill, *On liberty and utilitarianism* (New York: Alfred A. Knopf – Everyman's Library, 1992) pp. 113–72.

———, *Three essays on religion* (Amherst N.Y.: Prometheus Books, 1998 [1874]).

Mitchell, Joshua, 'Tocqueville on democratic religious experience', in *The Cambridge companion to Tocqueville*, ed. Cheryl B. Welch (Cambridge and New York: Cambridge University Press, 2006) pp. 276–302.

Mitchell, Timothy, *Colonising Egypt* (Cambridge: Cambridge University Press, 1988).

Molière, *Le bourgeois gentilhomme* (Paris: Classiques Larousse, 1990).

Moravscik, Andrew, 'In defence of the "democratic deficit": reassessing the legitimacy of the European Union', *Journal of Common Market Studies*, 40 (2002) pp. 603–24.

Mouffe, Chantal, *Dimensions of radical democracy* (London: Verso Books, 1992).

Neem, Johann N., 'Squaring the circle', *The Tocqueville Review/La Revue Tocqueville*, 27.1 (2006) pp. 99–121.

Nef, John, 'Truth, belief and civilization: Tocqueville and Gobineau,' *Review of Politics*, 25 (1963) pp. 460–82.

Nicolaïdis, Kalypso and Robert Howse, *The federal vision. Legitimacy and levels of governance in the United States and the European Union* (Oxford: Oxford University Press, 2001).

Nicolaïdis, Kalypso, 'We ... the Peoples of Europe', *Foreign Affairs*, 83 (2004) pp. 97–110.

——, 'UE: un moment tocquevillien', *Politique étrangère*, 3 (2005) pp. 497–509.

Nielsen, Kai, 'Ethics without religion', in *Philosophy of religion. Selected readings*, eds, Michael Peterson, William Hasker, Bruce Reichenbach, David Basinger (New York and Oxford: Oxford University Press, 1996) pp. 536–44.

Nietzsche, Friedrich, *Der Antichrist*, in Friedrich Nietzsche, *Sämtliche Werke. Band 6*, eds, Giorgio Colli and Mazzino Montinari (München: De Gruyter – Deutscher Taschenbuch Verlag, 1999).

Novalis, *Die Christenheid oder Europa* (Ditzingen: Reclam, 1984).

Ossewaarde, Ringo, *Tocqueville's moral and political thought: new liberalism* (London: Routledge, 2004).

——, 'Tocqueville's Christian citizen', *Logos: A Journal of Catholic Thought and Culture*, 8 (2005) pp. 5–17.

Pascal, Blaise, *Pensées*, ed. Leon Brunschvicg (Paris: Flammarion, 1993).

Pascal, Blaise, 'The wager', in *Philosophy of religion. Selected readings*, ed. Michael Peterson E.A., William Hasker, Bruce Reichenbach, David Basinger (New York and Oxford: Oxford University Press, 1996) pp. 77–9.

Pierson, George Wilson, *Tocqueville in America* (Baltimore: John Hopkins University Press, 1996).

Pocock, John G. A., *The Machiavellian moment. Florentine political thought and the Atlantic republican tradition* (Princeton: Princeton University Press, 1975).

Philip, Alston, Mara R. Bustelo, and James Heenan, eds, *The EU and human rights* (Oxford: Oxford University Press, 1999).

Putnam, Robert D., *Making democracy work: civic tradition in modern Italy* (Princeton, Princeton University Press, 1993).

——, *Bowling alone. The collapse and revival of American community* (New York: Simon and Schuster, 2000).

Quinn, Philip, 'The recent revival of divine command ethics', *Philosophy and phenomenological research*, 50 (1990) pp. 345–65.

Rémusat, Charles de, *L'habitation de Saint Domingue ou l'insurrection*, ed. J. R. Derré (Paris: Editions du CNRS, 1977).

Riesman, David, *The lonely crowd* (New Haven: Yale University press, 1950).

Russell, Bertrand, *Why I am not a Christian, and other essays on religion and related subjects* (London and New York: Routledge, 2004).

Riker, William H., 'Federalism', in *Handbook of political science vol.5, governmental institutions and processes*, eds, Fred Greenstein and Nelson Polsby (Reading, MA: Addison-Wesley, 1975) pp. 93–172.

Riker, William H. *The development of American federalism* (Boston: Kluwer, 1987).

Roldan, Dario, *Charles de Rémusat: certitudes et impasses du libéralisme doctrinaire* (Paris: Editions L'Harmattan, 1999).

Rousseau, Jean-Jacques, *Discourse on the sciences and the arts (First Discourse) and Polemics*, trans. Judith R. Bush, Roger D. Masters, and Christopher Kelly, eds, Roger D. Masters & Christopher Kelly (Hanover, NH: University Press of New England, 1992).

Sandel, Michael, *Democracy's discontent. America in search of a public philosophy* (Cambridge, MA: Harvard University Press, 1996).

Scharpf, Fritz W., 'The joint-decision trap: lesson from German federalism and European integration', *Public Administration*, 66 (1988) pp. 239–78.

——, *Governing in Europe. Effective and democratic?* (Oxford: Oxford University Press, 1999).

Schaub, Diana, 'On slavery: Beaumont's *Marie* and Tocqueville's *Democracy in America*,' *The Legal Studies Forum*, 22:4 (1996) pp. 607–27.

Schleifer, James, 'Tocqueville's *Democracy in America* reconsidered', in *The Cambridge companion to Tocqueville*, ed. Cheryl Welch (Cambridge: Cambridge University Press, 2006) pp. 121–38.

Sennett, Richard, *The fall of public man* (New York: Knopf, 1977).

Schmitter, Philippe, 'Is Euro-federalism a solution or a problem? Tocqueville inverted, perverted or subverted', in *Political theory and the European constitution*, eds, Lynn Dobson and Andreas Follesdal (London: Routledge, 2004) pp. 10–22.

Skach, Cindy, 'We, the Peoples? Constitutionalizing the European Union', *Journal of Common Market Studies*, 43 (2005) pp. 149–70.

Siedentop, Larry, *Tocqueville* (Oxford University Press, 1994).

——, *Democracy in Europe* (London: Allen Lane – The Penguin Press, 2000).

Stone-Sweet, Alex, *Governing with judges. Constitutional politics in Europe* (Oxford: Oxford University Press, 2000).

Smith, Page, *Rediscovering Christianity. A history of modern democracy and the Christian ethics* (New York: St. Martin's Press, 1994).

Spandri, Francesco, 'Le rôle de l'imagination dans l'idéal égalitaire', in *Tocqueville et la littérature*, eds, Françoise Mélonio and José-Luis Diaz (Paris: PUPS, 2005) pp. 181–92.

Songy, Benedict Gaston, 'Alexis de Tocqueville and slavery: judgments and predictions' (Unpublished dissertation, Saint Louis University, 1969).

Talmon, Jacob Leib, *Romanticism and revolt. Europe 1815–1848* (London: Thames and Hudson, 1967).

Sullivan, Antony Thrall, *Thomas-Robert Bugeaud* (Hamden: Archon, 1983).

Swenden, Wilfried, 'Is the European Union in need of a competence catalogue? Insights from comparative federalism', *Journal of Common Market Studies*, 42 (2004) pp. 371–92.

Richter, Melvin, 'Tocqueville on Algeria', *Review of Politics*, 25 (1963) pp. 362–98.

Taylor, A.E., *Plato. The man and his work* (London: Methuen & Co, 1977).

Taylor, Charles, *Sources of the self* (Cambridge, MA: Harvard University Press, 1989).

——, Charles Taylor, 'Modes of civil society', *Public Culture*, 3 (1990) pp. 95–118.

——, *The ethics of authenticity* (Cambridge, Mass.: Harvard University Press, 1992).

——, *Charles Taylor et l'interprétation de l'identité moderne, entretien avec Philippe de Lara* (Paris: Cerf, 1998).

Todorov, Tzvetan, *On human diversity: nationalism, racism, and exoticism in French thought* (Cambridge: Harvard University Press, 1994).

Tocqueville, Alexis de, *Correspondence and conversations of Alexis de Tocqueville with Nassau William Senior from 1834 to 1859*, ed. M.C.M. Simpson (London: King, 1872).

——, *Oeuvres complètes*, ed. Gustave de Beaumont (Paris: Michel Lévy-frères, 1864–66).

——, *Oeuvres complètes*, ed. J.-P. Mayer (Paris: Gallimard, 1951–).

——, *Democracy in America*, trans. George Lawrence, ed. J.P. Mayer (New York: Harper & Row, 1966).

——, *L'Ancien Régime et la Révolution*, ed. J.-P. Mayer (Paris: Gallimard, 1967).

——, *Selected letters on politics and society*, trans. James Toupin & R. Boesche, ed. Roger Boesche (Berkeley: University of California Press, 1985).

——, *De la démocratie en Amérique, Souvenirs, l'Ancien Régime et la Révolution*, eds, F. Mélonio, J-C. Lamberti et J.T. Schleifer (Paris: Robert Laffont, 1986).

——, *Recollections: The French Revolution of 1848*, eds, J.P. Mayer and A.P. Kerr (Oxford: Transaction Publishers, 1990).

——, *De la démocratie en Amérique*, ed. Eduardo Nolla (Paris: J. Vrin, 1990, 2 vols.)

——, *Recollections*, trans. George Lawrence, eds, J.P. and A.P. Kerr Mayer (New Brunswick: Transaction, 1995).

——, *The old regime and the revolution*, trans. Alan S. Kahan, eds, François Furet and Françoise Mélonio (Chicago: University of Chicago Press, 1998).

——, *Democracy in America*, trans. Harvey C. Mansfield and Delba Winthrop (Chicago: University of Chicago Press, 2000).

——, *Writings on empire and slavery*, ed. and trans. Jennifer Pitts (Baltimore: Johns Hopkins University Press, 2001).

——, *The old regime and the French revolution. Volume II: Notes on the French revolution and Napoleon*, trans. Alan S. Kahan. (Chicago: University of Chicago Press, 2001).

——, *The Tocqueville reader. A life in letters and politics*, eds, Olivier Zunz & Alan S. Kahan (Malden, Mass.: Blackwell, 2002).

——, *Lettres choisies; Souvenirs*, eds, Françoise Mélonio and Laurence Guellec (Paris: Gallimard, 2003).

——, *Democracy in America*, trans. Arthur Goldhammer (New York: The Library of America, 2004).

——, *Notes sur le Coran et autres textes sur les religions*, ed. Jean-Louis Benoît (Paris: Bayard, 2007).

Tocqueville, Alexis de and Arthur Gobineau, *Correspondance entre Alexis de Tocqueville et Arthur de Gobineau. 1843–1859*, ed. L. Schemann (Paris: Librairie Plon, 1909).

Valet, René, *L'Afrique du Nord devant le parlement au XIXième siècle* (Alger: Imprimerie 'La typo-litho', 1924).

Voltaire, *Dictionnaire philosophique*, ed. René Pomeau (Paris: Garnier-Flammarion, 1964).

Wach, Joachim, 'The role of religion in the social philosophy of Alexis de Tocqueville', *Journal of the History of Ideas*, 7 (1946) pp. 74–90.

Walzer, Michael, *Just and unjust wars* (New York: Basic Books, 1977).

——, *Spheres of justice* (New York: Basic Books, 1983).

——, *Thick and thin: moral argument at home and abroad* (Notre Dame, Indiana: Notre Dame Press, 1994).

Walzer, Michael, *Pluralisme et démocratie* (Paris: Esprit/Seuil, 1997).

——, *Arguing about war* (New Haven: Yale University Press, 2004) pp. 12–25.

——, 'Un empire américain', *Raison publique*, 3 (2004).

Welch, Cheryl, 'Colonial violence and the rhetoric of evasion', *Political Theory*, 31 (2) (2003) pp. 235–63.

Whitton, David, *Molière: Le bourgeois gentilhomme* (London: Grant and Cutler, 1992).

Ziblatt, Daniel, *Structuring the state. The formation of Italy and Germany and the puzzle of federalism* (Princeton: Princeton University Press, 2006).

Zuckert, Catherine, 'Not by preaching: Tocqueville on the role of religion in American democracy', *Review of Politics*, 43 (1981) pp. 259–80.

Index